Table of Contents

DOMAIN III.   **SKILLS AND PROCESSES**

DOMAIN IV.   INSTRUCTION

DOMAIN V.   ASSESSMENT

Great Study and Testing Tips!

What to study in order to prepare for the subject assessments is the focus of this study guide but equally important is *how* you study.

You can increase your chances of truly mastering the information by taking some simple, but effective steps.

Study Tips:

1. **Some foods aid the learning process.** Foods such as milk, nuts, seeds, rice, and oats help your study efforts by releasing natural memory enhancers called CCKs (*cholecystokinin*) composed of *tryptophan*, *choline*, and *phenylalanine*. All of these chemicals enhance the neurotransmitters associated with memory. Before studying, try a light, protein-rich meal of eggs, turkey, and fish. All of these foods release the memory enhancing chemicals. The better the connections, the more you comprehend.

Likewise, before you take a test, stick to a light snack of energy boosting and relaxing foods. A glass of milk, a piece of fruit, or some peanuts all release various memory-boosting chemicals and help you to relax and focus on the subject at hand.

2. **Learn to take great notes.** A by-product of our modern culture is that we have grown accustomed to getting our information in short doses (i.e. TV news sound bites or USA Today style newspaper articles.)

Consequently, we've subconsciously trained ourselves to assimilate information better in neat little packages. If your notes are scrawled all over the paper, it fragments the flow of the information. Strive for clarity. Newspapers use a standard format to achieve clarity. Your notes can be much clearer through use of proper formatting. A very effective format is called the *"Cornell Method."*

> Take a sheet of loose-leaf lined notebook paper and draw a line all the way down the paper about 1-2" from the left-hand edge.

> Draw another line across the width of the paper about 1-2" up from the bottom. Repeat this process on the reverse side of the page.

Look at the highly effective result. You have ample room for notes, a left hand margin for special emphasis items or inserting supplementary data from the textbook, a large area at the bottom for a brief summary, and a little rectangular space for just about anything you want.

3. Get the concept then the details. Too often we focus on the details and don't gather an understanding of the concept. However, if you simply memorize only dates, places, or names, you may well miss the whole point of the subject.

A key way to understand things is to put them in your own words. If you are working from a textbook, automatically summarize each paragraph in your mind. If you are outlining text, don't simply copy the author's words.

Rephrase them in your own words. You remember your own thoughts and words much better than someone else's, and subconsciously tend to associate the important details to the core concepts.

4. Ask Why? Pull apart written material paragraph by paragraph and don't forget the captions under the illustrations.

Example: If the heading is "Stream Erosion", flip it around to read "Why do streams erode?" Then answer the questions.

If you train your mind to think in a series of questions and answers, not only will you learn more, but it also helps to lessen the test anxiety because you are used to answering questions.

5. Read for reinforcement and future needs. Even if you only have 10 minutes, put your notes or a book in your hand. Your mind is similar to a computer; you have to input data in order to have it processed. *By reading, you are creating the neural connections for future retrieval.* The more times you read something, the more you reinforce the learning of ideas.

Even if you don't fully understand something on the first pass, *your mind stores much of the material for later recall.*

6. Relax to learn so go into exile. Our bodies respond to an inner clock called biorhythms. Burning the midnight oil works well for some people, but not everyone.

If possible, set aside a particular place to study that is free of distractions. Shut off the television, cell phone, and pager and exile your friends and family during your study period.

If you really are bothered by silence, try background music. Light classical music at a low volume has been shown to aid in concentration over other types. Music that evokes pleasant emotions without lyrics is highly suggested. Try just about anything by Mozart. It relaxes you.

7. <u>Use arrows not highlighters</u>. At best, it's difficult to read a page full of yellow, pink, blue, and green streaks. Try staring at a neon sign for a while and you'll soon see that the horde of colors obscure the message.

A quick note, a brief dash of color, an underline, and an arrow pointing to a particular passage is much clearer than a horde of highlighted words.

8. <u>Budget your study time</u>. Although you shouldn't ignore any of the material, *allocate your available study time in the same ratio that topics may appear on the test.*

Testing Tips:

1. <u>Get smart, play dumb</u>. Don't read anything into the question. Don't make an assumption that the test writer is looking for something else than what is asked. Stick to the question as written and don't read extra things into it.

2. <u>Read the question and all the choices *twice* before answering the question</u>. You may miss something by not carefully reading, and then re-reading both the question and the answers.

If you really don't have a clue as to the right answer, leave it blank on the first time through. Go on to the other questions, as they may provide a clue as to how to answer the skipped questions.

If later on, you still can't answer the skipped ones . . . ***Guess.*** The only penalty for guessing is that you *might* get it wrong. Only one thing is certain; if you don't put anything down, you will get it wrong!

3. <u>Turn the question into a statement</u>. Look at the way the questions are worded. The syntax of the question usually provides a clue. Does it seem more familiar as a statement rather than as a question? Does it sound strange?

By turning a question into a statement, you may be able to spot if an answer sounds right, and it may also trigger memories of material you have read.

4. <u>Look for hidden clues</u>. It's actually very difficult to compose multiple-foil (choice) questions without giving away part of the answer in the options presented.

In most multiple-choice questions you can often readily eliminate one or two of the potential answers. This leaves you with only two real possibilities and automatically your odds go to Fifty-Fifty for very little work.

5. <u>Trust your instincts</u>. For every fact that you have read, you subconsciously retain something of that knowledge. On questions that you aren't really certain about, go with your basic instincts. **Your first impression on how to answer a question is usually correct.**

6. <u>Mark your answers directly on the test booklet</u>. Don't bother trying to fill in the optical scan sheet on the first pass through the test.

Just be very careful not to miss-mark your answers when you eventually transcribe them to the scan sheet.

7. <u>Watch the clock</u>! You have a set amount of time to answer the questions. Don't get bogged down trying to answer a single question at the expense of 10 questions you can more readily answer.

Foundations of Reading

"Any child, who doesn't learn how to read early and well, will not easily master other skills and knowledge and is unlikely to ever flourish in school or in life."
Reading is Rocket Science, American Federation of Teachers

"If our teaching of reading is to be an art, we need to draw from all we know, think and believe in order to create something beautiful."
Lucy Calkins

This guide was developed to serve the needs of test takers on the PreK-6 level who are preparing for the Foundations of Reading certification test. The quotes which introduce this work point to the crucial nature and significance of effective teaching of reading for our children and our nation's future.

The competencies and skills shared in this guide are also intended to support the educator new to reading certification, in ongoing teaching and learning in Reading. Therefore, sample strategies, web resources, student trade books, picture book citations, and explanations of ready-to-use practices are included.

This guide had a specified page limit and is designed for immediate use. The web resources and bibliographies provided will allow the reader to keep up with new research or investigate a particular strategy, referenced theorist, or term in a deeper, more detailed fashion. In addition, there is in the Appendix, a dictionary of words and terms essential to one's knowledge base as a reading teacher. Yet another study guide is a directory of key reading theorists included for your use as well.

It is my hope that this study guide will merit placement in your home or on your classroom professional library shelf for use as you begin your teaching career. Enjoy and share with your colleagues and parents, as we work together to nurture lifelong readers and writers.

Please let XAMonline know how you are able to use this guide to help you in your teacher certification experience and in your ongoing or future teaching and learning.

THIS PAGE BLANK

DOMAIN I.   **MEANING AND COMMUNICATION**

COMPETENCY 1.0   UNDERSTAND THE CONSTRUCTIVE, DYNAMIC PROCESS OF READING

Skill 1.1   **Describe the interaction between the reader's existing knowledge, the information suggested by the written language, and the context of the reading situation.**

Reading comprehension and reading fluently are necessary skills that students must acquire in order to become good readers. There are students that can read fluently, yet do not understand what they read, which means that teachers should ask questions about the text to ensure comprehension is taking place. When students do not read fluently, this can hamper comprehension because the student takes so long trying to figure out the words that the meaning is lost.

A lack of background knowledge is often one of the factors that affect comprehension. When students do not understand the topic at hand, they will have difficulty reading about the topic no matter how fluently they read. Other factors that affect the level of comprehension are:
1   Lack of word recognition skills
2   Inability to determine the meanings of words through context clues
3   Insufficient level of vocabulary development

Through assessment teachers can determine the instruction students need before reading a text so that comprehension can take place.

See skill 16.2 for additional information

Skill 1.2   **Distinguish among phonemic, morphemic, semantic, and pragmatic systems of language and identify their relationship to the reading process**

COMPONENTS OF LANGUAGE
Language learning is composed of five components. Children progress through developmental stages through each component.

Phonology
Phonology is the system of rules about sounds and sound combinations for a language. A phoneme is the smallest unit of sound that combines with other sounds to make words. A phoneme, by itself, does not have a meaning; it must be combined with other phonemes. Problems in phonology may be manifested as developmental delays in acquiring consonants, or reception problems, such as misinterpreting words because a different consonant was substituted.

Morphology

Morphemes are the smallest units of language that convey meaning. Morphemes are root words, or free morphemes that can stand alone (e.g. walk), and affixes (e.g. ed, s, ing). Content words carry the meaning in a sentence, and functional words join phrases and sentences. Generally, students with problems in this area may not use inflectional endings in their words, may not be consistent in their use of certain morphemes or may be delayed in learning morphemes such as irregular past tenses.

Syntax

Syntax rules, commonly known as grammar, govern how morphemes and words are correctly combined. Wood, (1976) describes six stages of syntax acquisition (Mercer, p 347).

- **Stages 1 and** 2- Birth to about 2 years: Child is learning the semantic system.
- **Stage 3** – Ages 2 – 3 years: Simple sentences contain subject and predicate.
- **Stage 4**- Ages 2 ½ to 4 years: Elements such as question words are added to basic sentences (e.g. where), word order is changed to ask questions. The child begins to use "and" to combine simple sentences, and the child begins to embed words within the basic sentence.
- **Stage 5**- About 31/2 to 7 years: The child uses complete sentences that include word classes of adult language. The child is becoming aware of appropriate semantic functions of words and differences within the same grammatical class.
- **Stage 6**- About 5 to 20 years: The child begins to learn complex sentences and sentences that imply commands, requests and promises.

Syntactic deficits are manifested by the child using sentences that lack length or complexity for a child that age. The child may have problems understanding or creating complex sentences and embedded sentences.

Semantics

Semantics is language content: objects, actions, and relations between objects. As with syntax, Wood (1976) outlines stages of semantic development:

- **Stage 1**- Birth to about 2 years: The child is learning meaning while learning his first words. Sentences are one-word, but the meaning varies according to the context. Therefore, "doggie" may mean, "This is my dog," or, "There is a dog," or "The dog is barking."
- **Stage 2**- About 2 to 8 years: The child progresses to two-word sentences about concrete actions. As more words are learned, the child forms longer sentences, until about age 7, things are defined in terms of visible actions. The child begins to respond to prompts (e.g. pretty/flower), and at about age 8, the child can respond to a prompt with an opposite (e.g. pretty/ugly).
- **Stage 3**- Begins at about age 8: The child's word meanings relate directly to experiences, operations and processes. Vocabulary is defined by the child's experiences, not the adult's. At about age 12, the child begins to give "dictionary" definitions, and the semantic level approaches that of adults.

Semantic problems take the form of:

- Limited vocabulary
- Inability to understand figurative language or idioms; interprets literally
- Failure to perceive multiple meanings of words, changes in word meaning from changes in context, resulting in incomplete understanding of what is read
- Difficulty understanding linguistic concepts (e.g. before/after), verbal analogies, and logical relationships such as possessives, spatial, and temporal
- Misuse of transitional words such as "although," "regardless"

Pragmatics

Commonly known as the speaker's intent, pragmatics is used to influence or control actions or attitudes of others. **Communicative competence** depends on how well one understands the rules of language, as well as the social rules of communication such as taking turns and using the correct tone of voice.

Pragmatic deficits are manifested by failures to respond properly to indirect requests after age 8 (e.g. "Can't you turn down the TV"? elicits a response of "No" instead of "Yes" and the child turning down the volume). Children with these deficits have trouble reading cues that indicate the listener does not understand them. Whereas a person would usually notice this and adjust one's speech to the listener's needs the child with pragmatic problems does not do this.

Pragmatic deficits are also characterized by inappropriate social behaviors such as interruptions or monopolizing conversations. Children may use immature speech and have trouble sticking to a topic. These problems can persist into adulthood, affecting academic, vocational and social interactions.

Problems in language development often require long-term interventions, and can persist into adulthood. Certain problems are associated with different grade levels:

Preschool and Kindergarten: The child's speech may sound immature, the child may not be able to follow simple directions, and often cannot name things such as the days of the week and colors. The child may not be able to discriminate between sounds and the letters associated with the sounds. The child might substitute sounds and have trouble responding accurately to certain types of questions. The child may play less with his peers or participate in non-play or parallel play.

Elementary School: Problems with sound discrimination persist, and the child may have problems with temporal and spatial concepts (e.g. before/after). As the child progresses through school, he may have problems making the transition from narrative to expository writing. Word retrieval problems may not be very evident because the child begins to devise strategies such as talking around the word he cannot remember, or using fillers, and descriptors. The child might speak more slowly, have problems sounding out words, and get confused with multiple-meaning words. Pragmatic problems show up in social situations such as failure to correctly interpret social cues and adjust to appropriate language, inability to predict consequences, and inability to formulate requests to obtain new information.

Secondary School: At this level, difficulties become more subtle. The child lacks the ability to use and understand higher-level syntax, semantics, and pragmatics. If the child has problems with auditory language, he may also have problems with short-term memory. Receptive and/or expressive language delays impair the child's ability to learn effectively. The child often lacks the ability to organize/ categorize the information received in school. Problems associated with pragmatic deficiencies persist but because the child is aware of them, he becomes inattentive, withdrawn, or frustrated.

See skill 13.1 for the relationship to reading

Skill 1.3   Analyze the social, cultural and dynamic nature of language

Identify variations in language across contexts and cultures.

The content in material to be presented orally plays a big role in how it is organized and delivered. For example, a literary analysis or a book report will be organized inductively, laying out the details and then presenting a conclusion, which will usually be what the author's purpose, message, and intent are. If the analysis is focusing on multiple layers in a story that will probably follow the preliminary conclusion.

On the other hand, keeping in mind that the speaker will want to keep the audience's attention, if the content has to do with difficult-to-follow facts and statistics, slides (or PowerPoint) may be used as a guide to the presentation, and the speaker will intersperse interesting anecdotes, jokes, or humor from time to time so the listeners don't fall asleep.

It's also important to take the consistency of the audience into account when organizing a presentation. If the audience can be counted on to have a high level of interest in what is being presented, little would need to be done in the way of organizing and presenting to hold interest. On the other hand, if many of those in the audience are there because they have to be, or if the level of interest can be counted on not to be very high, something like a PowerPoint presentation can be very helpful.

Also the lead-in and introduction need to be structured not only to be entertaining and interest-grabbing, it should create an interest in the topic. If the audience is senior citizens, it's important to keep the presentation lively and to be careful not to "speak down" to them. Carefully written introductions aimed specifically at this audience will go a long way to attract their interest in the topic.

No speaker should stand up to make a presentation if the purpose has not been carefully determined ahead of time. If the speaker is not focused on the purpose, the audience will quickly lose interest. As to organizing for a particular purpose, some of the decisions to be made are where it will occur in the presentation—beginning, middle, or end—and whether displaying the purpose on a chart, PowerPoint, or banner will enhance the presentation. The purpose might be the lead-in for a presentation if it can be counted on to grab the interest of the listeners, in which case, the organization will be deductive. If it seems better to save the purpose until the end, the organization, of course, will be inductive.

The occasion, of course, plays an important role in the development and delivery of a presentation. A celebration speech when the company has achieved an important accomplishment will be organized around congratulating those who were most responsible for the accomplishment and giving some details about how it was achieved and probably something about the competition for the achievement. The presentation will be upbeat and not too long.

On the other hand, if bad news is being presented, it will probably be the CEO who is making the presentation and the bad-news announcement will come first followed with details about the news itself and how it came about, and probably end with a pep talk and encouragement to do better the next time.

"Political correctness" is a new concept tossed around frequently in the 21st century. It has always existed, of course. The successful speaker of the 19th century understood and was sensitive to audiences. However, that person was typically a man, of course, and the only audience that was important was a male audience, and more often than not, the only important audience was a white one.

Many things have changed in discourse since the 19th century just as the society the speaker lives in and addresses has changed, and the speaker who disregards the existing conventions for "political correctness" usually finds himself/herself in trouble. Rap music makes a point of ignoring those conventions, particularly with regard to gender, and is often the target of very hostile attacks. On the other hand, rap performers often intend to be revolutionary and have developed their own audiences and have become outrageously wealthy by exploiting those newly-developed audiences based primarily on thumbing their noses at establishment conventions.

Even so, the successful speaker must understand and be sensitive to what is current in "political correctness." The "n word" is a case in point. There was a time when that term was thrown about at will by politicians and other public speakers, but no more. Nothing could spell the end of a politician's career more certainly than using that term in his campaign or public addresses.

These terms are called "pejorative"—A word or phrase that expresses contempt or disapproval. Such terms as _redneck_, _queer_, or _cripple_ may only be considered pejorative if used by a non-member of the group they apply to. For example, the "n word," which became very inflammatory in the 1960s, is now being used sometimes by African-American artists to refer to themselves, especially in their music, with the intention of underscoring their protest of the establishment.

References to gender have became particularly sensitive in the 20th century as a result of the women's rights movement, and the speaker who disregards these sensitivities does so at his/her peril. The generic "he" is no longer acceptable, and this requires a strategy to deal with pronominal references without repetitive he/she, his/her, etc. Several ways to approach this: switch to a passive construction that does not require a subject; switch back and forth, using the male pronoun in one reference and the female pronoun in another one, being sure to sprinkle them reasonably evenly; or switch to the plural. The last alternative is the one most often chosen. This requires some care, and the speaker should spend time developing these skills before stepping in front of an audience.

Dialect differences are basically in pronunciation. Bostoners say "pahty" for "party" and Southerners blend words like "you all" into "y'all." Besides the dialect differences already mentioned, the biggest geographical factors in American English stem from minor word choice variances. Depending on the region where you live, when you order a carbonated, syrupy beverage most generically called a soft drink, you might ask for a "soda" in the South, or a "pop" in the Midwest. If you order a soda in New York, then you will get a scoop of ice cream in your soft drink, while in other areas you would have to ask for a "float".

COMPETENCY 2.0 RECOGNIZE THE VARIOUS USES OF LANGUAGE

Skill 2.1   **Identify differences in language use in professional, personal and community environments.**

Journalistic Writing

News reporters generally become excellent writers because they get a lot of practice, which is a principle most writing teachers try to employ with their students. Also, news writing is instructive in skills for writing clearly and coherently.

Reporters generally write in two modes: straight reporting and feature writing. In both modes, the writer must be concerned with accuracy and objectivity. The reporter does not write his opinions. He/she does not write persuasive discourse. The topic is typically assigned, although some experienced reporters have the opportunity to seek out and develop their own stories.

A good news story is written as an "inverted pyramid." That is, the reasoning is deductive. The "thesis" or point is stated first and is supported with details. It reasons from general to specific. The lead sentence might be, "The body of John Smith was found in the street in front of his home with a bullet wound through his skull." The headline will be a trimmed-down version of that sentence and shaped to grab attention. It might read: "Murdered man found on Spruce Street." The news article might fill several columns, the first details having to do with the finding of the body, the next the role of the police; the third will spread out and include details about the victim's life, then the scope will broaden to details about his family, friends, neighbors, etc. If he held a position of prominence in the community, those details will broaden further and include information about his relationships to fellow-workers and his day-to-day contacts in the community. The successful reporter's skills include the ability to do thorough research, to maintain an objective stance (not to become involved personally in the story), and to write an effective "inverted pyramid."

While the headline is intended to contain in capsule form the point that an article makes, it is rarely written by the reporter. This can sometimes result in a disconnection between headline and article. Well-written headlines will provide a guide for the reader as to what is in the article; they will also be attention-grabbers. This requires a special kind of writing, quite different from the inverted pyramid that distinguishes these writers from the investigative or feature reporter.

Other Forms of Expository Writing

It may seem sometimes that the **business letter** is a thing of the past. Although much business-letter writing has been relegated to email communications, letters are still a valuable and potentially valuable form of communication. A carefully-written letter can be powerful. It can alienate, convince, persuade, entice, motivate, and/or create good-will.

As with any other communication, it's worthwhile to learn as much as possible about the receiver. This may be complicated if there will be more than one receiver of the message; in these cases, it's best to aim for the lowest common denominator if that can be achieved without "writing down" to any of those who will read and be affected or influenced by the letter. It may be better to send more than one form of the letter to the various receivers in some cases.

Purpose is the most powerful factor in writing a business letter. What is the letter expected to accomplish? Is it intended to get the receiver to act or to act in a specific manner? Are you hoping to see some action take place as the result of the letter? If so, you should clearly define for yourself what the purpose is before you craft the letter, and it's good to include a time deadline for the response.

Reasons for choosing the letter as the channel of communication include the following:
1. It's easy to keep a record of the transaction.
2. The message can be edited and perfected before it is transmitted.
3. It facilitates the handling of details.
4. It's ideal for communicating complex information.
5. It's a good way to disseminate mass messages at a relatively low cost.

The parts of a business letter are as follow: date line, inside address, salutation, subject line*, body, complimentary close, company name*, signature block, reference initials*, enclosure notation*, copy notation*, and postscript*.

Business letters typically use formal language. They should be straightforward and courteous. The writing should be concise, and special care should be taken to leave no important information out. Clarity is very important; otherwise, it may take more than one exchange of letters or phone calls to get the message across.

A complaint is a different kind of business letter. It can come under the classification of a "bad news" business letter, and there are some guidelines that are helpful when writing this kind of letter. A positive writing style can overcome much of the inherent negativity of a letter of complaint. No matter how much in the right you may be, maintaining self-control and courtesy and avoiding demeaning or blaming language is more likely to be effective. Abruptness, condescension, or harshness of tone will not help achieve your purpose, particularly if you are requesting a positive response such as reimbursement for a bad product or some help in righting a wrong that may have been done to you.

It's important to remember that you want to solve the specific problem and to retain the good will of the receiver if possible.

Induction is better than deduction for this type of communication. Beginning with the details and building to the statement of the problem generally has the effect of softening the bad news. It's also useful to begin with an opening that will serve as a buffer. The same is true for the closing. It's good to leave the reader with a favorable impression by writing a closing paragraph that will generate good will rather than bad.

News articles are written in the "inverted pyramid" format—they are deductive in nature: the opening statement is the point of the article; everything else is details. "Who, what, why, when, and where" are usually the questions to be answered in a news article.

A formal essay, on the other hand, may be persuasive, informative, descriptive, or narrative in nature. The purpose should be clearly defined, and development must be coherent and easy to follow.

Email has revolutionized business communications. It has most of the advantages of business letters and the added ones of immediacy, lower costs, and convenience. Even very long reports can be attached to an email. On the other hand, a two-line message can be sent and a response received immediately bringing together the features of a postal system and the telephone. Instant messaging goes even one step further. It can do all of the above—send messages, attach reports, etc.—and still have many of the advantages of a telephone conversation.

Email has an unwritten code of behavior that includes restrictions on how informal the writing can be. The level of accepted business conversation is usually also acceptable in emails. Capital letters and bolding are considered shouting and are usually frowned on.

See Skill 15.1 for more information

Skill 2.2 **Analyze texts to determine style, voice, and language choices and to evaluate their appropriateness for the context, purpose, and audience; and assessing how language choices may affect people.**

Students need to be able to interpret what they read in order for it to make sense to them. Teachers need to encourage students to look beyond the words and the literal meaning to determine the author's voice and style. By analyzing word choices in the text, students begin to develop their own style in writing and are able to choose words that say exactly what they want to say. In primary classrooms, strategies include using word charts related to the theme or words students can use to express feelings. A mini-lesson on overworked words is also helpful as students learn from an early age to try to avoid using words such as "nice", "beautiful" "good" etc. Teachers can help students choose better words for their writing. This is not something that will require only one lesson. It is something that students need to practice year after year.

Because students need to become meaning makers of what they read, teachers can facilitate the process by matching the instruction they provide in the classroom to the individual needs of the students.

Before reading:
1 Activate students' prior knowledge before starting to read by asking them what they know of the situation or the topic.
2 Provide background knowledge so that they understand the topic when they start reading
3 Discuss the conventions and language used by the author by reading sample pages from the text
4 Ask the students to skim the text and study the illustrations
5 Have the students pose questions they think the text will answer

During Reading:
1 Encourage students to become involved with the text
2 Model reading strategies by asking questions, such as "What does that phrase mean?" or "Why did the author use these words?"
3 Help students make their own meaning of the text by encouraging responses.

After Reading:

1. Encourage the students to share their ideas about the text through discussion
2. Encourage students to move beyond literal understanding and develop meaningful connections and understandings
3. Analyze the text in terms of author's style and voice
4. Discuss the mood of the text
5. Encourage students to think about what they would have changed in the text
6. Provide related reading, listening, speaking and writing activities to allow the students to expand and develop understandings

It is important to accept all student answers to allow them to take risks and provide them with the opportunity to discuss their analysis of the text.

COMPETENCY 3.0 UNDERSTAND THE PROCESSES OF LANGUAGE DEVELOPMENT AND READING ACQUISITION.

Skill 3.1   **Apply concepts of emergent literacy to describe a student's development as a reader**

The Alphabetic principle is sometimes called graphophonemic awareness. This term means that written words are composed of letter (graphemes) which represent the sounds (phonemes) of written words.

Development of the Understanding that Print Carries Meaning

This understanding is demonstrated every day in the elementary classroom as the teacher holds up a selected book to read aloud to the class. The teacher explicitly and deliberately talks aloud about how to hold the book, focuses the class on looking at its cover, points to where to start reading, and sweeps her hands in the direction to begin, left to right.

When writing the morning message on the board, the teacher reminds the children that the message begins in the upper left hand corner at the top of the board to be followed by additional activities and a schedule for the rest of the day.

When the teacher invites children to make posters of a single letter such as *b* and list items in the classroom, their home, or outside which start with that letter, the children are concretely demonstrating that print carries meaning.

Strategies for Promoting Awareness of the Relationship between Spoken and Written Language

- Writing down what the children say on a language chart.
- Highlighting the uses of print products found in the classroom such as labels, yellow sticky pad notes, labels on shelves and lockers, calendars, signs, and directions.
- Reading together big-print and oversized books to teach print conventions such as directionality.
- Practicing how to handle a book: How to turn pages, to find the top and bottom of pages, and how to tell the difference between the front and back covers.
- Discussing and comparing with children the length, appearance and boundaries of specific words. For example, children can see that
- the names Dan and Dora share certain letters and a similar shape.
- Having children match oral words to printed words by forming an echo chorus as the teacher reads poetry or rhymes aloud and they echo the reading.

- Having the children combine, manipulate, switch and move letters to change words.
- Working with letter cards to create messages and respond to the messages that they create.

The Role of Environmental Print in Developing Print Awareness

An environmental print book can be created by the children, which contains collaged symbols of their favorite lunch or breakfast foods. The children cut and clip symbols from the packaging of these foods and then place them in alphabetical order in their class-made book. Magazines and catalogues are another source of environmental print that is accessible with ads for child centered products. Supermarket circulars and coupons from the newspaper are also excellent for engaging children in using environmental print as reading, especially when combined with dramatic play centers or prop boxes.

What is particularly effective in using environmental print is that it immediately invites the child from ELL background into print awareness, through the familiarity of commercial logos and packaging symbols used.

Development of Book Handling Skills

Understanding the value and importance of the concepts of print for beginning readers developed out of the work of Marie Clay in New Zealand. Assessment of these skills typically occurs in kindergarten and into first grade as necessary. The following skills are part of the assessment process:

- <u>Print carries a message</u> – The students can demonstrate this skill even if unable to read the text by pretending to read. This may be demonstrated even if the child does not demonstrate any of the other concepts.
- <u>Book organization</u> – Students demonstrate an understanding of the organization of books by being able to identify the title, cover, author, left to right progression, top to bottom order, and one to one correspondence. Students may learn these skills individually as they become more familiar with books.
- <u>Print Consistencies-</u> This is the understanding that text is made up of letters, which then form words, which then are combined to form sentences. As the beginning reader makes these connections, they will next develop the concept of capital letters at the beginning and basic punctuation marks.
- <u>Letter Identification-</u> The final stage of the concepts of print assessment involves the identification of both upper- and lower- case letters. More advanced students may begin to recognize some of the most common spelling patterns in beginning texts.

Have the children identify the front cover, back cover, and title page of a specific book.

Model storytelling with the book held so that the audience can see the illustrations shown to them. Then have children demonstrate the skills for their peers.

Have children search through the class libraries for special features on the fronts or backs of books as they help return the books to their bins. Have the children display and talk about the special symbols they have found.

Review with the children, in an age and grade appropriate format, additional parts of the book as appropriate during mini lessons and read alouds. These additional parts of the book can include: title pages, dedication page, table of contents, and copyright date and glossary.

Strategies for Promoting an Understanding of the Directionality of Print

In order to become proficient readers, young students need to develop a complete understanding that all print is read from left to right and top to bottom. Modeling is one of the most important strategies a teacher can use to develop this understanding in children. The use of big books, poems, and charts are strategies teachers can use in both large and small group instruction. Simple questions can engage the students to pay closer attention to these skills (i.e. "We are going to read this passage, where should I put my pointer to start reading?").

Directionality of print should also be taught during the writing process. In language experience stories, interactive writing, and Kidwriting©, the teacher can incorporate explicit modeling and instruction in these skills. Sometimes it may be necessary to provide children with a dot at the top left corner of the paper in order to provide a visual reminder of where to begin.

Techniques for Promoting the Ability to Track Print in Connected Texts

Model directionality and one-to-one word matching by pointing to words, while using a big book, pocket chart, or poem written out on a chart. As you repeatedly lead the children in this reading, they can follow along and eventually track the print and make one to one matches on the connected text independently. They can also practice by using a pointer (all children love to use the pointer because then pleasure becomes associated with the reading) or their fingers to follow the words. Children happily volunteer to be the point person. Even before Vanna White, the joy of "signifying letters" existed and has tremendous appeal for children.

Copy down a brief, familiar rhyme (perhaps from a favorite book or song) and post it in the room at child's eye level, so the children can independently walk around and read it.

Copy down a brief or familiar rhyme or poem on individual word cards. Then challenge the children in small groups or independently to reassemble and display them on a pocket chart. As children "play" with constructing and reconstructing this pocket chart, they will develop an awareness of directionality, one on one matching of print to spoken words, spacing, and punctuation.

Model interactive emergent writing with the class. While the teacher is noting down the weather, deliberately ask and have the children suggest where the first word in that report should go, top or bottom of the board? Will the first letter be upper case or lower case? What goes at the end of the sentence?

Create with the children sing-song repetitions/rules for using capitals, periods, commas, etc. Encourage the children to begin reciting these sing-songs as soon as they identify specific concepts of print in connected texts.

Model for children how, when pointing at words, they can start at the top and move from left to right. Tell the children that if there are more words to the sentence they are reading under the first line of print, they must go back to the left and under the previous line. Young children enjoy practicing this kinesthetic "return sweep." You might want to teach them to identify the need to do this by saying "Don't fall asleep at the page" or "Time to get to the "return sweep" stage!!" Post this saying and encourage them to singsong as they joyously take ownership of their reading.

Have even beginning readers "read" through the text to find letters they recognize in the story and then share some of the text that includes these specific letters to whet their appetite for reading.

Strategies for Promoting Letter Knowledge and Letter Formation

Engage the children in a Tale Trail game. Use a story they have already heard or read. Ask the children to circle certain letters and then reread the story, sharing the letters they have circled.

Give the children lots of opportunities to do letter sorts. Pass out word cards which have the targeted letter on them. Ask the children to come up and display their answers to questions like these about the letter, say *R*.

*R as the first letter--rose, rise, ran,
*R as the last letter--car, star, far,
*R with a t after it--start, heart, part, smart
*R, two r's in the middle of a word-- carry, sorry, starry

Play "What's in a Name?"- Select a student's name "William." Copy it down on a sentence strip. Have the children count the number of letters in the name and how many of them appear twice. Allow them to talk about which letter is upper case and which letters are lower case. Have the students chant the name. Then rewrite the name on another sentence strip. Have the strip cut into separate letters and see if some one from the class can put the name back correctly.
As you read a book with or to children, ask that they show you specific letters or lower case or upper case letters. Read the text first and encourage as many children to come up and identify the letters as possible. Use a big book and have felt and sandpaper letters available for display as well. If grade, age and developmentally appropriate, have children then write the letter they identified themselves or even more fun, construct it using pipe cleaners, play dough or coded colored markers (different colors for upper and lower case letters).

Play "letter leap" with the children and have them look carefully at the room to identify labeled items that begin with a specific letter by "leaping" over to them and placing a large lettered placard next to them. Children who are advanced in letter formation can then be challenged to "leap" through the classroom when called upon to literally "letter" unlabeled objects.

Recognition that Phonemes are Represented by Letters and Letter Pairs

As young children begin to learn to read, connections are made between the printed letters on the page and the sounds they have heard in language. Phonemic awareness activities are crucial for building this bridge. Students have engaged in many auditory activities. At this time, it is important the teacher use explicit and systematic methods to demonstrate to the students how these auditory sounds are represented on a page by letters or sometimes letter pairs. As this occurs, students can begin to decode text and move toward becoming proficient readers.

The Alphabetic principle is sometimes called graphophonemic awareness. This term means that written words are composed of letter (graphemes) which represent the sounds (phonemes) of written words.

Development of the Understanding that Print Carries Meaning

This understanding is demonstrated every day in the elementary classroom as the teacher holds up a selected book to read aloud to the class. The teacher explicitly and deliberately talks aloud about how to hold the book, focuses the class on looking at its cover, points to where to start reading, and sweeps her hands in the direction to begin, left to right.

When writing the morning message on the board, the teacher reminds the children that the message begins in the upper left hand corner at the top of the board to be followed by additional activities and a schedule for the rest of the day.

When the teacher invites children to make posters of a single letter such as *b* and list items in the classroom, their home, or outside which start with that letter, the children are concretely demonstrating that print carries meaning.

Skill 3.2   **Recognize the stages of literacy development on a continuum (e.g., phonemic awareness, accuracy and fluency, self-monitoring and self-correction strategies)**

There are several different factors that influence early literacy and language acquisition. They include:
1. The intellectual, social and emotional development of the child
2. The culture of the family
3. Socio- economic circumstances
4. The support the child receives in reading development in the home – presence of print, books and the reading level of the parents
5. Prior experience with printed materials
6. Parental attitudes toward reading
7. Attendance in a pre-school setting

Children learn more readily at an early age. This is why teaching the basic skills of reading at an early age is so important in reading development. So many children enter school with a deficiency in prior knowledge because they haven't been read to at home. In Kindergarten, teachers need to surround the children with print, read to them at every opportunity and balance the reading with instruction about letters and sounds.

The stages of literacy development are:
0 to 4 years
  - enjoys having an adult read to them
  - likes to pretend reading books
  - reads pictures of familiar books
  - recognizes some of the letters of the alphabet
  - practices printing their own name
  - starts to sound out letters

Beginning Literacy – 5 – 7 years
  - Starts to develop phonemic awareness
  - Can associate letters with sounds
  - Starts to sound out words
  - Can recognize some sight words
  - Uses picture clues
  - Starts to use context clues when reading
  - Uses invented spelling when writing

Literacy – 9 – 12 years
  - Reads fluently
  - Comprehends what is read
  - Has an expanded vocabulary
  - Writes for various purposes
  - Can use a dictionary for help with spelling
  - Can express personal tastes in reading

The typical variation in literacy backgrounds that children bring to reading can make teaching more difficult. Often a teacher has to choose between focusing on the learning needs of a few students at the expense of the group or focusing on the group at the risk of leaving some students behind academically. This situation is particularly critical for children with gaps in their literacy knowledge who may be at risk in subsequent grades for becoming "diverse learners."
Phonological awareness means the ability of the reader to recognize the sound of spoken language. This recognition includes how these sounds can be blended together, segmented (divided up), and manipulated (switched around). This awareness then leads to phonics, a method for teaching children to read. It helps them "sound out words."

Development of phonological skills may begin during pre-K years. Indeed by the age of 5, a child who has been exposed to rhyme can recognize a rhyme. Such a child can demonstrate phonological awareness by filling in the missing rhyming word in a familiar rhyme or rhymed picture book. I surprised my mother by filling in missing rhymes in a familiar nursery rhyme book at the age of four. She was trying to rush ahead to complete the book, but I wouldn't be cheated of even one rhyme!! Little did I know that I was phonologically aware at four!!

.

You teach children phonological awareness when you teach them the sounds made by the letters, the sounds made by various combinations of letters and to recognize individual sounds in words. Phonological Awareness Skills include:

1. Rhyming and syllabification
2. Blending sounds into words—such as pic-tur-bo-k
3. Identifying the beginning or starting sounds of words and the ending or closing sounds of words
4. Breaking words down into sounds-also called "segmenting" words
5. Recognizing other smaller words in the big word, by removing starting sounds, "hear" to ear

On a continuum, such as that used in First Steps, the stages of literacy development are defined as:

1. Role Play Reading
2. Experiential Reading
3. Early Reading
4. Transitional Reading
5. Independent Reading

When students some to school they are at varying degrees of the first three stages depending on their experience with reading in the home. The key indicators of each stage are:
1. Role Play – students can imitate reading behaviors, such as holding the book upright, reading the pictures to tell a story and understanding stories they listen to. During this time, students also start to develop a favorites list of books that they like to hear again and again.
2. Experiential – students realize that print carries meaning. During this phase they are more concerned with getting the meaning of the words rather than reading the words correctly. They also start to use prior knowledge to predict which words come next.
3. Early reading – students are beginning to reread familiar texts with ease and recognize different forms of writing, such as a letter, a story, a recipe, etc. They can talk about the illustrations in a book and can retell a story in their own words, giving details about the setting, character and plot.
4. Transitional reading – students can integrate many of the features of the text to construct meaning. They can recognize stereotyping and prejudice in a text and can select different reading material to suit different purposes.

5. Independent reading – students can recognize various forms of writing and express their response in writing. They can comprehend abstract topics and can make connections between sections of the text.

Self-Monitoring- When students self-monitor, they are able to keep track of all the factors themselves involved in the process. In this way, they are able to process the information in the manner that is best for them.

Additionally, the teacher can look at the student's ability to monitor their own reading and comprehension. Noting these self-monitoring attempts, allows the teacher to see if the student recognizes when they make a mistake which does not make sense. This is a very important skill for readers to develop. Once they realize something does not make sense, are they able to go back and then apply a correction strategy so as to not hinder comprehension. This becomes more important as the complexity of text increases.

Self-corrections by students begin to show a maturity of reading skills. However, students who make a tremendous amount of self-corrections lack fluency in reading and will eventually lose some comprehension. It is an important step to begin for readers, but as with any other learning process, we want students to pass through it rapidly, leaving in its place fluent, well comprehended reading.

In the instruction of reading, fluent reading has often been an overlooked, undertaught skill in schools. It was with the research review from the work of the National Reading Panel, that fluency came to the forefront.

The research has indicated that there is a correlation that a child who reads fluently will be more likely to comprehend the text than a child who does not demonstrate fluent reading. Since the end result of all reading is comprehension, or the understanding of what one has read, this body of research cannot be ignored.

Reading fluency is a broad term that is used to describe reading that has a high degree of accuracy, appropriate phrasing, is smooth and is paced fittingly for the text. In order to achieve all of these areas, it requires the child to be able to decode words in a very automatic and rapid way.

As reading is a complex task, it requires many cognitive processes to occur simultaneously. Efficient and automatic decoding of text allows the student to free up some of these cognitive processes to better address other areas, particularly comprehension. The child who struggles with decoding spends so much mental energy attempting to decode words that there is not enough of a reserve to be able to adequately address the comprehension issues.

Fluency develops over time and with much repetition and practice. The analogy is often drawn to learning to drive a car. When an individual is first learning to drive a car, they must concentrate on every little aspect involved. Which foot is the accelerator, how much pressure to place on the pedal, how to keep the car within the lane, etc. Often distractions such as pedestrians or radio noise cause large over corrections or require additional time for the newer drivers to respond correctly. However, as the driver becomes more skilled, he spends less energy on those more rote tasks previously described. He now has more time to devote to anticipating events. In some cases, he can use his mental energy to think about things unrelated to driving completely. How many times have you driven somewhere and not remembered how you got there? This is because for you driving has become automatic and freed you up for other more complex cognitive thoughts.

This automatic nature in reading is essential as the amount of information in texts grows and students are required to comprehend more and more information in order to be successful. Imagine trying to proceed through a college level course or text if you had to spend time decoding every word presented. You would gain nothing from the work and time you devoted, thus it is vital that students develop automaticity with decoding.

Skill 3.3 Analyze major theories of language development, cognition, and learning

Over the years, theories regarding language development have been very vocal and disagreed in many levels. The major disagreement can be tracked back to the 1950's where two predominant theories emerged.

Behaviorism developed and believed that language was the direct result of the situations surrounding the child. Behaviorists believed that the environment controlled all language and solely these outside forces influenced its development.

On the other hand, nativism theorists believed that all language was similar to genetic traits. They believed that language was determined before birth and developed in a similar manner to other innate characteristics. They ruled out that any outside factors could influence the development process.

Currently, these two opposing viewpoints have been combined to form the interactionist theories. This term indicates that children's language skills are a direct result of inherent predetermined skills and the surrounding environment.

It is this combination approach that is most accepted in today's society. In relation to reading, it is important to understand the fact that reading is language based. Children who struggle in language developmental will almost certainly have difficulty obtaining a solid foundation in reading skills.

As language developments, students begin to understand how sounds blend together to form words, how words go together to form sentences, and how sentences go together to form stories. It is through these stories and sentences that meaning is conveyed from one party to another.

If a student is unable to convey that meaning or draw conclusions from the message that someone else is sending, they miss a key component of language development. With this skill missing, the natural progression that text conveys meaning is also missed. Since the ultimate goal of reading is comprehension or understanding, one can see the significant deficit these children experience.

Speech pathologists who specialize in language development can therefore be an essential component to preventing and helping children with language disorders. In this way, these trained specialists can also help in preventing and remediating language issues, which will help reading skills.

In summary, language development is crucial to the progress students will experience in reading. Language and reading go hand in hand and this fact should be remembered when bringing in professionals with expertise to help work with children who are struggling.

Skill 3.4   Describe experiences that support literacy

Reading for enjoyment makes it possible to go to places in the world we will never be able to visit, or perhaps when we learn about the enchantments of a particular place, we will set a goal of going there someday. When *Under the Tuscan Sun* by Frances Mayes was published, it became a best seller. It also increased tourism to Italy. Many of the readers of that book visited Italy for the first time in their lives.

In fiction, we can live through experiences that we will never encounter. We delve into feelings that are similar to our own or are so far removed from our own that we are filled with wonder and curiosity. In fact, we read because we're curious— curious to visit, experience, and know new and different things. The reader lives with a crowd of people and a vast landscape. Life is constantly being enriched by the reading, and the mind is constantly being expanded. To read is to grow. Sometimes the experience of reading a particular book or story is so delicious that we go back and read it again and again, such as the works of Jane Austen. We keep track of what is truly happening in the world when we read current best-sellers because they not only reflect what everyone else is interested in right now, they can influence trends. We can know in-depth what television news cannot cram in by reading publications like *Time* and *Newsweek*.

How do we model this wonderful gift for our students? We can bring those interesting stories into our classrooms and share the excitement we feel when we discover them. We can relate things that make us laugh so students may see the humor and laugh with us. We can vary the established curriculum to include something we are reading that we want to share. The tendency of students nowadays is to receive all of their information from television or the internet. It's important for the teacher to help students understand that television and the internet are not substitutes for reading. They should be an accessory, an extension, a springboard for reading.

Another thing teachers can do to inspire students to become readers is to assign a book that you have never read before and read along with them, chapter by chapter. Run a contest and the winner gets to pick a book that you and they will read chapter by chapter. If you are excited about it and are experiencing satisfaction from the reading, that excitement will be contagious. Be sure that the discussion sessions allow for students to relate what they are thinking and feeling about what they are reading. Lively discussions and the opportunity to express their own feelings will lead to more spontaneous reading.

You can also hand out a reading list of your favorite books and spend some time telling the students what you liked about each. Make sure the list is diverse. It's good to include nonfiction along with fiction. Don't forget that a good biography or autobiography may encourage students to read beyond thrillers and detective stories.

When the class is discussing the latest movie, whether formally as a part of the curriculum or informally and incidentally, if the movie is based on a book, this is a good opportunity to demonstrate how much more can be derived from the reading than from the watching. Or how the two combined make the experience more satisfying and worthwhile.

Share with your students the excitement you have for reading. Successful writers are usually good readers. The two go hand-in-hand.

In the past teachers have assigned reports, paragraphs and essays that focused on the teacher as the audience with the purpose of explaining information. However, for students to be meaningfully engaged in their writing, they must write for a variety of reasons. Writing for different audiences and aims allows students to be more involved in their writing. If they write for the same audience and purpose, they will continue to see writing as just another assignment. Listed below are suggestions that give students an opportunity to write in more creative and critical ways.

* Write letters to the editor, to a college, to a friend, to another student that would be sent to the intended audience.

* Write stories that would be read aloud to a group (the class, another group of students, to a group of elementary school students) or published in a literary magazine or class anthology.

* Write plays that would be performed.

* Have students discuss the parallels between the different speech styles we use and writing styles for different readers or audiences.

* Allow students to write a particular piece for different audiences.

* Expose students to writing that is on the same topic but with a different audience and have them identify the variations in sentence structure and style.

Make sure students consider the following when analyzing the needs of their audience.

1. Why is the audience reading my writing? Do they expect to be informed, amused or persuaded?
2. What does my audience already know about my topic?
3. What does the audience want or need to know? What will interest them?
4. What type of language suits my readers?

Remind your students that it is not necessary to identify all the specifics of the audience in the initial stage of the writing process but that at some point they must make some determinations about audience.

1. **Values**- What is important to this group of people? What is their background and how will that affect their perception of your speech?
2. **Needs**- Find out in advance what the audience's needs are. Why are they listening to you? Find a way to satisfy their needs.
3. **Constraints**- What might hold the audience back from being fully engaged in what you are saying, or agreeing with your point of view, or processing what you are trying to say?
4. These could be political reasons, which make them wary of your presentation's ideology from the start, or knowledge reasons, in which the audience lacks the appropriate background information to grasp your ideas. Avoid this last constraint by staying away from technical terminology, slang, or abbreviations that may be unclear to your audience.
5. **Demographic Information**- Take the audience's size into account, as well as the location of the presentation.

Creation of an environment that promotes love of reading

The physical layout of the classroom can also promote literacy and a love of reading. For example, the creation of a meeting area with a reading chair (sometimes a rocking chair) with throw pillows around it, promotes a love of reading. Beyond that, some classrooms have adopted a author's hat, decorated with the pictures of famous authors and book characters which children wear when they read from their own works.

Many classrooms also have children's storyboards, artwork, story maps, pop-up books, and "in style ofs" inspired by specific authors displayed. Some teachers buy calendars for the daily schedule, which celebrate children's authors or types of literature. In addition, the Read Aloud selection is generally attractively displayed against an easel. Children are also encouraged to bring in public library books and special books from their home libraries.

The teacher can model this habit of sharing beautiful books and inviting stories from his or her home library.

In addition, news stories about children's authors, series books, television versions of books, theatrical film versions of books, stuffed toy book character decorations and other memorabilia related to books can be used to decorate the room.

Various chain book stores including Barnes and Nobles and Borders give out free book marks and promotional display materials related to children's books which can be available in the room for children to use as they read independently or in their guided groups. They might even use these artistic models to inspire their own book themed artifacts or souvenir design.

Skill 3.5   Recognize the value of responding personally, analytically, and critically to a variety of written texts

Define author's purpose: to inform, to entertain, to persuade. Student activity: A title can often set the tone of the passage. Reading newspaper headings is one way to practice determining the author's purpose.

Cause and effect: Cause and effect may occur in fiction, nonfiction, poetry, and plays. Sometimes one cause will have single or multiple effects. Other times, multiple causes lead to a single effect. Creating cause and effect diagrams helps you identify these components.

Chronological order: Recognizing the order of events in a selection. A text that is chronologically organized features a sequence of events that unfold over a period of time. Student activity: Read a passage to the students then complete a timeline by matching the major events to their corresponding dates.

Graphic organizers: Graphic organizers help readers think critically about an idea, concept, or story by pulling out the main idea and supporting details. These pieces of information can then be depicted graphically through the use of connected geometric shapes. Readers who develop this skill can use it to increase their reading comprehension. An example of a graphic organizer is below.

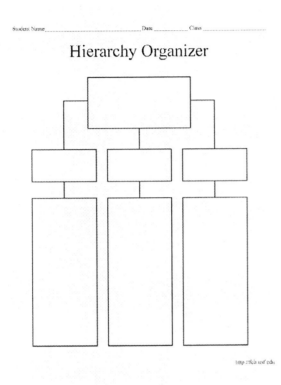

Student Name .... Date .... Class ....

Hierarchy Organizer

http://fcit.usf.edu

Probable passage: Probable passage is a strategy to improve comprehension, develop an awareness of story structure, and increase vocabulary development. Student activity: Have a story prepared to read to the students. Then put together a chart similar to the one below. Ask the students, "Can you predict the story you will be reading? Use the vocabulary words from your story frame to complete the probable passage by placing words into the blanks."

Vocabulary:
   Zeus
   recognized
   pardoned
   arena
   forest
   bound
   freed
   capture
   lion

Setting: _____

Characters: _____

Problem: _____

Solution: _____

Ending: _____

Selective underlining: Selective underlining is an effective tool for enhancing the recall of facts. It can be used both for initial reading and response, and as a reference when studying for tests. Have students identify the main idea of various short stories and articles.

Story mapping: Story mapping is a technique used after a story has been read. It includes identifying the main elements and categorizing the main events in sequential order. A graphic representation is often used to illustrate the story structure and sequence of events.

When preparing to read a book, the analyst should become acquainted with the elements of the story such as setting, characterization, style (language, both technically with regard to dialect but also structurally with regard to use of description, length of sentences, phrases, etc.), plot (particularly conflicts and pattern), tone (what is the *attitude* of the writer toward characters, theme, etc.) and particularly theme (the message or point the story conveys). It's not essential to know the writer's biography, but it is often helpful, especially in responding from the analyst's point of view.

Literature is written to evoke a personal response in readers. This is why so many books are sold. Once the analyst has a grip on the story—a thorough understanding of the story—then an analysis of one's own response to it is in order.

The following questions are useful:

1. Do you respond emotionally to one of the characters? Why? Is a character similar to someone you know or have known?
2. Is the setting evocative for you because of a place, situation, or milieu that you have experienced and that had meaning for you? Why?
3. Did the vocabulary, descriptions, or short or long sentences have impact on you? Why? For example, short, simple sentence after short, simple sentence may be used deliberately, but do you find it annoying?
4. Do you agree with the author's attitude toward the characters, setting, story, etc.? For example, has a character been written unsympathetically that you felt deserved more consideration? Does the author demonstrate a distaste for the setting he has chosen, and do you feel he is being unjust? Or do you experience the same distaste? Etc.

See Skill 16.2 for more information.

Skill 3.6 **Identify past and present literacy leaders and describing their contributions to the knowledge base**

Directory of Theorists and Researchers

<u>Introduction</u>
Many questions on the teacher certification examinations can only be correctly answered if you know the theorist or the research that is referenced. The teaching of reading owes much to the work, principles and guidelines of teacher educators and university field researchers who have changed the style, methods and practice of teaching reading. While those listed in this directory are by no means all the major researchers (page constraints would make a complete listing impossible), the individuals listed below are those whose contributions are frequently referenced on the certification tests and whose work is evident in today's elementary classroom teaching and learning of reading.

PHONICS CENTERED APPROACH

In 1955 Rudolph Flesch gained national prominence when he publishedx *Why Johnny Can't Read*. This book went on to become a best seller and has now become a classic which is readable and speaks to current concerns. Flesch became the spokesperson for a war that periodically resurfaces in the reading world.

Flesch, Chall (1967) Stahl (1992), Adams (1990), and Johnson and Bauman (1984) believe that a phonics-based approach is crucial for reading success. Flesch and others feel that the balanced literacy advocates are seriously undermining the crucial role that phonics plays in the children's development as successful decoding readers. However, it must be noted that while balanced literacy does emphasize the use of literature based reading programs, it in no way dismisses phonics from its reading program; indeed phonics is included in the crucial "word work" component of the reading and writing workshop.

The phonics advocates point to the fact that most research shows that early and systematic instruction in phonics skills results in superior reading achievement in elementary school and beyond.

Adams (1990) detailed what type of phonics instruction is needed.

To learn to read skillfully, children need practice in seeing and understanding decodable words in real reading situations and with connected text.... phonics instruction {needs to be} part of a reading program that provides ample practice in reading and writing. Encouraging children with connected text can also show them the importance of what they are learning and make the lessons in phonics relevant and sensible. Phonics centered advocates believe that children should begin to learn letter associations in kindergarten with most useful phonics skills being taught by first grade. These basic skills should then be reviewed in second grade and beyond.

Consonant sounds should be taught first, since they are more reliable in their letter-sound associations.

Short vowel sounds appear more frequently in beginning reading materials, so they should be introduced before long vowels. Phonics advocates believe that most beginning readers need to be taught letter sound associations explicitly. Phonics advocates also believe that beginning readers need to read stories that have words to which phonics skills apply. This allows them to practice their phonics skills as they write and spell words. They should also play lots of letter-sound association games.

Phonics advocates claim that when phonics is abandoned reading scores drop and balanced literacy advocates counter with the fact that they have never advocated abandoning the teaching of phonics.

As Jeanne Chall, a professor at Harvard's Graduate School of Education notes: "a beginning reading program that does not give children knowledge and skill in recognizing and decoding words will have poor results."

Theorists and Researchers:

Adams, Marilyn Jager

Noted for her research on early reading, Adams lists five basic types of phonemic awareness tasks which should be covered by the end of first grade. These include: ability to hear rhymes and alliterations, ability to do oddity tasks, ability to orally blend words, ability to orally segment words, ability to do phonemic manipulation tasks.

Clay, Marie M. Marie

A New Zealand born researcher, in the field of special needs emergent literacy and in the development of assessment tools for these children. Her research in this field is felt throughout the Reading Recovery movement and involves the use of her, *Reading Recovery: A Guidebook for Teachers in Training,* in the majority of graduate emergent literacy courses and in many classrooms in the US including those that do not have a Reading Recovery teacher.

Her doctoral thesis focused on what was to become her life's work, emergent reading behavior. At the crux of her research for the dissertation, Clay reviewed and detailed the progress week by week of one hundred children during their first year of school (1966). An important outcome of the dissertation was her development of reliable observation tools for the assessment and analysis of changes over time in children's literacy learning. These assessments are the crux of *An Observation Survey of Early Literacy Achievement* (1993) which is an essential work for the primary school educator. The assessments have been validated and reconstructed for learners from the Spanish, Maori and French languages. A special appendix in this guide includes the *Record of Reading Behavior* tool she created with Kenneth Goodman.

Reading Recovery is a key Clay contribution to the field of foundations of reading teaching. The movement, which is discussed in detail in this section, was born out of the concerns of classroom educators who were upset that even with excellent programs and expert teaching, they were not able to positively influence the literacy progress of some of their young children. Clay posed the question of investigating what would happen if the design and delivery of traditional reading education were changed for these struggling young learners.

The whole thrust of the Reading Recovery movement has been to improve the early identification and instructional delivery for these struggling young readers. Her goal was to develop a system which would bring those children scoring the lowest in assessment measures to the level of the average readers within their classes.

With the support of Barbara Watson and others, the program was developed in three years. The first field tests of the program took place in the late 1970's in Auckland schools. To date, circa 2005, the program is operating in most English speaking countries and has been reconstructed for use in Spanish and French.

Janet S. Gaffey and Billie Askew have said of Marie Clay (l991) that her contribution "has been to change what is possible for individual learners when teaching permits different routes to be taken for desired outcomes."

Reading Recovery has been identified by the International Reading Association as a program that not only teaches children how to read, but also reduces the number of children who are labeled as "learning disabled." It further lowers the number of children who are placed in remedial reading programs and classes.

Clay Reading Recovery lessons are designed to promote accelerated learning so that children can catch up to their peers and continue to learn independently.

The hallmark of the Reading Recovery program is that the Reading Recovery teacher works with one student at a time over a 12 to 20 week period. Each daily 30 minute lesson is tailored to address the needs of the individual student. Therefore Reading Recovery teachers generally teach no more than four or five students per day in individual lessons.

The Clay Observation of Early Childhood Achievement (l993) is used to assess children's strengths and weaknesses. Reading Recovery teachers devote the first ten minutes of their sessions with individual children to assessment as the children engage in reading and writing. A running record of the child's progress is taken every day and is used to plan future lessons.

The lessons themselves include the use of familiar stories. Children engage in assembling and in sequencing cut up stories. They work with letters or write a story. Teaching style involves the teacher demonstrating strategies and the child then developing effective strategies to continue reading independently. Key components of each lesson include: phonemic awareness, phonics, spelling, and comprehension study. Much time is devoted to problem solving so that the children's decoding is purposeful. Children are given time to practice and demonstrate fluency skills.

Ultimately what sets Reading Recovery aside is the fact that it is one-to-one tutoring. This is also what makes it effective for children, and of course, what raises issues about it are costs for the school systems which may want to adopt it. Obviously the districts and education systems have to decide whether they want to pay the costs of this and other individualized tutoring systems now in the primary school years or pay later as these children become adults whose literacy skills are not sufficient for proactive citizenship.

Fountas, Irene C and Gay Su Pinnell

These two researchers have developed a leveling system for reading texts, which arranges them by level of difficulty. Beyond a specific analysis of set titles, the theorists have explained in several published works how to use their leveling system to meet and assess the progress of various readers. They also provide detailed explanations and support for reading teachers of young children K-3 in using reading records and benchmark texts.

They are the key articulators of the balanced literacy model that includes reading and writing workshop. Among their other contributions to the field are: guidelines for creating sets of leveled books, assessment rubrics, strategies for fostering "word solver" skills in child readers, and methods for teaching phonics and spelling in the literacy classroom.

Routman, Regie

Routman's contributions to Reading Foundations are the result of over three decades of experience as an elementary school teacher, a reading specialist, a learning disabilities tutor, a Reading Recovery teacher, a language arts and mentor teacher and a staff developer. Due to these various experiences, her insights into reading resonate with a broad spectrum of school community members.

Routman's works are conversational, teacher to teacher sharings of her daily experiences in classrooms. In her published books on the teaching of reading (i.e. *Reading Essentials*-Heinemann, 2002), Regie shows teachers how to teach consistent with the findings in reading research, yet also with highly practical "scripted lessons" and teaching tips which make the classroom come alive. She advocates literature based teaching and meaning centered approaches for learning.

In addition, she is a strong advocate of using poetry from grades one and beyond as an integral thread for a reading program. She is the author of *Kids' Poems: Teaching Children to Love Writing Poetry* (Scholastic, 2000) which includes separate volumes of poetry for grades K-4.

Routman believes in teaching reading to meet specific children's needs regardless of the particular reading program in place. She is a strong advocate for the use of small guided reading groups and reading for understanding. Phonics and other word analysis strategies are part of her reading framework, but not at its core. Her focus for the reading classroom is on the development and the use of the classroom library as the center for an independent reading program, shared reading and reading aloud.

Routman has designed informal reading evaluations on books/texts her students are reading (her published works are known for their appendices replete with templates for evaluations, projects, reports, book lists, suggested texts by topics etc.). Her classroom model includes matching children with specific library books as well as linking assessment with instruction. Finally she is a researcher who sees reading as intimately linked to writing.

Routman is also involved with the politics of literacy. This vision of literacy involves the image of the teacher, as an informed professional, who regularly reads the latest professional books, collaborates with colleagues in school and beyond, and deals with the most recent research developments. Interestingly, Routman is one researcher who also feels that an informed professional can and should know when to question research. Other aspects of the politics of literacy as Routman conceptualizes them are: communicating effectively with parents and dealing with testing and standards mandates.

Two of her published works, *Conversations: Strategies for Teaching, Learning, and Evaluating* (Heinemann, 2000) and *Invitations: Changing as Teachers and Learners k-12* (Heinemann, 1991 and 1994) are essential for the elementary reading teacher's bookshelf and can take the teacher through several years of work.

Taberski, Sharon
Taberski is an experienced elementary teacher educator who is also a member of the Primary Literacy Standards Committee run by the National Center on Education and the Economy and the University of Pittsburgh. Her works in the field are served up as wonderfully accessible and necessary advice from "the veteran teacher across the hall" who loves her students and is delighted to help a new colleague.

Unlike many theorists in the field of reading, Taberski's work is not focused around a prescribed set of skills, but rather around a series of interconnected interactions with the learner.

Among these interactions which are detailed and clearly communicated in her book *On Solid Ground* (2000-Heinemann) are:

- Assessment- Procedures for assessing children's reading, and to inform teaching, scheduling and managing reading conferences, taking oral reading records, and using retellings as discussion tools.
- Demonstration- Taberski developed and field tested strategies for using shared reading and read aloud as platforms for figuring out words and comprehending texts. She is a strong advocate of small group work- guided reading, word-study groups and teaching children one on one.
- Practice- In the Taberski framework, independent reading is used as a time for practice. Students play key roles in this practice and Sharon has a set of detailed and easily adaptable guidelines for matching children with books for independent reading. Her work includes booklists and ready to use information that is available for reproduction.
- Response- It's important for students to know that they are doing well and where they must focus their efforts to improve skills. Taberski explains how her students use writing and dialogue as tools for independent reading.

Vail, Priscilla

Noted for her research in the study of dyslexia and its myths, Vail has articulated ways in which children can develop their reading skills as they cope with this disorder and techniques parents and educators can use to support reading development. She has also worked on specific test taking skills for children coping with dyslexia and other special needs. Her strategies can be infused in the regular education program to enhance all students' reading achievement schools. She is a proponent of phonics instruction and skills within the context of an integrated whole language approach (once called integrated language arts).

Another focus of Vail's research is the link between language and thinking. She is concerned with how a child's receptive language, expressive language and metacognition can be fostered. She has developed assessment methods for each of these capacities and activities to help strengthen them in children grades k-4.

COMPETENCY 4.0 ANALYZE THE INTEGRATED NATURE OF THE ENGLISH LANGUAGE ARTS

Skill 4.1   Identify and compare individual English language arts

In order to take students from where they are in English language arts to the next level of reading and writing, teachers need to know the individual levels of the students. Both formal and informal assessment should be a regular part of the classroom. Assessment for learning will help to lead the direction that the instruction needs to take. All students will not be at the same level or need the same supports. By using the balanced literacy model, teachers are better able to individualize their lessons to provide the instruction that all students need.

A comprehensive English language arts program should contain the following components:
1 Skills mini-lessons
2 Reading based on the skills lessons
3 Independent reading
4 Work with words
5 Shared and independent writing
6 Read alouds
7 Author and novel studies
8 Student projects
9 Language arts integration with the content areas
10 Student conferencing (with teacher and with peers)

Teachers should also be familiar with current research with regards to integrating all the components of language arts. The Internet is a valuable source of information in this regard with respect to the International Reading Association, best practices for teachers in language arts and in specific grades. Two sites of interest are www.teachersfirst.com and www.literacyuconn.edu.

See skill 3.1 for more information

Reading emphasis in middle school

Reading for comprehension of factual material - content area textbooks, reference books, and newspapers - is closely related to study strategies in the middle/junior high. Organized study models, such as the SQ3R method, a technique that makes it possible and feasible to learn the content of even large amounts of text (Survey, Question, Read, Recite, and Review Studying), teach students to locate main ideas and supporting details, to recognize sequential order, to distinguish fact from opinion, and to determine cause/ effect relationships.

Strategies

1. Teacher-guided activities that require students to organize and to summarize information based on the author's explicit intent are pertinent strategies in middle grades. Evaluation techniques include oral and written responses to standardized or teacher-made worksheets.

2. Reading of fiction introduces and reinforces skills in inferring meaning from narration and description. Teaching-guided activities in the process of reading for meaning should be followed by cooperative planning of the skills to be studied and of the selection of reading resources. Many printed reading for comprehension instruments as well as individualized computer software programs exist to monitor the progress of acquiring comprehension skills.

3. Older middle school students should be given opportunities for more student-centered activities - individual and collaborative selection of reading choices based on student interest, small group discussions of selected works, and greater written expression. Evaluation techniques include teacher monitoring and observation of discussions and written work samples.

4. Certain students may begin some fundamental critical interpretation - recognizing fallacious reasoning in news media, examining the accuracy of news reports and advertising, explaining their reasons for preferring one author's writing to another's. Development of these skills may require a more learning-centered approach in which the teacher identifies a number of objectives and suggested resources from which the student may choose his course of study. Self-evaluation through a reading diary should be stressed. Teacher and peer evaluation of creative projects resulting from such study is encouraged.

5. Reading aloud before the entire class as a formal means of teacher evaluation should be phased out in favor of one-to-one tutoring or peer-assisted reading. Occasional sharing of favored selections by both teacher and willing students is a good oral interpretation basic.

Reading emphasis in high school

Students in high school literature classes should focus on interpretive and critical reading. Teachers should guide the study of the elements of inferential (interpretive) reading - drawing conclusions, predicting outcomes, and recognizing examples of specific genre characteristics, for example - and critical reading to judge the quality of the writer's work against recognized standards. At this level students should understand the skills of language and reading that they are expected to master and be able to evaluate their own progress.

Strategies

1. The teacher becomes more facilitator than instructor - helping the student to make a diagnosis of his own strengths and weaknesses, keeping a record of progress, and interacting with other students and the teacher in practicing skills.

2. Despite the requisites and prerequisites of most literature courses, students should be encouraged to pursue independent study and enrichment reading.

3. Ample opportunities should be provided for oral interpretation of literature, special projects in creative dramatics, writing for publication in school literary magazines or newspapers, and speech/debate activities. A student portfolio provides for teacher and peer evaluation.

When preparing to read a book, the analyst should become acquainted with the elements of the story such as setting, characterization, style (language, both technically with regard to dialect but also structurally with regard to use of description, length of sentences, phrases, etc.), plot (particularly conflicts and pattern), tone (what is the *attitude* of the writer toward characters, theme, etc.) and particularly theme (the message or point the story conveys). It's not essential to know the writer's biography, but it is often helpful, especially in responding from the analyst's point of view.

Literature is written to evoke a personal response in readers. This is why so many books are sold. Once the analyst has a grip on the story—a thorough understanding of the story—then an analysis of one's own response to it is in order.

Skill 4.2   Recognize the value of students integrating their use of reading, writing, listening, speaking, viewing, and visually representing (e.g. mutual reinforcement of complementary skills, building on the students' authentic uses of language)

Over the years, theories regarding language development have been very vocal and disagreed in many levels. The major disagreement can be tracked back to the 1950's where two predominant theories emerged.

Behaviorism developed and believed that language was the direct result of the situations surrounding the child. Behaviorists believed that the environment controlled all language and solely these outside forces influenced its development.

On the other hand, nativism theorists believed that all language was similar to genetic traits. They believed that language was determined before birth and developed in a similar manner to other innate characteristics. They ruled out that any outside factors could influence the development process.

Currently, these two opposing viewpoints have been combined to form the interactionist theories. This term indicates that children's language skills are a direct result of inherent predetermined skills and the surrounding environment.

It is this combination approach that is most accepted in today's society. In relation to reading, it is important to understand the fact that reading is language based. Children who struggle in language developmental will almost certainly have difficulty obtaining a solid foundation in reading skills.

As language developments, students begin to understand how sounds blend together to form words, how words go together to form sentences, and how sentences go together to form stories. It is through these stories and sentences that meaning is conveyed from one party to another.

If a student is unable to convey that meaning or draw conclusions from the message that someone else is sending, they miss a key component of language development. With this skill missing, the natural progression that text conveys meaning is also missed. Since the ultimate goal of reading is comprehension or understanding, one can see the significant deficit these children experience.

Speech pathologists who specialize in language development can therefore be an essential component to preventing and helping children with language disorders. In this way, these trained specialists can also help in preventing and remediating language issues, which will help reading skills.

In summary, language development is crucial to the progress students will experience in reading. Language and reading go hand in hand and this fact should be remembered when bringing in professionals with expertise to help work with children who are struggling.

See skill 6.1 for more information

Skill 4.3   Describe the benefits of students acting in all aspects of literacy (e.g., as readers, writers, responders)

See Skills 4.1 and 4.2

COMPETENCY 5.0   DEMONSTRATE KNOWLEDGE OF THE EFFECTS OF VARIOUS FACTORS ON LANGUAGE DEVELOPMENT, READING ACQUISITION, AND THE PROMOTION OF LITERACY.

Skill 5.1   Describe the effects of factors (e.g., emotional, perceptual, environmental) on a student's learning, language development, and reading acquisition

Learning is the ultimate goal of all schooling systems. When a student has an exceptionality in one or more areas quite often learning is impacted. In cases where learning is impacted, special education services are warranted. Various exceptionalities can impact learning in a variety of ways, all of which are unique to each student individually. However, there are some overriding generalizations which can be drawn.

Language Disorders: Students with language disorders have difficulty understanding language, expressing themselves, or communicating. When this occurs, learning is impacted significantly. As language of some form is the main method in which information to be learned is conveyed to the student, a breakdown is imminent. Students with language disorders may need specific clarification, visual cuing and support, and other modifications to overcome these difficulties.

Processing Deficits: Processing deficits affect the manner in which students take the information presented and transfer it into something meaningful to themselves. When a student has difficulties processing information, they often will arrive at misconceptions. These misconceptions require specific clarification for the correct learning to occur.

Cognitive Disorders: Cognitive disorders affect the ability the student has to acquire new information. There are many different levels of cognitive disorders all of which affect the types and amount of new information which can be learned by these students.

Behavior/Emotional/Social Disorders: Students who struggle in these domains often have difficulty learning. The difficulties arise from the inability of the more basic needs the student may have being met before more higher level (learning) can take place. For these students, management of the behavior and emotions needs to occur and be secure before students are able to take in the more academic concepts.

Physical/Sensory Disabilities: Students with physical disabilities alone may need accommodations to be able to access the information presented. Learning needs to be maneuvered in such a manner as to allow the student to have equal opportunity to engage in the same learning experiences as those with no physical issues. Once these opportunities are presented, learning will follow in a manner similar to those without physical disabilities.

A positive self-concept for a child or adolescent is a very important element in terms of the students' ability to learn and to be an integral member of society. If students think poorly of themselves or have sustained feelings of inferiority, they probably will not be able to optimize their potentials for learning. It is therefore part of the teacher's task to ensure that each student develops a positive self-concept.

A positive self-concept does not imply feelings of superiority, perfection, or competence/efficacy. Instead, a positive self-concept involves self-acceptance as a person, liking himself or herself, and having a proper respect for oneself. The teacher who encourages these factors has contributed to the development of a positive self-concept in students.

Teachers may take a number of approaches to enhancement of self-concept among students. One such scheme is the process approach, which proposes a three-phase model for teaching. This model includes a sensing function, a transforming function, and an acting function. These three factors can be simplified into the words by which the model is usually given: reach, touch, and teach. The sensing, or perceptual, function incorporates information or stimuli in an intuitive manner. The transforming function conceptualizes, abstracts, evaluates, and provides meaning and value to perceived information. The acting function chooses actions from several different alternatives to be set forth overtly. The process model may be applied to almost any curricular field.

An approach that aims directly at the enhancement of self concept is designated Invitational Education. According to this approach, teachers and their behaviors may be inviting or they may be disinviting. Inviting behaviors enhance self-concept among students, while disinviting behaviors diminish self-concept.

Disinviting behaviors include those that demean students, as well as those that may be chauvinistic, sexist, condescending, thoughtless, or insensitive to student feelings. Inviting behaviors are the opposite of these, and characterize teachers who act with consistency and sensitivity. Inviting teacher behaviors reflect an attitude of "doing with" rather than "doing to." Students are "invited" or "disinvited" depending on the teacher behaviors.

Invitational teachers exhibit the following skills (Biehler and Snowman, 394):

   a) reaching each student (e.g., learning names, having one-to-one contact)
   b) listening with care (e.g., picking up subtle cues)
   c) being real with students (e.g., providing only realistic praise, "coming on straight")
   d) being real with oneself (e.g., honestly appraising your own feelings and disappointments)
   e) inviting good discipline (e.g., showing students you have respect in personal ways)
   f) handling rejection (e.g., not taking lack of student response in personal ways)
   g) inviting oneself (e.g., thinking positively about oneself)

Cooperative learning situations, as practiced in today's classrooms, grew out of searches conducted by several groups in the early 1970's. Cooperative learning situations can range from very formal applications such as STAD (Student Teams-Achievement Divisions) and CIRC (Cooperative Integrated Reading and Composition) to less formal groupings known variously as "group investigation," "learning together," "discovery groups." Cooperative learning as a general term is now firmly recognized and established as a teaching and learning technique in American schools. Since cooperative learning techniques are so widely diffused in the schools, it is necessary to orient students in the skills by which cooperative learning groups can operate smoothly, and thereby enhance learning. Students who cannot interact constructively with other students will not be able to take advantage of the learning opportunities provided by the cooperative learning situations and will furthermore deprive their fellow students of the opportunity for cooperative learning.

These skills form the hierarchy of cooperation in which students first learn to work together as a group, so they may then proceed to levels at which they may engage in simulated conflict situations. This cooperative setting allows different points of view to be constructively entertained.

Effective teaching and learning for students begins with teachers who can demonstrate sensitivity for diversity in teaching and relationships within school communities. Student portfolios include work that has a multicultural perspective and inclusion where students share cultural and ethnic life experiences in their learning. Teachers are responsive to including cultural and diverse resources in their curriculum and instructional practices.

Exposing students to culturally sensitive room decorations and posters that show positive and inclusive messages is one way to demonstrate inclusion of multiple cultures. Teachers should also continuously make cultural connections that are relevant and empowering for all students and communicate academic and behavioral expectations. Cultural sensitivity is communicated beyond the classroom with parents and community members to establish and maintain relationships.

Diversity can be further defined as the following:
1 Differences among learners, classroom settings and academic outcomes
2 Biological, sociological, ethnicity, socioeconomic status psychological needs, learning modalities and styles among learners
3 Differences in classroom settings that promote learning opportunities such as collaborative, participatory, and individualized learning groupings
4 Expected learning outcomes that are theoretical, affective and cognitive for students

(a) Teachers establish a classroom climate that is culturally respectful and engaging for students. In a culturally sensitive classroom, teachers maintain equity and fairness in student interactions and curriculum implementation. Assessments include cultural responses and perspectives that become further learning opportunities for students. T
Other artifacts that could reflect teacher/student sensitivity to diversity might consist of the following:

1 Student portfolios reflecting multicultural/multiethnic perspectives
2 Journals and reflections from field trips/ guest speakers from diverse cultural backgrounds
3 Printed materials and wall displays from multicultural perspectives
4 Parent/guardian letters in a variety of languages reflecting cultural diversity
5 Projects that include cultural history and diverse inclusions
6 Disaggregated student data reflecting cultural groups
7 Classroom climate of professionalism that fosters diversity and cultural inclusion

The target of diversity allows teachers a variety of opportunities to expand their experiences with students, staff, community members and parents from culturally diverse backgrounds, so that their experiences can be proactively applied in promoting cultural diversity inclusion in the classroom. Teachers are able to engage and challenge students to develop and incorporate their own diversity skills in building character and relationships with cultures beyond their own. In changing the thinking patterns of students to become more cultural inclusive in the 21st century, teachers are addressing the globalization of our world.

Skill 5.2 Recognize the influence of culture and language on a student's instructional needs

Adolescent literature, because of the age range of readers, is extremely diverse. Fiction for the middle group, usually ages ten/eleven to fourteen/fifteen, deals with issues of coping with internal and external changes in their lives. Because children's writers in the twentieth century have produced increasingly realistic fiction, adolescents can now find problems dealt with honestly in novels.

Teachers of middle/junior high school students see the greatest change in interests and reading abilities. Fifth and sixth graders, included in elementary grades in many schools, are viewed as older children while seventh and eighth graders are preadolescent. Ninth graders, included sometimes as top dogs in junior high school and sometimes as underlings in high school, definitely view themselves as teenagers. Their literature choices will often be governed more by interest than by ability; thus, the wealth of high-interest, low readability books that have flooded the market in recent years. Tenth through twelfth graders will still select high-interest books for pleasure reading but are also easily encouraged to stretch their literature muscles by reading more classics.

Because of the rapid social changes, topics that once did not interest young people until they reached their teens - suicide, gangs, homosexuality - are now subjects of books for even younger readers. The plethora of high-interest books reveals how desperately schools have failed to produce on-level readers and how the market has adapted to that need. However, these high-interest books are now readable for younger children whose reading levels are at or above normal. No matter how tastefully written, some contents are inappropriate for younger readers. The problem becomes not so much steering them toward books that they have the reading ability to handle but encouraging them toward books whose content is appropriate to their levels of cognitive and social development. A fifth-grader may be able to read V.C. Andrews book *Flowers in the Attic* but not possess the social/moral development to handle the deviant behavior of the characters. At the same time, because of the complex changes affecting adolescents, the teacher must be well versed in learning theory and child development as well as competent to teach the subject matter of language and literature.

Each child in the classroom, whether it is a primary grade or a high school grade, is at different learning points in his/her development of literacy development. Teachers need to be cognizant of these differences and tailor the instructional experiences to match each learner. In a literature based classroom, students choose books that match their interest. They also read books chosen by the teacher and from books that match their individual reading levels. Thus the teacher becomes a facilitator providing help to the children that need it in phonics, writing and comprehension. Teachers value the differences that children bring to their classrooms and consider different objectives to suit their needs.

Children need to experience success in reading and teachers should celebrate the successes. The teachers also need to realize that parents have different ways of supporting their children in literacy depending on their culture. The teachers provide the models for children reading and writing in the classroom. They do need to communicate the models to the parents so that both of them are on the same page.

Skill 5.3   Analyze the reciprocal relationship between language, culture and individual identity.

See Skills 5.1 and 5.2

Skill 5.4   Determine how contextual factors in the classroom can influence students' learning and reading (e.g., grouping procedures, types of reading tasks, assessment)

There are a variety of assessments, tasks and grouping procedures which will need to be utilized within classrooms to ensure the success of students with their reading instruction. As the teacher, it is imperative to understand the benefits of each type as well as possible drawbacks. For example, some programs are meant to be delivered in a one-on-one setting. Perhaps a student is uncomfortable being pulled out of the regular classroom into this type of setting, in this case, this type of instruction may not be the most appropriate for that particular student.

It is important to know the needs of your students and match them with the most effective strategies for instruction including grouping, tasks and assessments. When considering grouping look at the duration, intensity and size of the group. In considering tasks, it is essential to look at the mode and method for implementation. Is there a learning modality which can be incorporated into the lesson to make it more meaningful for the student? Taking the time to plan and design your instruction well ahead of presenting it to the students will ensure a more productive time for all parties.

DOMAIN II.   GENRES AND CRAFT OF LITERATURE AND LANGUAGE

COMPETENCY 6.0   DEMONSTRATE AN UNDERSTANDING OF LITERATURE WRITTEN FOR STUDENTS.

Skill 6.1   Recognize classic and contemporary children's and young adults' literature, easy-reading fiction, and nonfiction at appropriate levels

Awareness of Text Leveling

The classroom library in the context of the balanced literacy approach to reading instruction is focused on leveled books. These are books which have been leveled with the support of Fountas and Pinnell's Guided Reading: *Good First Teaching for All Children* and *Matching Books to Readers: Using Leveled Reading in Guided Reading,* K-3.

The books which are leveled according to the designations in these reference books need to be stored in bins or crates with front covers facing out. This makes them much easier for the children to identify. In that way the children can go through the appropriate levels and find those books that they are particularly interested in which are also at the right level for them to read. These are those books which the children can read with the right degree of reading accuracy. When young children can see the cover of a book, they are more likely to flip through the book until they can independently identify an appealing book. Then they will read a little bit of the book to see if it's "just right."
"Just right" leveled books, that children can read on their own, need to be available for them to read during independent reading. The goal is for the more fluent readers to select books on their own. Ultimately the use of leveled books helps the children, in addition to the teacher, decide which books are "good" or "just right" for them.

Levels are indicated by means of blue, yellow, red, and green dot stickers at their right upper corners which parallel emergent, early, transitional, and fluent reading stages. They are then kept in containers with other "blue," "yellow," "red," and "green" books.

Other lists and resources other than Fountas and Pinnell which can be used to match children with "just right" books include the Reading Recovery level list. Ultimately, the teacher has to individualize whatever leveling is used in the library to address the individual child learners' needs.

Awareness of the Challenges and Supports in a Text

Illustrations can be key supports for emergent and early readers. Teachers should not only use wordless stories (books which tell their narratives through pictures alone), but can also make targeted use of Big Books for read-alouds, so that young children become habituated to the use of illustrations as an important component for constructing meaning. The teacher should model for the child how to reference an illustration for help in identifying a word in the text the child does not recognize. Of course, children can also go on a picture walk with the teacher as part of a mini-lesson or guided reading and anticipate the story (narrative) using the pictures alone to construct meaning.

Decodability: Use literature which contains examples of letter sound correspondences you wish to teach. First, read the literature with the children or read it aloud to them. Then take a specific example from the text and have the children reread it as the teacher points out the letter-sound correspondence to the children. Then ask the children to go through the now familiar literature to find other letter-sound correspondences. Once the children have correctly made the letter-sound correspondences, have them share similar correspondences they find in other works of literature.

Cooper (2004) suggests that children can become word detectives so that they can independently and fluently decode on their own. The child should learn the following word detective routines so that he or she can function as an independent fluent reader who can decode words on his/her own. First the child should read to the end of a sentence. Then the child should search for word parts which he or she knows. The child should also try to decode the word from the letter sounds. As a last resort, the child should ask someone for help or look up the word in the dictionary.

Techniques for Determining Students' Independent, Instructional and Frustration Reading Levels

Instructional reading is generally judged to be at the 95 percent accuracy level, although, Taberski places it at between 92 and 97 percent. Taberski tries to enhance the independent reading levels by making sure that readers on the instructional reading levels read a variety of genres, and have a range of available and interesting books within a particular genre to read.

Taberski's availability for reading conferences helps her to both assess first hand her children's frustration levels and to model ongoing teacher/reader book conversations by scheduling child-initiated reading conferences when she personally replenishes their book bags.

In order to allay children's frustration levels in their reading and to foster their independent reading, it is important to some children that the teacher personally take time out to hear them read aloud and to check for fluency and expression. Children's frustration level can be immeasurably lessened if they are explicitly told by the teacher after they have read aloud that they need to read without pointing and that they should try chunking words into phrases which mimic their natural speech.

Strategies for Selecting and Using Meaningful Reading Materials at Appropriate Levels of Difficulty

Matching young children with "just right" books fosters their reading independently, no matter how young they are. The teacher needs to have an extensive classroom library of books. Books that emergent readers and early readers can be matched with should have fairly large print, appropriate spacing, so that the reader can easily see where word begins and ends, and few words on each page so that the young reader can focus on all important concerns of top-to-bottom, left-to-right, directionality, and the one-to-one match of word to print.

Illustrations for young children should support the meaning of the text and language patterns and predictable text structures should make these texts appealing to young readers. Most important of all the content of the story should relate to the children's interests and experiences as the teacher knows them.

Only after all these considerations have been addressed, can the teacher select "just right" books from an already leveled bin or list. In a similar fashion, when the teacher is selecting books for transitional and fluent readers, the following ideas need to be taken into account:

The book should take at least two sittings to read, so children can get used to reading longer books. The fluent and transitional reader needs to deal with more complex characters and more intricate plotting. Look for books that set the stage for plot development with a compelling beginning. Age appropriateness of the concepts, plot and themes is important so that the child will sustain interest in the book. Look for book features such as a list of chapters to help children navigate through the book.

Series books are wonderful to introduce at this point in the children's development.

Skill 6.2   Analyze key issues and recurring themes in literature in a variety of cultural contexts

See Skill 6.1

Skill 6.3   Understand the importance of respecting students' reading choices

Although there may be times when teachers do not want students to read certain books or types of texts, it important to respect their choice in reading material. Students who have difficulty in reading may not want to read lower level books because it reinforces the knowledge that they cannot read as well as their peers. Then they experience failure because they are unable to read the text. On the other hand, good readers often choose to read easy material simply because they do not want to be challenged.

Teachers should try to have adequate reading material in the classroom library to meet the needs of the varying reading levels in the class. There should be a variety of reading material matching the themes and topics. By letting students know what their reading level is and pointing them in the right direction, it will help them experience success and therefore keep them reading.

The most important thing is that students are reading. Comic books in the classroom are perfectly acceptable as long as students are reading.

Skill 6.4   Applying ways to cultivate students' enthusiasm for reading

Creation of an Environment that Promotes Love of Reading

The aforementioned creation of the meeting area and the reading chair (sometimes a rocking chair) with throw pillows around it promotes a love of reading. Beyond that, some classrooms have adopted an author's hat, decorated with the pictures of famous authors and book characters which children wear when they read from their own works.

Many classrooms also have children's storyboards, artwork, story maps, pop-up books, and "in the style of" writing inspired by specific authors. Some teachers buy calendars for the daily schedule which celebrate children's authors or types of literature. Children are also encouraged to bring in public library books and special books from their home libraries. The teacher can model this habit of sharing beautiful books and inviting stories from his or her home library.

In addition, news stories about children's authors, series books, television versions of books, theatrical film versions of books, stuffed toy book character decorations and other memorabilia related to books can be used to decorate the room.

Various chain book stores including Barnes and Nobles and Borders give out free book marks and promotional display materials related to children's books which can be available in the room for children to use as they read independently or in their guided groups. They might even use these artistic models to inspire their own book themed artifacts.

Strategies for Promoting Independent Reading in the Classroom and at Home

Pre-select books for the children that are just right for them. Provide the children with a quiet, relaxing space within the classroom where they can go to read these books. Don't get upset if they seem to take a break or wander around the room after fifteen minutes. Adults take breaks as well.

Make certain that the children who are reading independently fill in their weekly logs. Beyond telling what books they were reading and how many pages they have read, have the children respond to the following prompts:

This week I was successful at ...

Next week I plan to...

A response can also be an illustration or a sentence or two about the book.

Deliberately assign a child or a pair of children to read big books. These are a guaranteed success for the children because they have already been shared in class. Some children enjoy reading these independently using big rulers to point at words. This provides them with a sense of mastery over the words and ownership of their independent reading.

Some children enjoy working on their own strategy sheet such as a story map, character map, or storyboard panel, to demonstrate how they can apply a strategy to their own independent learning.

COMPETENCY 7.0 APPLY KNOWLEDGE OF METHODS FOR USING LITERATURE IN READING INSTRUCTION

Skill 7.1   Apply ways to use oral, visual, and written texts to address issues and problems in communities beyond the classroom

See Skill 16.3

Skill 7.2   Describe how to help students investigate examples of distortion and stereotypes through literature and other texts

The five types of expository texts to which the children should be introduced to through modeled reading and a teacher facilitated walk through. These are:

Description process: This usually describes a particular topic or provides the identifying characteristics of a topic. It can be depended upon to be factual. Within this type of text, the child reader has to use all of his or her basic reading strategies, because these types of expository texts do not have explicit clue words.

Causation or Cause- Effect text: This is one where faulty reasoning may come into play and the child reader has to use the inferential and self-questioning skills already mentioned to help assess whether the stated cause-effect relationship is a valid and correct one. This text appears in content area textbooks, newspapers, magazines, advertisements, and on some content area and general information web sites. Clue words, which the reader must note and then decide whether or not the evidence available or presented in the excerpt is sufficient, are: "therefore", "the reasons for", "as a result of", "because", "in consequence of", and "since."

Comparison text: This is an expository text which is centered on the reader's noting the contrasts and similarities between two or more objects and ideas. Many social studies, art, and science text books in class and non-fiction books include this contrast. Sometimes newspaper columnists use it as well in their editorial commentary.

Again, strategies for supporting children in being able to first comprehend the comparison and contrast intended by the author and then in being able to decide if this comparison is correctly taken, lies in focusing them on the use of key clue words and phrases. Among these are: like, unlike, resemble, different, different from, similar to, in contrast with, in comparison to, and in a different vein. It is important that as children examine texts which are talking about illustrated or photographed entities. They can also review the graphic representations for clues to support or contradict the text.

Collection text: This is an expository text that presents ideas in a group. The writer's goal is to present a set of related points or ideas. Another name for this structure of expository writing is a listing or a sequence. The author frequently uses clue words such as first, second, third, finally, and next to alert the reader to the sequence. Based on how well the writer structures the sequence of points or ideas, the reader should be able to make connections. It is important the writer make clear in the expository text how the items are related and why they follow in that given sequence.

Simple collection texts that can be literally modeled for young children include recipe making. A class of first graders, beginning readers and writers, were literally spellbound by the author's presentation of a widely known copyrighted collection text. The children were thrilled as the author followed the sequences of this collection text and finally took turns stirring it until it was creamy and smooth. After it had cooled, they each had a taste using their plastic spoons. Can you guess what it was? No? What gourmet children's delight would have first graders begging for a taste? Can't guess? Cream Farina from a commercial cereal box which had cooking directions on it (a.k.a known as a collection text).

You can bet that the children had constructed meaning from this five minute class demonstration and that they would pay close attention to collection texts on other food and product instruction boxes now because this text had come to be an authentic part of their lives.

Response structure expository texts present a question or response followed by an answer or a solution. Of course, entire mathematics text books and some science and social studies text books are filled with these types of questions. Again it is important here to walk the child reader through the excerpt and to sensitize the child to the clue words which signal this type of structure. These words include, but are not limited to: the problem is, the questions is, you need to solve for, one probable solution would be, an intervention could be, the concerns is, and another way to solve this would be.

Newspapers provide wonderful features which can be used by the teacher as read-alouds to introduce children grades 3-6 to point of view distinctions, specifically, editorials, editorial cartoons and key sports editorial cartoons (i.e. Bill Gallo of the New York Daily News). Children can also come to understand the distinction between fact and fiction, when they examine a newspaper advertisement or a supermarket circular for a product they commonly use, eat, drink or wear which includes exaggerated claims about what the product can actually do for or with the individual in question.

Finally the fact versus opinion distinction can be nicely explored if a teacher takes the children online to look at some star web sites and walks them through some exaggerated claims made about their particular movie star favorites. It is very important at some point, if the children have access to the internet, that the teacher show them how to examine web sites, look at who developed a particular web site and consider how credible (to be trusted and believed that individual or individuals are) the developers of the site are or are not.

See also Silll 16.3

Skill 7.3 Understand how to help students draw parallels and contrasts among varied ideas, concepts, and perspectives in multiple texts ; and describing how to help students identify differing views presented in text, support an opinion, and base conclusions on that opinion

See Skill 4.2

COMPETENCY 8.0 UNDERSTAND CHARACTERISTICS OF VARIOUS LITERARY GENRES

Skill 8.1 Describe various narrative genres and analyzing how they are used to convey ideas and perspectives

Authors use various ways to tell a story while employing various literary techniques. If teachers want students to understand the technique, they need to teach them the characteristics of each narrative genre. It may be necessary to draw the students' attention to the elements and structure of narratives as well the strategies they can use for reading each of the genres. Before students actually read a selection, the teacher can address the literary techniques, forms and vocabulary in mini-lessons to provide the students with knowledge about what they will be reading about. This helps them to become more engaged with the text and to have an idea of what they should think about as they are reading.

Narrative genres:

Prose fiction - this is literature about imaginary people, places and events. The purpose of this narrative genre is to stimulate the students' imaginations and to present the author's view of the world. This genre includes novels, short stories and plays, each of which has its own distinctive characteristics. They all have a setting, conflict, plot, climax and resolutiuon to varying degrees.

- Short story - this narrative usually has only one focus and a smaller world view. The students do have to determine whether the person telling the story is a narrator or is a character within the story. They do have to take note of the central conflict and determine why the characters act as they do. As a response to the story, they can decide how they feel about the characters and their actions and ask questions about the message that the author is trying to convey in the story.
- Novel - a novel is a longer version of the short story, often with sub-plots. During the reading the students have to be able to keep the subplots separated and understand their relationship to the main plot of the novel. They must be aware of the motives of the various characters and of their reactions to the characters' actions.

Prose non-fiction - this is literature that is about real events, times and places. It includes essays, journals, articles, letters, biographies and autobiographies. Much of the contemporary nonfiction reads like fiction with suspense, expression and ingenuity of style. Because it is vivid and personal, it can provide the students with a model for their own writing. When students are reading for information, they need to keep this purpose in mind and may need time and instruction to help them summarize or restate the main ideas.

Poetry - this form of literature helps the author communicate ideas and feelings through an arrangement of words and sounds. Poetry can be used to capture a mood, tell a story or explore different ideas. There are various literary techniques authors use in writing poetry which the teacher can discuss withy the class through mini-lessons.

Plays - these can be read for the purpose of performance or for literary effect. Students pay attention to the literary devices that the author uses. When reading a play, students can work on putting expression into their reading so that they can bring the characters to life.

Students should be aware of the purpose for reading so that they know what thinking is expected of them. When reading any text, students need to employ certain strategies. Therefore teachers need to engage the students in the reading process and model the appropriate strategies of:
- connecting
- making meaning
- questioning
- predicting
- inferencing
- reflecting
- evaluating

Skill 8.2   Analyze how characteristics of various informational genres and elements of expository text structure are used to convey ideas; and determining how textual aids have been used to convey meaning in a specific passage.

See Skills 4.2 and 7.2

COMPETENCY 9.0   UNDERSTAND THE APPROPRIATE USE OF
MECHANICS AND CRAFT TO CONVEY MEANING IN
THE ENGLISH LANGUAGE ARTS

Skill 9.1   Use mechanics (e.g., grammar, spelling, punctuation,
figurative and descriptive language) to facilitate understanding
in all of the language arts; and analyzing how aspects of the
craft of the speaker, writer, and illustrator are used to
formulate and express ideas artistically

Generalization of tasks from specific skill instruction to broader areas is a
complex skill that some students have difficulty obtaining. Understanding how
English grammar, spelling and the other language conventions previously
discussed cross all of the language arts disciplines is a skill students need to be
successful.

Reading. In reading students will be exposed to all of the grammar, spelling and
other conventions on a regular basis. As the teacher, it is important to take time
to point out these areas to the students who may otherwise pass them by without
a second thought. One important strategy for helping in this area is called
Directed Reading Thinking Activities (DRTA). This strategy developed by
Russell Stauffer (1969) allows the teacher to guide the thinking of the student
usually in making predictions and improving comprehension. An adaptation to
this strategy would allow the teacher to guide the thinking of the students to
recognize and identify the conventions.

Writing. Since writing is a more formal skill than oral language, the conventions
will be slightly different. Many times students will write the same way they speak
which is usually unacceptable for written language. The editing process is
probably the most effective method for helping students achieve improved use of
grammar, spelling, syntax and semantics. Peer editing and teacher editing
provide excellent tools for students.

Listening. Listening is an art. Many times it is obvious that students are hearing
what the speaker is saying, but are not truly listening. Setting the purpose for an
oral presentation and providing graphic organizers are strategies that help
structure listening activities. Having a purpose for listening with a graphic
organizer, allows the students to better filter out relevant and irrelevant
information. Demonstration of correct language conventions and incorrect ones
would provide the students with the opportunity to complete a comparison and
contrast situation.

Speaking. When orally presenting information, it is important the student realize
the necessity of using correct language. Having the students practice the
presentation out loud into a tape recorder is a technique that will allow the
students the opportunity to critique themselves or others and provide valuable
feedback.

When considering the assessment of students' understanding of English language structures and conventions, the most commonly used method is rubrics.

Rubrics can be commercially, teacher, or even student created to be used as an assessment tool. A rubric is a tool that defines in writing the teacher's expectations for assignments. The language on rubrics should be clearly thought out and leave little room for misinterpretations. Rubrics provide different levels of criteria to obtain different levels of proficiency. In this way, students clearly understand why their work was assessed in the manner it was without needing further clarification.

Rubrics also provide consistency when assessing assignments that could otherwise be viewed subjectively, as is the case with English language and conventions, particularly style.

Well-developed rubrics tell the criteria for evaluation while giving performance expectations, ratings and descriptors. They cover a range from the unacceptable to the acceptable providing students with a clear picture of all possible scores.

Another assessment method to use with considering English language structures and conventions is a list of essential questions to refer to as the evaluator. When using this strategy, the teacher prepares a list of essential questions that he feels when answered affirmatively will demonstrate the appropriate skills to show master of these skills.

When developing these questions, most teachers derive them as yes or no questions directly from the curriculum and/or state standards that specifically pertain to their grade level. In this way, the teacher can use one piece of writing or one oral presentation and be able to show others how he determined the proficiency level of a student.

The use of yes and no questions limits the variability of ratings and tying it directly to the curriculum ensures that what is to be taught has been taught.

Both methods of assessment discussed provide the opportunity for the teacher to go back and determine what if any skills or information may need to be retaught in order for students to achieve competence.

DOMAIN III.   **SKILLS AND PROCESSES**

COMPETENCY 10.0 DEMONSTRATE KNOWLEDGE OF WAYS TO CREATE
A LITERATE ENVIRONMENT IN THE CLASSROOM

Skill 10.0   Identify methods teachers can use to promote learners'
motivation to read for information, pleasure, and personal
growth; analyzing ways texts can be used to stimulate
students' interest, promote their reading growth, and foster
their appreciation for the written word; describing way to give
students opportunities to respond creatively and personally to
literature; and specifying how instructional and information
technologies can be used to support literacy

There are many ways teachers can encourage reading for pleasure in their classrooms. One of the best ways is to read aloud from a novel each day, even with grades as young as Grade 2. For Kindergarten and Grade 1, choosing picture books by one author at a time will help students realize that different authors write on different topics and in different ways. Author studies in all grades will encourage students to seek out books by that author and read them on their own.

Even within the content areas, there is a wealth of fiction that relates to the theme at hand and provides the students with background information that will help them with their studies. For example, when studying Colonial America in Social Studies, there are many picture books that teachers can use as introductions for the lessons. Using part of the class to read aloud from a novel about that period in history will help students to develop an interest in reading about the themes and help them understand how much enjoyment that reading can bring.

Monthly book clubs are also an excellent way of getting age-appropriate reading material into the students' hands. Since these book clubs offer the books at fairly inexpensive prices, parents realize that they can get more value for their money when they order each month. Book fairs at school provide students with the chance to win books for themselves and their classrooms.

Read-a-thons encourages reading because the students realize that by reading they are helping a cause. Some of these offers include prizes for the students or the teacher or school could initiate this kind of motivation.

Responding to literature is one of the most important parts of reading. By the responses that students give to what they have read, teachers can determine the level of comprehension. It takes practice for students to be able to respond critically to a text because they have the idea that all published authors are perfect and they should not criticize what they write.

Some of the strategies that teachers can use to provide opportunities for students to give creative and personal responses to their reading include:

1 Reading conferences – ask a student to read a section of the text and then tell why he/she chose that section. Teachers can also ask students why they are reading a certain book or ask about their favorite author.

2 Reading Surveys – Teachers can devise a list of questions to find out what students are reading, how they decide what books to read, and how students feel about the topics or language used in the book.

3 Daily reading time – This could be a set time when everyone in the class is reading, including the teacher or it could be a center activity for a small group of children.

4 Literature Circles – using the role sheets developed by Harvey Daniels in Voice and Choice in a Student-Centered Classroom, students take on different roles each day. They discuss the chapter or book, find new vocabulary words, illustrate a scene or pose questions for the group.

5 Reader's Theatre – students adapt part of the book or story and make it into a choral reading with expression that shows how they felt about what they have read.

Responding to literature does not always take the form of written responses. In a Reader's Workshop, students can choose to respond to what they read in art, painting, song, dance or any number of ways to show an interpretation of the reading. Interviewing the author or asking them to change a scene so that the result is different are other examples of how students can give a personal response to reading.

Students who have a hard time coming up with a response would benefit from a sheet listing ideas for ways they can respond. These usually take the form of open-ended sentences such as:

1 The character I liked the best was

2 The character that is most like me is

3 If I were _____, I would have

COMPETENCY 11.0 APPLY KNOWLEDGE OF THE DEVELOPMENTAL NATURE OF THE LANGUAGE ARTS

Skill 11.1 Recognize the stages of oral language (listening and speaking), reading, writing, and spelling development

See Skill 3.1

Skill 11.2 Recognize why students progress through stages of literacy at different rates

The stages of literacy development are covered under Skill 3.1. In every grade there are students in various stages of this development. There are many reasons for the discrepancy teachers find in their classrooms. In some cases when the teacher reads a story to the class, this is the first interaction the child has had with this experience. Parents often don't realize the benefit of reading to students at an early age and do not spend money on books. On the other hand, there are also children that come to school already reading or ready to start reading. Then you have the majority of students who love to listen to stories and are starting to develop some phonetic skills.

There are also medical reasons why students are in the early stages of literacy development. Brain damage through birth defects can cause learning disabilities that hamper a child's development. These students may require specialized help so that they can progress, although it is at a slower rate.

In all cases, teachers need to take a look at where each child is on the literacy continuum and design lessons that will help each child progress to the next level. There is no one program that will suit all children. They need to be surrounded by print and allowed to read material at their own level so that they will experience success.

Skill 11.3   Identify the processes of second language acquisition and the implications for developing oral language, reading, and writing proficiency

Given the demographics of our country, which is becoming increasingly pluralistic and has burgeoning numbers of citizens who are from ELL –English Language learner backgrounds, the likelihood that currently or even with in the next few years of your teaching career, you will be teaching at least one, if not more children who are from a non-native English speaking background (even though they won't officially be classified as ELL students), is at least 75%, if not more. Therefore, as a conscientious educator, it is important that you understand the special factors involved in supporting their literacy development, which include fostering progress in native language literacy as a perquisite for second language (ENGLISH) reading progress.

Not all English phonemes are present in various ELL native languages. Some native language phonemes may and do conflict with English phonemes. It is recommended that all teachers of reading and particularly those who are working with ELL students use meaningful, student centered, and culture customized activities. These activities may include: language games, word walls, and poems. Some of these activities might also, if possible, be initiated in the child's first language and then reiterated in English.

See also skill 19.1

Skill 11.4   Describe the nature of the writing process

Students need numerous opportunities to write for various purposes. Writing should be a daily activity in all classrooms and students should be instructed in the writing process. The components of the writing process are:
- Pre-writing – brainstorming, webbing, story maps- these are a few ways that students can generate ideas for their writing. For younger writers, a picture can be the stimulus for writing. They draw a picture and then write a few sentences about the picture. For older writers, teachers can provide the picture or a prompt to generate ideas for writing.
- Drafting – Students get their ideas down on paper. Teachers should not worry about proper spelling or conventions. The main idea is to get the students writing. Correcting the mistakes is part of the editing process.
- Revising – in this stage of the writing process, students reread the writing to determine where they can add in ideas or delete some things. They can also change around parts of the writing so that it flows more smoothly.
- Editing – this section of the writing process sees the students correcting the writing for conventions of grammar and correct spelling
- Publishing – in this component, the students prepare the writing to be displayed on a bulletin board or to be published in some other way. It is important to note that not all writing needs to be brought to this stage.

Skill 11.5 Identify strategies for teaching each step of the writing process

When students are given a writing assignment, the first instinct is to start writing. They also want to finish the piece and pass it in without reading it over or editing it. It is a chore to rewrite a draft so teachers need to model this for them and to teach them that it is what all writers do.

Prewriting activities set the stage for writing in the classroom. Students need guidance in terms of how to plan for their writing and instruction in how to brainstorm, use a web, a story map or some other graphic organizer to help them organize their thoughts. Modelling by the teacher helps the students understand the steps they need to take to tackle different forms of writing. The instruction needs to be very explicit so that students can see and hear every action they should take with their own writing. The prewriting activities include planning the writing, considering the purpose and in the case of a research project, they can consider where they will get the information they will need.

During the drafting stage, students will be putting their ideas on paper. The quality of the text should not be a concern at this point as it is more important for the students to just write. Students may even used inventive spelling in this stage and not bother with capitalization or punctuation depending on their stage in the development of writing.

Revising and editing stages are the ones where teachers do have to spend the most time teaching the concepts. In revising, students have to look at the relationship of the sentences and decide whether or not the piece flows smoothly. They may have to read the text out loud as this is when they can really hear where the text does not make sense. Teachers can work with students to revise their work by asking them to add in information to clarify a point or to help them see where certain sentences do not fit together. Modelling is crucial here and the use of exemplars can really demonstrate how the students can improve their work.

Editing for grammatical structure, correct spelling, punctuation and capitalization is another issue in teaching the stages of writing. Here students need plenty of practice. Many teachers have mini-lessons as the need arises in student writing and provide practice in the form of worksheets. However, the students may get all the answers correct on the worksheets and still not edit their own work. For this reason, teachers should look for only specific things in a piece of writing so as not to confuse the students. Instead of marking the paper with red ink, ask the students to look for all the places where they should have used capital letters. On another occasion, ask the students to underline all the words they think may be spelled incorrectly. Do not overload them with too much editing all at once.

Peer editing also helps with revising and editing. Providing opportunities for students to work together in small groups or pairs to edit each others work not only helps the writer, but also the other student gains experience in editing and revising.

Once the writing has been revised and edited to the student's satisfaction, he./she can decide how to publish the work or even whether or not to publish. The student can rewrite the piece in good handwriting or even use a word processor. Colored paper and the use of colorful illustrations give the students the opportunity to take pride in their work and to display it for others to see.

COMPETENCY 12.0 UNDERSTAND METHODS FOR PROMOTING LITERACY AS A LIFELONG SKILL

Skill 12.1 Prompt learners to select from variety of written materials, read extended texts, and read for authentic purposes

Students need a purpose for reading whether it is for pleasure or to find information on a specific topic. Struggling readers and those that have not yet developing a love of reading may need to be prompted to select from a variety of texts or to read to find out more about a topic. If teachers create a purpose for students' reading, the student can create a specific goal for reading. This can include finding the author's point of view or finding the answer to the 5W's in a newspaper article. They could read movie reviews to determine whether or not they want to see the movie or read a book review to determine whether they would like to read a particular book.

There are other ways students can respond to their reading, but the purpose has to be communicated to them before they start. For example, students can illustrate a favorite scene form a story or create a different version of the story. Students can be prompted to read texts to look at how different author's approach the same subject or how an author uses different literary techniques to get his/her message across. Depending on the reading level of the student, teachers may have to redirect him/her to easier or more challenging texts.

Skill 12.2 Help students recognize how the craft of literacy expression can enhance their understanding and appreciation of varied text

Students can become better readers and writers when they practice writing in all three modes. They learn to adjust their style to suit the purpose and the audience. The three modes of writing are:

- Expressive

This is personal writing and the student does it mainly for himself/herself. This form of writing frees up the student to write down personal thoughts and ideas without having to worry about the conventions of language. This writing may be in the form of a personal journal, a learning log, or jot notes. It can also be in the form of a reading journal to record their responses to the texts they read.

- Transactional

Transactional writing is done for a specific purpose, such as to inform, instruct, advise, record, explain, speculate or persuade. This is a more formal type of writing in which the student has to present the ideas in a clear and organized manner. In order to produce this type of writing, students must have knowledge of how to organize their ideas, develop a thesis and to quote references or paraphrase information they read in other texts.

- Poetic

Poetic writing uses language as a medium to produce imaginary texts. Students learn how to use figurative and expressive language from the authors they read. They learn the form of poetry, plays and short stories from reading these texts. Through mini-lessons, teachers can help them develop characterization, plot and literary elements in their writing.

Skill 12.3   Analyze how the techniques and devices of expression influence a reader's, listener's, or viewer's responses

Learning to listen and view for specific reasons is a skill that students must learn and practice. By frequently having students respond to viewing and discussing their op-inions with their classmates, students can come to regard the art of discussion as being important. Viewing does not just refer to watching films in class. It also refers to looking at pictures and images and being able to discern a message in the medium. Students should also be able to represent texts in art painting and other mediums for their classmates to view.

Students can easily learn to recognize the techniques and devices of expression by being immersed in the reading, viewing and listening experience. When they know they have to respond in some way to what they are viewing or listening to, then they develop a sense of ownership of the text. They need to receive feedback on their responses, but most of all they need to see responding to viewing being modeled.

Students can demonstrate their learning through visual representations, such as
- Venn diagrams to compare two texts they have listened to or two pictures
- Story maps to tell the basics of a story the teacher has read
- Character Web
- Concept map
- Drawings of characters
- Charts

Skill 12.4 Describe methods for including parents, guardians, and surrogates as partners in the literacy development of their children

Quite often the only communication between the school and parents takes the form of end of term reports and parent-teacher interviews. Parents are often reluctant to come to the school because they feel that the teachers are more knowledgeable than they are. In order to have good literacy communication between the school and parents, teachers and reading specialists can employ different techniques. These include:

- Holding a curriculum night during the first two weeks of school. At this time the teacher can explain how the children will be taught and the textbooks and materials that will be used.
- Having an open door policy where parents can feel free to come into the classroom and observe what is happening.
- Telephoning or emailing the parents on a regular basis. Parents dread getting a call from the teacher because it usually means that their children have been in trouble or are experiencing problems in school. When you make these phone calls to report progress parents become an ally in helping their children at home.
- Notes to parents in the child's agenda are also helpful in keeping parents informed about how to help at home and about how well their children are doing.
- Inviting parents or members of the community into the classroom to help with literacy centers gives those outside the school a chance to experience what is happening in the classroom. This could be listening to children read, helping them revise and edit writing or even helping them choose books to take home

Skill 12.5 Identify ways for teachers to model reading and writing as valuable, lifelong activities

See Skills 1.1 and 1.2

SCHOOL OF EDUCATION
CURRICULUM LABORATORY
UM-DEARBORN

COMPETENCY 13.0 APPLY KNOWLEDGE OF READING COMPREHENSION STRATEGIES

Skill 13.1 **Describe word identification strategies (e.g., phonemic awareness, phonics, spelling, prior knowledge)**

Phonological Awareness

Phonological awareness means the ability of the reader to recognize the sounds or phonemes of spoken language. This recognition includes how these sounds can be blended together, segmented (divided up), and manipulated (switched around). This awareness eventually leads to phonics, a method for decoding language by unlocking letter-sound or grapheme-phoneme relationships.

Development of phonological skills for most children begins during the pre-K years. Indeed by the age of 5, a child who has been exposed to fingerplays and poetry can recognize a rhyme. Such a child can demonstrate phonological awareness by filling in the missing rhyming word in a familiar rhyme or rhymed picture book. The procedure of filling in a missing word is called the cloze procedure. It can be used in oral or print literacy activities.

One teaches children phonological awareness by directly pointing out the sounds made by letters singly (as in /b/) or in combination (as in /bl/), and to recognize individual sounds in words.

Phonological awareness skills include but are not limited to the following:

I. Rhyming and syllabification
2. Blending sounds into words—such as pic-tur-bo-k
3. Identifying beginning or initial phonemes and ending or final phonemes in short, one-syllable words
4. Breaking words down into sounds- which is also called "segmenting" words
5. Removing initial sounds, and substituting others. An example is /bat/ minus the /b/ with an /m/ substituted becomes /mat/.

The Role of Phonological Awareness in Reading Development

Instructional methods to teach phonological awareness may include any or all of the following:

1. Auditory games during which children recognize and manipulate the sounds of words, separate or segment the sounds of words, take out sounds, blend sounds, add in new sounds, or take apart sounds to recombine them in new formations.

2. Snap game- the teacher says two words. The children snap their fingers if the two words share a sound, which might be at the beginning, or end of the word. Children hear initial phonemes most easily, followed by final ones. Medial or middle sounds are most difficult for young children to discriminate. One sees this in their oral responses as well as in their invented spelling. Silence occurs if the words share no sounds. Children love this simple game and it also helps with classroom management.

3. Language games model for children identification of rhyming words. These games help inspire children to create their own rhymes.

4. Read books that rhyme such as *Sheep in A Jeep* by Nancy Shaw or *The Fox on a Box* by Barbara Gregorich.

5. Share books with children that use alliteration (words that begin with the same sound) such as *Avalanche, A to Z.*

Assessment of Phonological Awareness

These skills can be assessed by having the child listen to the teacher say two words. Then ask the child to decide if these two words are the same word repeated twice or two different words.

When making this assessment, when using two different words, make certain that they only differ by only one phoneme, such as /d/ and /g/.

Children can be assessed on words which are not real words that are familiar to them. Words used can be make-believe words.

The Role of Phonological Processing in the Development of Individual Students

Children who are raised in homes where English is not the first language and or where standard English is not spoken, may have difficulty with hearing the difference between similar sounding words like "send" and "sent." Any child who is not in a home, day care, or preschool environment where English phonology operates, may have difficulty perceiving and demonstrating the differences between English language phonemes. If children can not hear the difference between words that "sound the same" like "grow" and "glow," they will be confused when these words appear in a print context. This confusion will of course, sadly, impact their comprehension.

Considerations for teaching phonological processing to ELL children include recognition by the teacher that what works for the English language speaking child from an English language speaking family, does not necessarily work in other languages.

Research recommends that ELL children learn to read initially in their first language. It is critical for ELL learn to speak English before being taught to read English. Research supports that oral language development lays the foundation for phonological awareness.

All phonological instruction programs must be tailored to the children's learning backgrounds. Rhymes and alliteration introduced to ELL children should be read or shared with them in their first language, if at all possible.

Struggling Readers

"Students who cannot read by age 9 are unlikely to become fluent readers and have a greater tendency to drop out"
Beth Antunez

Among the causes of reading difficulties for some children (and adults) are auditory trauma or ear infections that affect their ability to hear speech. Such children need one-on-one support with articulation and perception of different sounds. When a child says a word such as "parrot" incorrectly, repeat it back as a question with the correct. If the child "gets" the sound correctly after your question, all is well. Extra support was needed. If the child still has difficulty with pronunciation after repeated instances, then consult with a speech therapist or audiologist. Early identification of medical conditions that affect hearing is crucial to reading development.

Points to Ponder

Phonological awareness is auditory.
It does not involve print.
It begins before children have learned letter-sound relationships.
It is the basis for the successful teaching of phonics and spelling.
It can and must be taught and nurtured.
It precedes and must be in place before the alphabetic principle can be taught.

Phonemic Awareness

"The two best predictors of early reading success are alphabetic recognition and phonemic awareness."
    Marilyn Jager Adams

"In order to benefit from formal reading instruction, children must have a certain level of phonemic awareness. . . phonemic awareness is both a prerequisite for and a consequence of learning to read."
    Hallie Kay Yopp

Phonemic awareness is a specific skill within the broader category of phonological awareness. Probably developing fairly late, it is the knowledge that words are comprised of individual phonemes that can be blended.
Theorist Marilyn Jager Adams who researches early reading has outlined five basic types of phonemic awareness tasks.

Task 1- Ability to hear rhymes and alliteration.
For example, the children would listen to a poem, rhyming picture book or song and identify the rhyming words heard which the teacher might then record or list on chart.

Task 2- Ability to do oddity tasks (recognize the member of a set that is different [odd} among the group.
For example, the children would look at the pictures of grass, a garden and a rose, answering, Which one starts with a different sound?

Task 3 –The ability to orally blend words and split syllables.
For example, the children can say the first sound of a word and then the rest of the word and put it together as a single word.

Task 4 –The ability to orally segment words.
For example, the ability to count sounds. The child would be asked to count or clap the sounds in "hamburger."
Task 5- The ability to do phonics manipulation tasks.
For example, replace the "r" sound in rose with a "p" sound.

The Role of Phonemic Awareness in Reading Development

Children who have problems with phonics generally have not acquired or been exposed to phonemic awareness activities at home or in preschool-2. This includes extensive songs, rhymes and read–alouds.

Instructional Methods

Since the ability to distinguish between individual sounds, or phonemes, within words is a prerequisite to association of sounds with letters and manipulating sounds to blend words—a fancy way of saying "reading," the teaching of phonemic awareness is crucial to emergent literacy (early childhood K-2 reading instruction). Children need a strong background in phonemic awareness in order for phonics instruction (sound –spelling relationship-printed materials) to be effective.

Instructional methods that may be effective for teaching phonemic awareness can include:

- Clapping syllables in words

- Distinguishing between a word and a sound

- Using visual cues and movements to help children understand when the speaker goes from one sound to another

- Incorporating oral segmentation activities which focus on easily distinguished syllables rather than sounds

- Singing familiar songs (e.g. Happy Birthday, Knick Knack Paddy Wack) and replacing key words those of a different ending

- Dealing children a deck of picture cards and having them sound out the words for the pictures on their cards or calling for a picture by asking for its first and last sound.

Consideration for ELL Students

Given the demographics of our country with its influx of New Americans, the likelihood it is likely that you will be teaching at least some children who are from a non-native English speaking background. Therefore, as a conscientious educator, it is important that you understand the special factors involved in supporting children's second language literacy development.

Not all English phonemes are present in various ELL native languages; for example, the sound of /th/ does not appear in Spanish. Some native language phonemes may and do conflict with English phonemes.

It is recommended that all teachers of reading and particularly those who are working with ELL students use meaningful, student centered, and culturally customized activities. These activities may include: language games, word walls, and poems. Some of these activities might, if possible, be initiated in the child's first language and then reiterated in English.

Reading and the ELL Learner

Research has shown that there is a positive and strong correlation between a child's literacy in his/her native language and his/her learning of English. The degree of native language proficiency and literacy is a strong predictor of English language development. Children who are literate and engaged readers in their native language can easily transfer their skills to a second language (i.e. English).

What this means is that teacher educators should not approach the needs of ELL learners in reading the same as they do native speakers. Those children whose families are not from a focused oral literacy and reading culture in the native language will need additional oral language rhymes, read-alouds, and singing as supports for reading skills development in both their native and the English language.

Assessment of Phonemic Awareness

Teachers can maintain ongoing logs and rubrics for assessment throughout the year of phonemic awareness for individual children. Such assessments would identify particular stated reading behaviors or performance standards, the date of observation of the child's behavior (in this context-phonemic activity or exercise), and comments. The rubric or legend for assessing these behaviors might include the following descriptors:

- demonstrates or exhibits reading behavior consistently,
- makes progress/strides toward this reading behavior, and
- has not yet demonstrated or exhibited this behavior.

Depending on the particular phonemic task the teacher models, the performance task might include:

- Saying rhyming words in response to an oral prompt
- Segmenting a word spoken by the teacher into its beginning, middle and ending sounds
- Counting correctly the number of syllables in a spoken word

Phonological awareness involves the recognition that spoken words are composed of a set of smaller units such as onsets and rimes, syllables, and sounds.

Phonemic awareness is a specific type of phonological awareness which focuses on the ability to distinguish, manipulate and blend specific sounds or phonemes within an individual word.

Think of phonological awareness as an umbrella and phonemic awareness as a specific spoke under this umbrella.

Phonics deals with printed words and the learning of sound-spelling correlations, while phonemic awareness activities are oral.

In reviewing reading research and theory, new distinctions and definitions appear often. The body of reading knowledge changes over time. The information and definitions in this guide are those accepted in the year of its publication and the time of its authoring and updating. As changes occur in accepted theories, they will be made in the guides and in the certification exams.

"If you believe that you learn to read by reading, you must learn to want to read. Reading to children, therefore models both the "how" and "why" of reading."
Helen Depree and Sandra Iversen-Early Literacy in the Classroom
"The long talk that parents have put off about the ways of the world might need to be an introduction to the facts about the English alphabet."
Terrence Moore-Ashbrook Center Fellow-Principal of Ridgeview Classical Schools in Fort Collins, Colorado

Use of Reading and Writing Strategies for Teaching Letter-sound Correspondence

Provide children with a sample of a single letter book (or create one from environmental sources, newspapers, coupons, circulars, magazines or your own text ideas). Make sure that your already published or created sample includes a printed version of the letter in both upper and lower case forms. Make certain that each page contains a picture of something that starts with that specific letter and also has the word for the picture. The book you select or create should be a predictable one in that when the picture is identified, the word can be read.

Once the children have been provided with your sample and have listened to it being read, challenge them to each make a one letter book. Often it is best to focus on familiar consonants for the single letter book or the first letter of the child's first name. Using the first letter of the child's first name, invites the child to develop a book which tells about him or her and the words that he or she finds. This is an excellent way to have the reading and writing workshop enhance the teaching of the alphabetic principle. Encourage children to be active writers and readers by finding words for their book on the classroom word wall, in alphabet books in the special alphabet book bin and in grade and age appropriate pictionaries, (dictionaries for younger children which are filled with pictures).

Of course, the richest resource within the reading and writing workshop classroom for teaching and fostering the alphabetic principle lies in the use of alphabet books as anchor books for inspiring students writing. While young children in grades K-1 will do better with the one letter book authoring activity, children in grades 2 and beyond can truly be inspired and motivated by alphabet books to enhance their own reading, writing and alphabetic skills. Furthermore, use of these books which have and are being produced in a variety of formats to enhance social studies, science and mathematical themes, provide an opportunity for even young children to create a meaningful product that authenticates their content study as it enhances alphabetic skills and, of course, print awareness

An annotated bibliography of selected alphabet books has been provided in the bibliography section of this guide. It was limited by space considerations, but the teacher can with no expense and with much pleasure catch up on the latest titles and identify those most appropriate for the grade taught, by visiting a bookstore. Hold the print book in hand and then consider selecting an alphabet book that has a particularly inviting concept, art style, or adaptable format within the children's capacity to use as a model.

For instance, Tina Hoban uses actual color photographs of letters in her *26 Letters and 99 Cents.* Children may want to make clay letters or create letter sculptures that develop their own alphabet book similar to Hoban's. If nutrition is the science topic, children might want to examine Ehlert's very accessible *Eating the Alphabet: Fruits and Vegetables from A to Z.* This, combined with an examination of the fruits and vegetables in a local store (perhaps a pleasant walk from the school and a quick break from the routine) can yield a wonderful alphabet book on fruits and vegetables which can also include those fruits and vegetables eaten in various cultures (i.e. mangos, plantains, pomegranates, etc).

The alphabet book can also offer the class a chance to work collaboratively using a template page created by the teacher. Completion of this collaborative work can be shared with peers in another class and parents and be kept in the classroom library as a model for the following year's class with their recognition and acceptance of the authors!

Assessment Throughout the Year of Graphophonemic Awareness

The teacher will want to maintain individual records of children's reading behaviors demonstrating alphabetic principle/graphophonemic awareness.

The following performance standards should be part of a record template form for each child in grades K-1 and beyond as needed (depending on ELL or special needs):

- Match all consonant and short vowel sounds.
- Read one's own name.
- Read one syllable words and high frequency words.
- Demonstrate ability to read and understand that as letters in words change, so do the sounds.
- Generate the sounds from all letters including consonant blends and long vowel patterns. Blend those different sounds into recognizable words.
- Read common sight words.
- Read common word families.
- Recognize and use knowledge of spelling patterns when reading: run/running, hop/hopping.

Any record kept of an individual child's progress should include each date of observation and some legend or rubric detailing the level of performance, standard acquisition, or mastery.

The following template can be used by teachers to record student progress for each child in grades K-1 and beyond as needed (depending on ELL or special needs):

Reading Progress

Skill Area	Mastered	Making Progress	Not Yet	Comments
Matches all consonant and short vowel sounds				
Reads one's own name				
Reads one syllable words and high frequency words				
Demonstrates ability to read and understand that as letters in words change, so do the sounds				
Generates the sounds from all letters including consonant blends and long vowel patterns. Blend those different sounds into recognizable words				
Reads common sight words				
Reads common word families				
Recognizes and uses knowledge of spelling patterns when reading: run/running, hop/hopping				

Any record kept of an individual child's progress should include each date of observation and some legend or rubric detailing the level of performance, standard acquisition, or mastery.

Development of Alphabetic Knowledge in Individual Students

Researchers Laura M. Justice and Helen K. Ezell (2002) evaluated alphabetic knowledge and print awareness in pre-school children from low income households. In their post-tests, children who had participated in shared reading sessions that emphasized a print focus outperformed their control group peers (other Head Start children) on three measures of print awareness: words in print, print recognition, and alphabetic knowledge.

Other researchers including Chaney (1994) have demonstrated a statistically significant and inverse relationship between household income and children's performance on measures of print awareness and the alphabetic principle. Lonigan (l999) found that substantial group differences existed on a variety of pre literacy tasks administered to 85 preschool children from lower and middle income households. The researchers looked at environmental print, print and book reading conventions, and alphabet knowledge. Results showed that preschool children from middle income households showed significantly higher levels of skill across all print awareness tasks in comparison with preschoolers from low income households.

Obviously this data highlights the importance of extensive alphabetic knowledge activities and print awareness opportunities for some children from low income households in grades K-1 and even beyond if necessary.

Two other studies undertaken by Ezell and Justice (in the year 2000) suggested that structuring adult-child shared book reading interactions to include an explicit print awareness and alphabetic principle focus resulted in a substantial increase in children's verbal interactions with print.

This work highlights the importance of not only classroom and preschool emphasis on print awareness and alphabetic principle routines, but also the need for teachers to reach out to parents and to model for them these shared reading experiences so that family life can parallel the classroom experiences. Many schools currently have parent volunteers and reading buddy programs. Training of these volunteers, particularly in high need, low economic income status communities is certainly warranted.

David J. Chard and Jean Osborn (l999) have reflected on the guidelines necessary for teachers to use in selecting supplemental phonics and word-recognition materials for addressing students with learning disabilities.
They note that an important way to help children with reading disabilities figure out the system underlying the printed word is leading them to understand the alphabetic principle. Children with learning disabilities (LD) in particular, benefit from organized instruction that centers on letters, sounds, and the relations between sounds and letters. They also benefit from word-recognition patterns instruction that offers practice with word families that share similar letter patterns.

Children who are LD also benefit from opportunities to apply what they are learning to the reading and re-reading of stories and other texts. Such texts contain a high portion of words which reflect the letters, sounds, and spelling patterns the children are learning.

For special needs children, a beginning reading program should include the following elements of alphabetic knowledge instruction:

1. A variety of alphabetic knowledge activities in which the children learn to identify and name both upper and lower case letters.
2. Games, songs, and other activities that help children to learn to name the letters quickly.
3. Writing activities that encourage children to practice the letters which they are writing.
4. A sensible sequence of letter introduction that can be adjusted to the needs of the children.

Sequence of Phonics Skills

- Letter Naming
    - Lower Case Letters
    - Upper Case Letters
- Letter Sounds
    - Continuous Sounds
    - Stop Sounds
    - Both Consonant and Vowel Sounds
- Short Vowels in CVC Words
- Short Vowels with Digraphs and –tch Trigraph
- Short Vowels and Consonant Blends
- Long Vowels
- Variant Vowels and Diphthongs
- R- and L- Controlled Vowels
- Multisyllabic Words

Explicit and Implicit Strategies for Teaching Phonics

Uta Frith has identified three phases which describe the progression of children's phonic learning from ages four through eight. These are:

Logographic Phase
Children recognize whole words that have significance for them such as their own names or the names of stores they frequent or products that their parents buy. Examples are McDonald's, SuperValu, and the like. Strategies which nurture development in this phase include explicit labeling of class room objects, components, furniture and materials and showing the children's names in print as often as possible. Toward the end of this phase children start to notice initial letters in words and the sounds that they represent.

Analytic Phase
During this phase the children begin to make associations between the spelling patterns in the words they know and new words-they encounter. Children in this phase of reading development are able to generalize that hat and cat are going to be read in a similar manner because they recognize that the /at/ portions of the words are the same. This is helpful with word families and can be transferred to encoding words through many activities. Some teachers find it helpful to add word families or family houses to their word walls around the room. In this way, students can begin to make these generalizations more rapidly. As the students find more complex words that fall into the family/house, they add them.

Orthographic Phase
In this phase, children recognize words almost automatically. They can rapidly identify an increasing number of words. Students are able to apply many different strategies in a seamless manner to help them decode unknown words. This may include: phonics, structural analysis, syntax, semantics, and contextual clues. Students at this level are fluent readers with good prosody. They are reading to make the shift from learning to read to reading to learn. It is a critical shift for children.

To best support these phases and the development of emergent and early readers, teachers should focus on elements of phonics learning which help children analyze words for their letters, spelling patterns, and structural components. The children need to be involved in activities in which they use what they know about words to learn new ones.

The teacher needs to build on what the children know to introduce new spelling patterns, vowel combinations, and short and long vowel investigations. The teacher must do this and be aware that these will be reintroduced again and again as needed.

Keep in mind that children's learning of phonics and other key components of reading is not linear, but rather falls back to review and then flows forward to build new understandings.

Among suggested activities to support phonics instruction to address the needs of these three phases of phonics learning are:

(These activities have specifically been provided in detail so that the educator can study them and use them in the sample constructed response questions which have been provided at the end of the guide. Since the role of phonics in promoting reading development is so crucial, it is highly likely that a constructed response question on the certification test will focus on the use of such strategies. Therefore it is a good idea for the certification candidate to study them closely. As a bonus, the detail with which these strategies are set forth also makes them readily useful with classes the teacher is currently teaching).

Sorting Words

This activity allows children to focus closely on the specific features of words and to begin to understand the basic elements of letter sound relationships. Start with one syllable (monosyllabic) words. Have the children group them by their length, common letters, sound, and/or spelling pattern.

Prepare for the activity by writing ten to fifteen words on oaktag strips and place them randomly on the sentence strip holder. These words should come from a book previously shared in the classroom or a language experience chart.

Next begin to sort out the words with the children, perhaps by where a particular letter appears in a word. While the children sort the place of a particular letter in a given word, they should also be coached (or facilitated) by the teacher to recognize that sometimes a letter in the middle of the word can still be the last sound that we hear and that some letters at the end of a word are silent (such as "e").

Children should be encouraged to make their own categories for word sorts and to share their own discoveries as they do the word sorts. The children's discoveries should be recorded and posted in the rooms with their names so they have ownership of their phonics learning.

Spelling Pattern Word Wall

One of the understandings emergent readers come to about a word is that if they know how to read, write, and spell one word, they can write, read, and spell many other words as well.

Create in your classroom a spelling pattern word wall. The spelling word wall can be created by stapling a piece of 3" x 5" butcher block paper to the bulletin board. Then attach spelling pattern cards around the border with thumbtacks, so that the cards can be easily removed to use at the meeting area.

Once you decide on a spelling pattern for instruction, remove the corresponding card from the word wall. Then take a 1"x 3" piece of a contrasting color of butcher block paper and tape the card to the top end of a sheet the children will use for their investigation.

After the pattern is identified the children can try to come up with other words that have the same spelling pattern. The teacher can write these on the spelling pattern sheet, using a different color marker to highlight the spelling pattern within the word. The children have to add to the list until the sheet is full, which might take two days or more.

After the sheet is full, the completed spelling pattern is attached to the wall.

Letter Holder Making Words

Use a 2" x 3" piece of foam board to make a letter holder. On the front of the board, attach 16 library pockets —one for each letter from A to P. Use the back of the board to attach another 10 pockets for the rest of the alphabet.

Write the letter name on each pocket and use clear bookbinding tape to secure each row of cards with clear tape. Make twelve cards for each letter. On the front of each 2"x 6" strip, make a capital letter and on its back write that letter in lower case. Write consonants in, say, black marker and vowels in red marker.

Through use of this letter holder, children can experience how letters can be rearranged, added, or removed to make new words. They can use these cards also to focus as needed on letter sequences and to support them in recognizing spelling patterns in words.

The words you choose to use for this activity can be selected from Patricia Cunningham and Dorothy P. Hall's, *Making Words* (1994). Select a word that is called the "secret word." Build up toward the creation of that word through a focus on the smaller words within it. Words should be chosen which reflect the spelling patterns being studied by the class.

You can create letter holders for the children by folding up the bottom third of a used manila file folder and taping the ends to form a shallow pocket. Give them

letter cards which are made of 2"x 6" oaktag. So, for example, if the secret word is bicycle, the children would be given the separate letter cards which would make up that word. The children keep the letters on the floor in front of them and only place them in the holder when they are actually making a word.
Making words should begin with making two letter words and then progress as the individual child is ready to make larger words. The teacher provides the instruction of which two letters the child is to use to make a word. After the instruction is given the children select the correct letters and make the word in their folder. The teacher then writes the word down and the children check their letter holder word against it. The teacher goes around checking through and reviewing the letter holders to see which children are "getting it" and then continues to build up words with more letters if the children are ready.

Word Splits

Splitting compound words. Through working with compound words, children can actually experience bigger words that are often made up of smaller words. By working with five to ten compound words on oaktag cards, children can analyze letter-sound relationships and meaning.

Before children meet in a group, write five to ten words on oaktag cards and arrange them on the sentence strip holder. After the words have been read, cut each of the words into its two smaller words and randomly arrange them on the sentence strip holder. Allow the children to randomly take turns arranging the small words back into the original compound words. Also, encourage them to form new compound words. For example, if one of two original compound words is "rainbow" and the other is "dropping," the children should be able to come with "raindrop." The new words the children come up with should be written on blank oaktag cards with the names of the children who came up with them attached. In this way the children can add to their growing bank of new words and have ownership in the words that they have added.

Role of Phonics in Developing Rapid, Automatic Word Recognition, Decoding, and Reading Comprehension

To decode means to change communication signals into messages. Reading comprehension requires that the reader learn the code within which a message is written and be able to decode it to get the message.

Although effective reading comprehension requires identifying words automatically (Adams, 1990, Perfetti, 1985), children do not have to be able to identify every single word or know the exact meaning of the every word in a text to understand it. Indeed, Nagy (1988) says that, children can read a work with a high level of comprehension even if they do not fully know as many as 15 percent of the words within a given text.

Children develop the ability to decode and recognize words automatically. They then can extend their ability to decode to multi-syllabic words.

J. David Cooper (2004) and other advocates of the Balanced Literacy Approach, feel that children become literate, effective communicators and able to comprehend, by learning phonics and other aspects of word identification through the use of engaging reading texts. Engaging text, as defined by the balanced literacy group, are those texts which contain highly predictable elements of rhyme, sound patterns, and plot. Researchers, such as Chall (1983) and Flesch (1981), support a phonics-centered foundation before the use of engaging reading texts. This is at the crux of the phonics versus whole language/ balanced literacy/ integrated language arts, teaching of reading controversy.

It is important for the new teacher to be informed about both sides of this controversy, as well as the work of theorists who attempt to reconcile these two perspectives, such as Kenneth Goodman (1994). There are powerful arguments on both sides of this controversy, and each approach works wonderfully with some students and does not succeed with others.

As far as the examinations go, all that is asked of you is the ability to demonstrate that you are familiar with these varied perspectives. If asked on a constructed response question, you need to be able to show that you can talk about teaching some aspect of reading using strategies from one or the other or a combination of both approaches.

This guide is designed to provide you with numerous strategies representing both approaches.

The working teacher can, depending on the perspective of his /her school administration and the needs of the particular children he or she serves, choose from the strategies and approaches which work best for the children concerned.

Blending Letter Sounds

Prompts for Graphophonic Cues

You said (the child's incorrect attempt). Does that match the letters you see?
If it were the word you just said, (the child's incorrect attempt), what would it have to start with?

If it were the word you just said (the child's incorrect attempt), what would it have to end with?

Look at the first letter/s . . . look at the middle letter/s
. . . the last letter. . What could it be?

If you were writing (the child's incorrect attempt) what letter would you write first?
What letters would go in the middle?
What letters would go last?

A good strategy to use in working with individual children is to have them explain how they finally correctly identified a word that was troubling them. If prompted and habituated through one on one teacher/tutoring conversations, they can be quite clear about what they did to "get" the word.

If the children are already writing their own stories, the teacher might say to them: "You know when you write your own stories, you would never write any story which did not make sense. You wouldn't and probably this writer didn't either. If you read something that does make sense, but doesn't match the letters, then it's probably not what the author wrote. This is the author's story, not yours right now, so go back to the word and see if you can find out the author's story. Later on, you might write your own story."

Letter Sound Correspondence and Beginning Decoding

Use this procedure for letter-sound investigations that support beginning decoding.

First, focus on a particular letter/s which you want the child to investigate. It is good to choose one from a shared text which the children are familiar with. Make certain that the teachers' directions to the children are clear and either focuses them on looking for a specific letter or listening for sounds.

Next, begin a list of words that meet the task given to the children. Use chart paper to list the words that the children identify. This list can be continued into the next week as long as the children's focus is maintained on the list. This can be easily done by challenging the children with identifying a specific number of letters or sounds and "daring" them as a class team to go beyond those words or sounds.

Third, continue to add to the list. Focus the children at the beginning of the day on the goal of their individually adding to the list. Give them an adhesive note (sticky pad sheet) on which they can individually write down the words they find. Then they can attach their newly found words with their names on them to the chart. This provides the children with a sense of ownership and pride in their letter-sounding abilities. During shared reading, discuss the children's proposed additions and have the group decide if these meet the directed category. If all the children agree that they do meet the category, include the words on the chart.

Fourth, do a word sort from all the words generated and have the children put the words into categories that demonstrate similarities and differences. They can be prompted to see if the letter appeared at the beginning of the word, or in the end of the word. They might also be prompted to see that one sound could have two different letter representations. The children can then "box" the word differences and similarities by drawing colors established in a chart key.

Finally, before the children go off to read, ask them to look for new words in the texts which they can now recognize because of the letter sound relationships on their chart. During shared reading, make certain that they have time to share these words they were able to decode because of their explorations.

Strategies for Helping Students Decode Single Syllable Words that Follow Common Patterns and Multi-syllable Words

(This activity is presented in detail so it can actually be implemented with children in an intermediate classroom and also to provide detail for a potential constructed response question on a certification examination.)

The CVC phonics card game developed by Jackie Montierth, a computer teacher in South San Diego for use with 5th and 6th grade students, is a good one to adapt to the needs of any group with appropriate modifications for age, grade level and language needs.

The children use the vehicle of the card game to practice and enhance their use of consonants and vowels. Their fluency in this will increase their ability to decode words. Potential uses beyond whole classroom instruction include use as part of the small group word work component of the reading workshop and as part of cooperative team learning. This particular strategy also is particularly helpful for grade four and beyond English Language learners who are in a regular English Language classroom setting.

The card game works well because the practice of the content is implicit for transfer as the children continue to improve their reading skills. In addition, the card game format allows "instructional punctuation" using a student centered high interest exploration.

Card Design: The teacher can use the computer or use 5"x 8" index cards or actual card deck sized oaktag cards to create a deck. For repeated use and durability, it is recommended that the deck be laminated.

The deck should consist of the following:
44 consonant cards (including the blends)
15 vowel cards (including 3 of each vowel)
5 wild cards (which can be used as any vowel)
6 final e cards

The design of this project can also focus on particular CVC words that are part of a particular book, topic or genre format. In advance of playing the game, children can also be directed to review the words on the word wall or other words on a word map.

Procedure:

The game is best introduced first as part of a mini lesson with the teacher reading the rules, and a pair of children demonstrating step by step, when the game is played before the class for the first time. Have the children divide into pairs or small groups of no more than 4 per group. Each group needs one deck of C-V-C cards.

Have each group choose a dealer. The dealer shuffles the cards and deals 5 cards to each player. The remaining cards are placed face down for drawing during the play. One card is turned over to form the discard pile. Players may not show their cards to the other players. The first player to the left of the dealer looks at his/her cards and if possible, puts down three cards which make a consonant-vowel-consonant word. For more points, four cards forming a consonant-vowel-consonant word can be placed down. The player must then say the word and draw the number of cards he or she laid down. If he or she is unable to form a word, he/she draws either a card from either the draw or discard pile. The player then discards one card. All players must have 5 cards at all times. Play moves to the left.

The game continues until one or more of the following happens:
1. There are no more cards in the draw pile
2. All players run out of cards.
3. All players cannot form a word

The winner is the player who has laid down the most cards during the game.

Players may only lay down words at the beginning of their turn.
Proper names may not be counted as words.

Other ways the game may be played:

The game can be played with teams of individuals in a small group of four or fewer competing against one another (Excellent for special needs or resource room students). It can also be done as a whole class activity where all the students are divided into cooperative teams or small groups who compete against one another. This second approach will work well with a heterogeneous classroom that includes special needs and/or ELL children.

Teachers of ELL learners can do this game in the native language first and then transition it into English, facilitating native language reading skills and second language acquisition. They can develop their own appropriate decks to meet the vocabulary needs of their children and to complement the curricula.

Using Phonics to Decode Words in Connected Text

Identifying New Words

Some strategies to share with children during conferences or as part of shared reading include the following prompts:

- Look at the beginning letter/s... What sound do you hear?
- Stop to think about the text or story. What word with this beginning letter would make sense here?
- Look at the book's illustrations. Do they provide you with help in figuring out the new word?
- Think of what word would make sense, sound right, and match the letters that you see. Start the sentence over, making your mouth ready to say that word.
- Skip the word, read to the end of the sentence, and then come back to the word. How does what you've read help you with the word?
- Listen to whether what you are reading makes sense and matches the letters (asking the child to self-monitor). If it doesn't make sense, see if you can correct it on your own.
- Look for spelling patterns you know from the spelling pattern wall.
- Look for smaller words you might know within the larger word.
- Read on a little, and then return to the part that confused you.

Skill 13.2   Analyze the relationships among print sound code, word identification and meaning, fluency, and comprehension; identifying the characteristics of fluent readers; analyzing strategies that promote comprehension (e.g., modeling a variety of questions, connecting prior knowledge with new information)

See Skill 3.4

Skill 13.3   Identify multiple, metacognitive fix-up strategies for monitoring comprehension

See Skill 3.2

COMPETENCY 14.0 APPLY KNOWLEDGE OF VARIOUS STUDY STRATEGIES

Skill 14.1 Identify uses of print, nonprint, and electronic reference sources

Teachers should have a toolkit of instructional strategies, materials and technologies to encourage and teach students how to problem solve and think critically about subject content. With each curriculum chosen by a district for school implementation, comes an expectation that students must master benchmarks and standards of learning skills. There is an established level of academic performance and proficiency in public schools that students are required to master in today's classrooms. Research of national and state standards indicate that there additional benchmarks and learning objectives in the subject areas of science, foreign language, English language arts, history, art, health, civics, economics, geography, physical education, mathematics, and social studies that students are required to master in state assessments (Marzano & Kendall, 1996).

In the Florida Teacher Certification Standards, code 6A-5.065, critical thinking is the number 4 assessment criteria for effective teacher performance on the three levels below:

(4) Accomplished Practice Four - Critical Thinking.

  (a) Accomplished level. The accomplished teacher uses appropriate techniques and strategies, which promote and enhance critical, creative, and evaluative thinking capabilities of students.
  (b) Professional level. The professional teacher will use a variety of performance assessment techniques and strategies that measure higher order thinking skills in students and can provide realistic projects and problem solving activities, which will enable all students to demonstrate their ability to think creatively.

  (c) Preprofessional level. The preprofessional teacher is acquiring performance assessment techniques and strategies that measure higher order thinking skills in students and is building a repertoire of realistic projects and problem solving activities designed to assist all students in demonstrating their ability to think creatively. (www.floridateachercertificationstandards.org)

A critical thinking skill is a skill target that teachers help students develop to sustain learning in specific subject areas that can be applied within other subject areas.

For example, when learning to understand algebraic concepts in solving a math word problem on how much fencing material is needed to build a fence around a backyard area that has a 8' x 12," a math student must understand the order of numerical expression in how to simplify algebraic expressions. Teachers can provide instructional strategies that show students how to group the fencing measurements into an algebraic word problem that with minor addition, subtraction and multiplication can produce a simple number equal to the amount of fencing materials needed to build the fence.

Students use basic skills to understand things that are read such as a reading passage or a math word problem or directions for a project. However, students apply additional thinking skills to fully comprehend how what was read could be applied to their own life or how to make comparatives or choices based on the factual information given. These higher-order thinking skills are called critical thinking skills as students think about thinking and teachers are instrumental in helping students use these skills in everyday activities:

- Analyzing bills for overcharges
- Comparing shopping ads or catalogue deals
- Finding the main idea from readings
- Applying what's been learned to new situations
- Gathering information/data from a diversity of sources to plan a project
- Following a sequence of directions
- Looking for cause and effect relationships
- Comparing and contrasting information in synthesizing information

Teachers who couple diversity in instructional practices with engaging and challenging curriculum and the latest advances in technology can create the ultimate learning environment for creative thinking and continuous learning for students. Teachers who are innovative and creative in instructional practices are able to model and foster creative thinking in their students. Encouraging students to maintain journals and portfolios of their valued work from projects and assignments will allow students to make conscious choices on including a diversity of their creative endeavors in a filing format that can be treasured throughout the educational journey.

The ability to create a personal and professional charting of student's academic and emotional growth found within the performance-based assessment of individualized portfolios becomes a toolkit for both students and teachers. Teachers can use semester portfolios to gauge student academic progress and personal growth of students who are constantly changing their self-images and worldviews on a daily basis.

When a student is studying to master a math concept and is able to create visual of the learnings that transcend beyond the initial concept to create a bridge connecting a higher level of thinking and application of knowledge, then the teacher can share a moment of enjoyable math comprehension with the student.

The idea of using art concepts as visual imagery in helping students process conceptual learning of reading, math and science skills creates a mental mind mapping of learning for students processing new information. Using graphic organizers and concept web guides that center around a concept and the applications of the concept is an instructional strategy that teachers can use to guide students into further inquiry of the subject matter. Imagine the research of the German chemist Fredrich August Kekule when he looked into a fire one night and solved the molecular structure of benzene and you can imagine fostering that same creativity in students. Helping students understand the art of "visualization" and the creativity of discovery may impart a student visualizing the cure for AIDS or Cancer or how to create reading programs for the next generation of readers.

Helping students become effective note-takers and stimulating a diversity of perspectives for spatial techniques that can be applied to learning is a proactive teacher strategy in creating a visual learning environment where art and visualization become natural art forms for learning. In today's computer environment, students must understand that computers cannot replace the creative thinking and skill application that comes from the greatest computer on record, the human mind.

Using the Florida Standard Code to understand the three levels of professionalism and practice in technology listed below can also be simulated in the creative diversity of learning in the classroom.

Skill 14.2 Analyze how reading rate should vary depending on the purpose and difficulty of the material

Fluency is the ability to read a text quickly and accurately. In silent reading, readers can recognize words automatically and they fully comprehend what they read. If comprehension is not immediate, these readers can use context clues to grasp the meaning of the sentence or paragraph. When reading aloud, fluent readers display confidence and they read effortlessly and with expression (prosody). This is in contrast to readers that are not fluent – they read slowly, often one word at a time so that meaning is lost in an effort to read words with accuracy.

Fluency is an important skill when learning to read because it helps readers to develop from the word recognition stage to one where they can understand what they read. When readers don't have to spend time focusing on reading individual words, they can group words together to form ideas, which leads to comprehension. Not only can they grasp the main idea of the text, but they can make connections between the text and their prior knowledge and events in their own lives.

Fluency is a skill that readers have to develop over time with repeated practice and exposure to literature and opportunities to read for various purposes. Early readers read words rather than phrases and sentences and the act of reading often appears to be laborious rather than enjoyable. In order to become fluent, readers have to decode the letters and words. Eventually this leads to comprehension of ideas.

Even when readers do have a repertoire of words that they recognize easily, they may not be fluent readers. This is because the expression is missing from the reading. Reading fluently with expression means that the reader must be able to chunk the text into meaningful segments – phrases and clauses. Fluency changes over time as readers are exposed to more difficult texts. The most fluent readers at one level may read slowly when they are first introduced to a more difficult text because they need time for comprehension.

Some techniques to use when teaching students to read fluently include:
- repeated reading of the same text
- oral reading practice using audiotapes
- provide models of what fluent reading looks and sounds like
- read to students
- choral reading
- partner reading
- Readers' Theatre

Automaticity

Automaticity is not the same as fluency. This is the fast and effortless recognition of words that only comes through repeated practice. Automaticity refers to accurate reading of words. It does not refer to reading with expression or reading with comprehension. It deals with word recognition only. It is necessary for fluency, but it is not the only factor that determines whether or not a student can read fluently.

Skill 14.3 Identify techniques for managing time, organizing and recalling information, and test taking

Teacher's main job is to impart their own knowledge on students by guiding them to and through various pieces of information presented. There is so much information to be shared to the new students, these students must find some way to manage the large amount. Helping students find ways to be able to access all of the information presented is mutually beneficial and should be encouraged. There are many different types of study skills and helping techniques, which can be useful.

Time Management:
One of the hardest skills for students to learn is time management. Face it; it's difficult for many adults to manage their time well. Teaching this skill to students is important to start at a young age so they are better able to transfer this at a later time far into adulthood. Using a timer can be one step to start with younger children, helping them to complete assignments in a defined time frame. For older students, setting long term assignments for students to complete works on time management. Providing a calendar with due dates is a technique to help the students keep track.

Organization:
From the elementary years through high school, students need to have some method for keeping track of assignments and other materials. Many classes use a day planner type of system to help keep track of assignments. Colored folders are another strategy to help students keep track of their work. Assigning a different color to each subject provides with a built in organization tool. Organizing notes and other information through the use of graphic organizers can also be helpful to students.

Recalling Information:
Teaching students different memory techniques is critical to helping them file the new information in their internal file cabinets. The brain enjoys novelty and many of the memory techniques help provide just that. In addition, the brain generally only has about seven slots for new information to fill at any one time, so the more condensed information can be, the easier it will be for students to recall. Mnemonic devices are a good strategy for helping students to recall information.

Test Taking Strategies:
Teaching to the test is a phrase that will set push many teacher's buttons in a negative manner. However, it is important students understand generalities of how to approach the different types of tests. Preparing students with the understanding of weeding out answers they know are wrong immediately helps the student to be better approach a task. This type of teaching is important for all levels and grades, especially in the era of NCLB and accountability.

Skill 14.4   Analyze the process of learning through genuine inquiry

Throughout their career in education, few learning experiences are as meaningful as those completed through genuine inquiry. Students, who are able to discover the answers to questions they may have about various topics throughout their education, are more likely to become the life-long learners of the future.

Children are naturally curious creatures. They begin from the time they begin to explore their environment through touch, taste and their other senses as infants. This exploration can sometimes be stifled during school due to the fact that teachers have a set curriculum to cover, which may or may not be related to the things the children are actually interested in learning.

The process of inquiry involves more than simply asking a question and finding the answer to said question. Students involved in genuine inquiry are engaged in all facets of learning. They are researching various topics, finding truths and non-truths, comparing and contrasting, as well as combining new knowledge with prior knowledge.

The process can be very unstructured or structured depending on the teacher, student and the information to be gained. An unstructured approach usually involves one student's personal interests. This student has the desire to learn more about a topic and takes the initiative to use a library, the internet, or other sources of information to do some research to try and find the answers to their questions. Often times, the answers are found with little to no support from adults. Additional questions also tend to arise during this process, which most times lead to further answers in a continuing cycle of constant learning.

A structured approach is more often utilized in a school setting. Teachers want to feed the interests and excitement of their students and will often include projects where the students are able to choose their own methods of learning. For students who are proficient readers and writers, they are able to complete these types of more independent projects with less direct teacher input. Usually, the overall project has guidelines that are general enough to allow for a large variety of topics. Rubrics are most often the tool utilized for grading these projects.

Students, who struggle with reading and learning, often require more teacher support. Also, it is imperative for the teacher to find materials written on a level the student can read independently but match the topic. This can be a challenge for the teacher and the student. More specific guidance may also need to be provided as to the completion of the projects. These students, though they struggle with learning to read, have the same curious nature. They want to learn and have questions to ask. If the right teacher can tap into this wonderful spark and desire to learn, the process itself will encourage other skills to build and develop, including reading skills. After all, reading about something that interests you is what we adults do on a regular basis.

Skill 14.5   Specify ways to guide students as they set their own goals, select resources, investigate topics, organize and interpret data, draw inferences, and present their conclusions

Throughout the inquiry process, students need to understand how to manage their own work in progress. Staying on track to complete an assigned project can be overwhelming to children. It is important before leading children down the path of independent inquiry tasks, the teacher take the time to provide specific guidance and suggestions for possible management.

The first step is to help the student to determine realistic goals. This can be particularly hard for students, especially young children. They have a hard time setting appropriate attainable goals. It is the role of the teacher to help students whittle down over-reaching goals and find a middle ground or priority of goals.

Once the goal is set, the next phase of the project generally involves identifying appropriate resources. Teachers generally rely on the library and the librarian to help provide resources. Now that the Internet and computers are available to most students, they are often utilized as part of the resources available. Additionally, it may be necessary for the teacher or student to do some outreach into the community to find experts or other people with knowledge on the area for interview.

After resources have been located, it is the responsibility of the student to now gathers the necessary information related to their goal and topics. This may become overwhelming for them. Most times, students need organizational aides to be successful at gathering notes and the information. Teachers can provide guiding questions, outlines, or other graphic organizers to help students be successful during this process. Once all of the data is gathered, it needs to be organized into a more manageable manner. In this way, students can begin to weed out erroneous information and better focus on the more specific information, which relates directly to their goal or hypothesis. In this way, the students will be able to review all gathered information and begin to make their own interpretations. Mind mapping is a graphic organizing tool, which incorporates pictures and words to help students organize numerous concepts, thoughts and ideas.

Organization of the data allows the student to be able to draw conclusions and then make other inferences that can be explored at a later time as part of future inquiries. In the process of making inferences and drawing conclusions, the student needs to understand how to complete both of these activities. Modeling through oral reading activities and practice prior to the process of inquiry begin is a fundamental factor in the success of the student's with this process.

Finally, it is important for the students to be able to present in some manner the results they have gained throughout the process. This can be done in writing, orally or using other media formats.

<u>**DOMAIN IV.**</u>   **INSTRUCTION**

COMPETENCY 15.0 APPLY LITERACY INSTRUCTION THEORIES

Skill 15.1   Identify developmentally appropriate instructional practices that are based on learning theory and are supported by current research

Knowledge of the Significant Theories, Approaches, Practices and Programs for Developing Reading Skills and Reading Comprehension

Decoding

In the late l960's and the l970's, many reading specialists, most prominently Fries (l962), believed that successful decoding resulted in reading comprehension. This meant that if children could sound out the words, they would then automatically be able to comprehend the words. Many teachers of reading and many reading texts still subscribe to this theory.

Asking questions

Another theory or approach to the teaching of reading that gained currency in the late sixties and the early seventies was the importance of asking inferential and critical thinking questions of the reader which would challenge and engage the children in the text. This approach to reading went beyond the literal level of what was stated in the text to an inferential level of using text clues to make predictions and to a critical level of involving the child in evaluating the text. While asking engaging and thought-provoking questions is still viewed as part of the teaching of reading, it is only viewed currently as a component of the teaching of reading.

Comprehension "Skills"

As various reading theories, practices, and approaches percolated during the l970's and l980's, many educators and researchers in the field came to believe that the teacher of reading had to teach a set of discrete "Comprehension Skills" (Otto et al, l977). Therefore the reading teacher became the teacher of each individual comprehension skill. Children in such classrooms came away with: main idea, sequence, cause and effect, and other concepts that were supposed to make them better comprehenders. However, did it make them lifelong readers?

Transactional Approach

During the late 1970's and early 1980's, researchers in the field of education, psychology and linguistics, began to examine how the reader comprehends. Among them was Louise Rosenblatt who posited that reading is a transaction between the reader and the text. It is Rosenblatt (1978) who explained successful reading as the reader constructing a meaning from the text that reflected both the reader and the text. She described two general purposes for reading: *efferent* and *aesthetic*. Efferent reading is looking for and remembering information to use functionally. Examples would be filling out a job application, reading a story in preparation for a test, or reading a newspaper article to find out who won the state basketball championship. Aesthetic reading is done to connect one's own life to the text, to be swept away by the beauty of a poem, or to respond emotionally to a book such as *Bridge to Terabithia.*

These differing purposes call for somewhat different reading strategies: one might skim the newspaper article for basketball information but read a poem closely ten times and create mental images of different passages. Lastly, when children are asked to read all fiction efferently (What's the setting? What's the main conflict in the plot? There will be a test on this on Thursday!), it can thwart a child's joy in the written word and work against the student's desire to be a lifelong reader.

Bottom-up, Top-down, Interactional Theories of Reading

Bottom-up theories of reading assume that children learn from part-to-whole starting with the smallest segments possible. Instruction begins with a strong phonics approach, learning letter-sound relationships and often using basal readers or *decodable books*. Decodable books are vocabulary-controlled using language from word families with high predictability. Thus we get sentences like "Nan has a tan fan." Reading is seen as skills-based, and the skills are taught one at a time.

Top-down theories of reading suggest that reading begins with the reader's knowledge, not the print. Children are seen as having a drive to construct meaning. This stance views reading as moving from the whole to the parts. An early top-down theory was the *whole word* approach. Children memorized high-frequency words to assist them in reading the Dick and Jane books of the 30s. Then teachers helped children discover letter-sound correpondences in what they read. A more recent top-down theory is the *whole language* approach. This approach was influenced by research on how young children learned language. It was thought that children could learn to read as naturally as they learned to talk. Children were surrounded by print in their classrooms, using quality literature often printed in Big Books and were viewed as writers from the start. Hence journals kept by kindergarten children. Advocates of whole language viewed the "skill'em-drill'em-and kill'em" approach based on bottom-up theories as a deadly dull introduction to the world of reading.

Interactive theories of reading combine the strengths of both bottom-up and top-down approaches. Teachers need to be able to teach decoding, vocabulary, and comprehension skills to support children's drive for meaning and desire for a stimulating exchange with high-quality literary texts from their earliest days in school. Strategies include shared, guided, and independent reading, Big Books, reading and writing workshops, and the like. Today this approach is called the *balanced literacy approach*. It is considered to be a synthesis of the best from bottom-up and top-down methods.

Literacy and Literacy Learning

To be literate in the 21st century world means more than being able to read and write. To live well and happily in today's society an individual has to be able to read, not only newspapers and books, but emails, blogs, directions for how to use one's cell phone, and the like. There has evolved a "disconnect" between the isolated reading comprehension skills the schools were teaching and the literacy skills including listening and speaking that are crucial for employment and personal and academic success. Thornburg (1992, 2003) has also noted that technology capacities and the ability to communicate online are now integral parts of our sense of literacy.

Cooper (2004) views literacy as reading, writing, thinking, listening, viewing, and discussing. These are not viewed as separate activities or components of instruction, but rather as developing and being nurtured simultaneously and interactively. Children learn these abilities by engaging in authentic explorations, readings, projects and experiences.

Just as in learning how to ride a bike, the learner goes through various approximations before learning how to actually ride the bike, so too does the reader with the scaffold (support) of the teacher go through various approximations before developing his/her own independent literacy skills and capacities.

Emergent Literacy: the concept that young children are emerging into reading and writing with no real beginning or ending point. Children are introduced into the word of print as soon as their parents read board books to them at the age of one or two. When children scribble write or use invented spelling during the preschool years, they reveal themselves as detectives of the written word, having watched parents and teachers make lists, write thank-you notes, or leave messages. This view of the reader assumes that all children have a drive to make meaning in print and will begin doing it almost on their own if surrounded by a print-rich environment.

Reading Readiness: an approach which is antithetical to emergent literacy in that it assumes that all children must have mastered a sequence of reading skills before they can begin to read. This approach stands in contrast to emergent literacy.

Language Acquisition: continuous and never-ending. From the perspective of this theory and research, all children come to school with a language base which the school must build on. As a consequence of the connection between oral language and reading, it is important that schools build literacy experiences around the language the child brings to the school.

Prior Knowledge, Schemata, Background, and Comprehension

Schemata are structures which represent generic concepts stored in our memory (Rumelhart, l980). Young children develop their schemata through experiences. Prior knowledge and the lack of experiences in some cases influence comprehension. The more closely the reader's experiences and schemata approximate those of the writer, the more likely the reader is to comprehend the text. It is obvious that for many children from non-native English language speaking backgrounds and perhaps for those from struggling socio-economic family structures schemata deficits indicate the need for intense teacher support as these children become emergent and early readers.

Often the teacher will have to model and scaffold for the child the steps to form a schemata from the information provided in a text.

Comprehension: Cooper defines comprehension as: "a strategic process by which readers construct or assign meaning to a text by using the clues in the text and their own prior knowledge. " We view comprehension as a process where the reader transacts with the text to construct or assign meaning. Reading and writing are both interconnected and mutually supportive. Comprehension is a strategic process in which readers adjust their reading to suit their reading purpose and the type or genre of text they are reading. Narrative and expository texts require different reading approaches because of their different text structures.

Strategic readers also call into play their metacognitive capacities as they analyze texts so that they are self aware of the skills needed to construct meaning from the text structure.

The Role of Literature in Developing Literacy

The balanced literacy approach advocates the use of "real literature"—recognized works of the best of children's fiction and non-fiction trade books and winners of such awards as the Newberry and Caldecott medals for helping children develop literacy. Balanced literacy advocates argue that:

- Real literature engages young readers and assures that they will become lifelong readers.
- Real literature also offers readers a language base that can help them expand their expressiveness as readers and as writers.
- Real literature is easier to read and understand than grade-leveled texts

There are districts in the United States where the phonics-only approach is heavily embedded. However, the majority of school districts would describe their approach to reading as the balanced literacy approach which includes phonics work as well as the use of real literature texts. To contrast the phonics and balanced literacy approaches as opposite is inaccurate, since a balanced approach includes both.

It is important to go online and to visit the key resources of the NCTE, National Council of Teachers of English, and the IRA, International Reading Association, to keep abreast of the latest research in the field.

Skill 15.2 Analyze approaches and strategies that represent principles of authentic instruction (e.g., higher-order thinking, connections to the world beyond the classroom)

The interdisciplinary curriculum planning approach to student learning creates a meaningful balance inclusive of curriculum depth and breadth. Take for instance the following scenario: Mrs. Jackson presents her 9A Language Arts class with an assignment for collaborative group work. She provides them with the birthdate and death of the infamous author Ernest Hemingway and asks them to figure how old he was when he died. She gives them five minutes as a group to work on the final answer. After five minutes, she asked each group for their answer and wrote the answers on the board. Each group gave a different answer. When Mrs. Jackson came to the last group, a female student stated, "Why do we have to do math in a Language Arts class?"

The application of knowledge learned from a basic math class would have problem-solved the Language Arts' question. Given the date of his birth and the date of his death, all students needed to do was subtract his birth from his death year to come up with a numerical answer = age when he died. Providing students with a constructivist modality of applying knowledge to problem-solve pertinent information for a language arts' class should be an integral part of instructional practice and learning in an interdisciplinary classroom.

Historically, previous centuries of educational research have shown a strong correlation between the need for interdisciplinary instruction and cognitive learning application. Understanding how students process information and create learning was the goal of earlier educators. Earlier researchers looked at how the brain connected information pieces into meaning and found that learning takes place along intricate neural pathways that formulate processing and meaning from data input into the brain. The implications for student learning are vast in that teachers can work with students to break down subject content area into bits of information that can be memorized and applied to a former learning experience and then processed into integral resources of information.

The brain learning theorists believe that students formulate schematic structures of hundreds, oftentimes thousands, of interconnected and integrated bits of information that provide a framework for learning and meaning. The research of Ausubel (1968) understood the schematic structure of processing and "cognitive hooks" where students create links of connection in applying prior knowledge to new learning experiences.

Providing students with learning toolkits like clustering/mind mapping techniques that provide organizational tools for large quantities of information and establish associations between major and minor thematic context is vital to the visual or tactile-kinesthetic learner. Figure 1 (next page) shows a cluster of how students would understand the current events in Irag:

Figure 1. The Making of a Conflict-Iraq

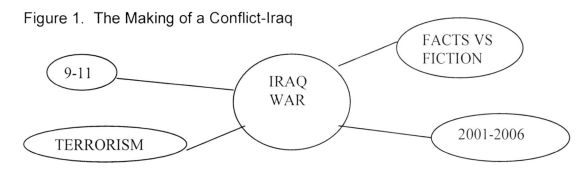

When students are provided opportunities in brainstorming sessions to construct meaning around a specific subject area, they are able to create new meaning and expand upon prior cognitive knowledge of an event. Teachers who utilize a diversity of instructional strategies in the classroom provide students with multiple styles of learning modalities, which for students can translate into academic and life successes.

There are many factors that affect student learning including how students learn and how learning is presented and/or based on background knowledge or experiences. There are several educational learning theories that can be applied to classroom practices. One classic learning theory is Piaget's stages of development which consist of four learning stages: sensory motor stage (from birth to age 2); pre-operation stages (ages 2 to 7 or early elementary); concrete operational (ages7 to 11 or upper elementary); and formal operational (ages 7-15 or late elementary/high school). Piaget believed children passed through this series of stages to develop from the most basic forms of concrete thinking to sophisticated levels of abstract thinking.

Some of the most prominent learning theories in education today include brain-based learning and the Multiple Intelligence Theory. Supported by recent brain research, brain-based learning suggests that knowledge about the way the brain retains information enables educators to design the most effective learning environments. As a results, researchers have developed twelve principles that relate knowledge about the brain to teaching practices. These twelve principles are:

- The brain is a complex adaptive system
- The brain is social
- The search for meaning is innate
- We use patterns to learn more effectively
- Emotions are crucial to developing patterns
- Each brain perceives and creates parts and whole simultaneously
- Learning involves focused and peripheral attention
- Learning involves conscious and unconscious processes
- We have at least two ways of organizing memory
- Learning is developmental
- Complex learning is enhanced by challenged (and inhibited by threat)
- Every brain is unique

(Caine & Caine, 1994, Mind/Brain Learning Principles)

Educators can use these principles to help design methods and environments in their classrooms to maximize student learning.

The Multiple Intelligent Theory, developed by Howard Gardner, suggests that students learn in (at least) seven different ways. These include visually/spatially, musically, verbally, logically/mathematically, interpersonally, intrapersonally, and bodily/kinesthetically.

The most current learning theory of constructivist learning allows students to construct learning opportunities. For constructivist teachers, the belief is that students create their own reality of knowledge and how to process and observe the world around them. Students are constantly constructing new ideas, which serve as frameworks for learning and teaching. Researchers have shown that the constructivist model is comprised of the four components:

1. Learner creates knowledge
2. Learner constructs and makes meaningful new knowledge to existing knowledge
3. Learner shapes and constructs knowledge by life experiences and social interactions
4. In constructivist learning communities, the student, teacher and classmates establish knowledge cooperatively on a daily basis.

Kelly (1969) states "human beings construct knowledge systems based on their observations parallels Piaget's theory that individuals construct knowledge systems as they work with others who share a common background of thought and processes." Constructivist learning for students is dynamic and ongoing. For constructivist teachers, the classroom becomes a place where students are encouraged to interact with the instructional process by asking questions and posing new ideas to old theories. The use of cooperative learning that encourages students to work in supportive learning environments using their own ideas to stimulate questions and propose outcomes is a major aspect of a constructivist classroom.

The metacognition learning theory deals with "the study of how to help the learner gain understanding about how knowledge is constructed and about the conscious tools for constructing that knowledge" (Joyce and Weil 1996). The cognitive approach to learning involves the teacher's understanding that teaching the student to process his/her own learning and mastery of skill provides the greatest learning and retention opportunities in the classroom. Students are taught to develop concepts and teach themselves skills in problem solving and critical thinking. The student becomes an active participant in the learning process and the teacher facilitates that conceptual and cognitive learning process.

Social and behavioral theories look at the social interactions of students in the classroom that instruct or impact learning opportunities in the classroom. The psychological approaches behind both theories are subject to individual variables that are learned and applied either proactively or negatively in the classroom. The stimulus of the classroom can promote conducive learning or evoke behavior that is counterproductive for both students and teachers. Students are social beings that normally gravitate to action in the classroom, so teachers must be cognizant in planning classroom environments that are provide both focus and engagement in maximizing learning opportunities.

Skill 15.3 Evaluate ways to help students apply individual, shared, and academic standards according to the purpose of the communication context

As technology invades all aspects of our work, students must be exposed to and expected to develop some level of proficiency with using various forms of communication. The communication context requires teachers to help the students to realize the many different formats of communication available to them. It allows students: to explore different media, provide current information and skills related to the various formats for communication.

The teacher must keep in mind that it important to utilize various methodologies as well as communication methods. An example might include having the students create a web page then at a later time correspond with pen pals in a different country via email.

Whatever process or technology used, the teacher needs to encourage a variety of different applications for the students. Having the students work alone sometimes and other times with peers is a useful strategy to help master the content.

Along those same lines, it is also important for students to create products that will sometimes be shared with others, while other products may be made for their own personal use. Knowing the purposes for various projects or assignments will help the students to better plan and create their products.

As the instructor it is important to understand how academic area standards can be incorporated into these different projects or assignments. As a reading specialist, it is of particular interest to see how reading and technology can work together. Employing various media to encourage reading or as an assessment tool can be powerful for all parties. Current innovations, like web quests, can provide an almost unlimited manner for all academic areas. If you are not familiar with web quests you can view various ones designed by other educators on any variety of academic topics at http://www.teach-nology.com/teachers/lesson_plans/computing/web_quests/ .

Students and teachers can work together to incorporate other communication contexts into the classroom to ensure students are prepared for the future and all it has to offer.

Skill 15.4 Analyze the use of various methodologies to teach reading, writing, listening, speaking, viewing, and visually representing

There are numerous methodologies for teaching the combined integrated language arts skills. There is no one approach, which will meet the needs of all students in a classroom or building. It is important to be aware of various methods to be able to utilize as many different strategies as possible to meet the needs of students within the classroom.

Reading: There are several main approaches to teaching reading in today's society. They include:
- Balanced Literacy – wherein the students will spend portion of each day reading to themselves, to the teacher, listening to the teacher read, and reading with the teacher
- Phonics – wherein the majority of reading instruction is accomplished by using systematic sequential phonics instruction
- Whole Language- wherein the instruction is managed through a reader's workshop and learning is accomplished by reading authentic literature
- Combination Approach-wherein authentic literature is combined with phonics instruction

Writing: Teachers generally teach writing through a process of grammar and more holistic writing assignments. Generally, the process involves explicit grammar instruction and specific spelling instruction. The holistic writing can include specific writing assignments from the various forms of writing (persuasive, narrative, expository, letters, etc.) and journaling. Most teaching of writing includes the writing process with brainstorming, rough drafts, peer editing and teacher editing being a complete part of the process. Students sometimes write for publication as well.

Listening and Speaking: Listening and speaking are generally not a subject for which you will find specific lesson plans for in a teacher's plans. They are usually incorporated through reading and presentation activities. Listening skills assessed and developed through the shared reading or other activities. Speaking skills are assessed through classroom discussion and oral presentations required throughout the curriculum. If there are difficulties in these areas, students may require specific instruction from a speech pathologist in these areas, at this point more intensive and specific skill development will occur.

Viewing: As technology has increased and become an integral part of the society, students are required more and more often to view information and respond in some format. Students can gain and gather more information than ever before using the Internet in addition to the traditional movies, slides and filmstrips. Using these media information tools, students may respond in a variety of formats (written response, graphic organizers, oral presentations, etc.).

Visual Representation: Students need to understand how to use the visual formats to represent thoughts and ideas. Mind mapping is a technique involving visually recording notes instead of a traditional outline. This allows more complex ideas to be recorded and specifically personalized to individual students experiences. Creation of charts and graphs is also a method used which bridges math and reading and can cross content areas. This mode of teaching should be combined with all of the above referenced methods to help students process information, as manipulating data or information to represent it in a different format requires a higher level of thinking.

COMPETENCY 16.0 APPLY METHODS FOR ENHANCING STUDENTS' READING COMPREHENSION

Skill 16.1 Describe appropriate uses of direct instruction

Direct Instruction

Siegfried Engelmann and Dr. Wesley Becker, and several other researchers proposed what they call direct instruction, a teaching method that emphasizes well-developed and carefully-planned lessons with small learning increments. It assumes that clear instruction that eliminates misinterpretations will improve outcomes. Their approach is being used by thousands of schools. It recommends that the popular valuing of teacher creativity and autonomy be replaced by a willingness to follow certain carefully prescribed instructional practices. At the same time, it encourages the retention of hard work, dedication, and commitment to students. It demands that teachers adopt and internalize the belief that all students, if properly taught, can learn.

There are many ways to evaluate a child's knowledge and assess his/her learning needs. In recent years, the emphasis has shifted from "mastery testing" of isolated skills to authentic assessments of what children know. Authentic assessments allow the teacher to know more precisely what each individual student knows, can do, and needs to do. Authentic assessments can work for both the student and the teacher in becoming more responsible for learning.

One of the simplest most efficient ways for the teacher to get to know his/her students is to conduct an entry survey. This is a record that provides useful background information about the students as they enter a class or school. Collecting information through an entry survey will give valuable insights into a student's background knowledge and experience. Teachers can customize entry surveys according to the type of information considered valuable. Some of the information that may be incorporated include student's name and age, family members, health factors, special interests, strengths, needs, fears, etc., parent expectations, languages spoken in the home, what the child likes about school, etc.

At the beginning of each school term the teacher will likely feel compelled to conduct some informal evaluations in order to obtain a general awareness of his/her students. These informal evaluations should be the result of a learning activity rather than a "test" and may include classroom observations, collections of reading and writing samples, and notations about the students' cognitive abilities as demonstrated by classroom discussions and participation including the students' command of language. The value of these informal evaluations cannot be underestimated. These evaluations, if utilized effectively, will drive instruction and facilitate learning.

After initial informal evaluations have been conducted and appropriate instruction follows, teachers will need to fine tune individual evaluations in order to provide optimum learning experiences. Some of the same types of evaluations can be used on an ongoing basis to determine individual learning needs as were used to determine initial general learning needs. It is somewhat more difficult to choose an appropriate evaluation instrument for elementary-aged students than for older students. Therefore, teachers must be mindful of developmentally appropriate instruments. At the same time, teachers must be cognizant of the information that they wish to attain from a specific evaluation instrument. Ultimately, these two factors—students' developmental stage and the information to be derived—will determine which type of evaluation will be most appropriate and valuable. There are few commercially designed assessment tools that will prove to be as effective as the tool that is constructed by the teacher.

A simple-to-administer, information-rich evaluation of a child's reading strengths and weaknesses is the running reading record. "This technique for recording reading behavior is the most insightful, informative, and instructionally useful assessment procedure you can use for monitoring a child's progress in learning to read;" (Traill, 1993) The teacher uses a simple coding system to record what a child does while reading text out loud. At a later time the teacher can go back to the record and assess what the child knows about reading and what the teacher needs to address in an effort to help the student become a better reader.

If the teacher is evaluating a child's writing, it is a good idea to discourage the child from erasing his/her errors and to train the child to cross out errors with a single line so that the teacher can actually see the process that the student went through to complete a writing assignment. This writing becomes an important means of getting to know about students' writing and is an effective, valuable writing evaluation.

Mathematics skills can be evaluated informally by observing students as they work at their seats or perform at the board. Teachers can see if the students know basic computation skills, if they understand place value, or if they transpose numbers simply by watching them as they solve computation problems. Some teachers may prefer to administer some basic computation "tests" to determine a student's mathematics strengths and weaknesses. Although these "tests" are not as effective or thorough in assessing students, they are quick and easy to administer.

One of the most valuable and effective assessment tools available to any teacher is the classroom observation. As instructional decision makers, teachers must base their instructional strategies upon students' needs. An astute observer of student behaviors and performance is most capable of choosing instructional strategies that will best meet the needs of the learners. Classroom observations take place within the context of the learning environment thus allowing the observer the opportunity to notice natural behaviors and performances.

Classroom observations should be sensitive and systematic in order to permit a constant awareness of student progress. One of the shortcomings of classroom observations is that they are often performed randomly and frequently are focused on those students whose behaviors are less than desirable. If the teacher establishes a focused observation process then observations become more valuable. It has been suggested that a teacher focus his/her observations on five or six students at a time for a period of one to two weeks.

In order for observations to truly be useful, teachers must record the information obtained from observations. When doing a formal behavioral observation, the teacher will write what the child is doing for a designated time period. At times the teacher will tally the occurrences of specific behaviors within a designated time period. When making focused observations that are ongoing, the teacher may simply use a blank piece of paper with only the student's name and date written on it and space for the teacher to write anecdotal notes. Other teachers might write on post-it notes and put the information in a student's file. If it is not possible to record the information as it occurs and is observed, it is critical that it be recorded as soon as possible in order to maintain accuracy.

Sometimes it is helpful to do an observation simply to watch for frequency of a specific behavior. An observation can answer questions such as: Is the student on-task during independent work time? Is the student interacting appropriately with peers? Is the student using materials appropriately? These behaviors can be tallied on a piece of paper with the student's name and date of observation.

Classroom observations can provide the teacher with one of the most comprehensive means of knowing their students. Teachers can observe students to see how they interact with their peers, to see which activities they choose, what they like to read, and how frequently they choose to work alone. "Everything you hear a child say and see a child do is a glimpse into a mind and a source of information to 'know' from." (Traill, 1993)

Skill 16.2   Determine when and how to use multiple comprehension strategies in a variety of texts

The Relationship Between Oral and Written Vocabulary Development and Reading Comprehension

Biemiller's (2003) research documents that those children entering 4th grade with significant vocabulary deficits demonstrate increasing reading comprehension problems. Evidence shows that these children do not catch up, but rather continue to fall behind.

Strategy One: Word Map Strategy

This strategy is useful for children grades 3-6 and beyond. The target group of children for this strategy includes those who need to improve their independent vocabulary acquisition abilities. The strategy is essentially teacher-directed learning where children are "walked through" the process. They are helped by the teacher to identify the type of information that makes a definition. They are also assisted in using context clues and background understanding to construct meaning.

The word map graphic organizer is the tool teachers use to complete this strategy with children. Word map templates are available online from the Houghton Mifflin web site and from READWRITETHINK, the web site of the NCTE (see webliography section). The word map helps the children to visually represent the elements of a given concept.

The children's literal articulation of the concept can be prompted by three key questions: What is it?; What is it like? What are some examples?

For instance, the word "oatmeal" might yield a word map with "What?", and in a rectangular box a hot cereal you eat in the morning, "What is it like?"; hot, mushy, salty, "What are some examples?", instant oatmeal you make in a minute, apple-flavor oatmeal, Irish Oatmeal.

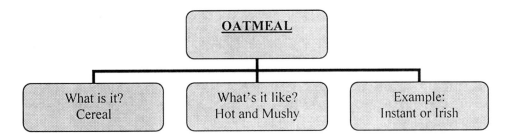

The procedure to be used in sharing this strategy with children is to select three concepts the children are familiar with. Then show them the template of a word map. Tell them that the three questions asked on the map and the boxes to fill in beneath them helps readers and writers to see what they need to know about a word. Next, help the children to complete at least two word maps for two of the three concepts that were pre-selected. Then have the children select a concept of their own to map either independently or in a small group. As the final task for this first part of the strategy, have the children, in teams or individually, write a definition for at least one of the concepts using the key things about it listed on the map. Have the children share these definitions aloud and talk about how they used the word maps to help them with the definitions.

For the next part of this strategy, the teacher should pick up an expository text or a textbook the children are already using to study mathematics, science or social studies. The teacher should either locate a short excerpt where a particular concept is defined or use the content to write model passages of definition on his/her own.

After the passages are selected or authored, the teacher should duplicate them. Then they should be distributed to the children along with blank word map templates. The children should be asked to read each passage and then to complete the word map for the concept in each passage. Finally, have the children share the word maps they have developed for each passage. Give them a chance to explain how they used the word in the passage to help them fill out their word map. End by telling them that the three components of the concept-class, description, example- are just three of the many components for any given concept.

This strategy has assessment potential because the teacher can literally see how the students understand specific concepts by looking at their maps and hearing their explanations. The maps the students develop on their own demonstrate whether they have really understood the concepts in the passages. This strategy serves to ready students for inferring word meanings on their own. By using the word map strategy, children develop concepts of what they need to know to begin to figure out an unknown word on their own. It assists the children in grades 3 and beyond to connect prior knowledge with new knowledge.

This word map strategy can be adapted by the teacher to suit the specific needs and goals of instruction. Illustrations of the concept and the comparisons to other concepts can be included in the word mapping for children grades 5 and beyond. This particular strategy is also one that can be used with a research theme in other content areas.

Strategy Two: Preview in Context

This is a direct teaching strategy which allows the teacher to guide the students as they examine words in context prior to reading a passage. Before beginning the strategy, the teacher selects only two or three key concept words. Then the teacher reads carefully to identify passages within the text that evidence strong context clues for the word.

Then the teacher presents the word and the context to the children. As the teacher reads aloud, the children follow along. Once the teacher has finished the read aloud, the children re-read the material silently. After the silent re-reading, the children will be coached by the teacher to a definition of one of the key words selected for study. This is done through a child-centered discussion. As part of the discussion, the teacher asks questions which get the children to activate their prior knowledge and to use the contextual clues to figure out the correct meaning of the selected key words. Make certain that the definition of the key concept word is finally made by the children.

Next, help the children to begin to expand the word's meaning. Do this by having them consider the following for the given key concept word: synonyms, antonyms, other contexts or other kinds of stories/texts where the word might appear. This is the time to have the children check their responses to the challenge of identifying word synonyms and antonyms by having them go to the thesaurus or the dictionary to confirm their responses. In addition, have the children place the synonyms or antonyms they find in their word boxes or word journals. The recording of their findings will guarantee them ownership of the words and deepen their capacity to use contextual clues.

The main point to remember in using this strategy is that it should only be used when the context is strong. It will not work with struggling readers who have less prior knowledge. Through listening to the children's responses as the teacher helps them to define the word and its potential synonyms and antonyms, the teacher can assess their ability to successfully use context clues. The key to this simple strategy is that it allows the teacher to draw the child out and to grasp through the child's responses the individual child's thinking process. The more talk from the child the better.

The Role of Systematic, Noncontextual Vocabulary Strategies

Strategy One: Hierarchical and Linear Arrays

The very complexity of the vocabulary used in this strategy description, may be unnerving for the teacher. Yet this strategy included in the Cooper (2004) literacy instruction is really very simple once it is outlined directly for children.

By using the term "hierarchical and linear" arrays, Cooper really is talking about how some words are grouped based on associative meanings. The words may have a "hierarchical" relationship to one another. For instance, an undergraduate or a first grader is lower in the school hierarchy than the graduate student and second grader. Within an elementary school, the fifth grader is at the top of the hierarchy and the pre K or kindergartener is at the bottom of the hierarchy. By the way, the term for this strategy obviously need not be explained in this detail to K-3 children, but might be shared with some grade and age appropriate modifications with children in grades 3 and beyond. It will enrich their vocabulary development and ownership of arrays they create.

Words can have a linear relationship to one another in that they run a spectrum from bad to good-for example from K-3 experiences, pleased-happy-overjoyed. These relationships can be displayed in horizontal boxes connected with dashes. Below is another way to display hierarchical relationships.

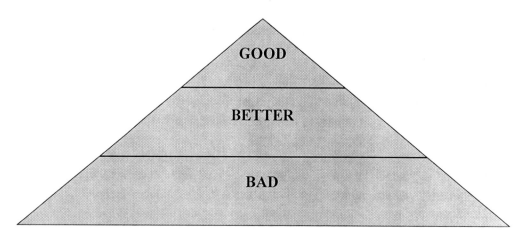

Once you get past the seemingly daunting vocabulary words, the arrays turn out to be another neat, graphic organizer tool which can help children "see" how words relate to one another.

To use this graphic organizer, the teacher should pre-select a group of words from a read aloud or from the children's writing. Show the children how the array will look using arrows for the linear array and just straight lines for the hierarchy. In fact invite some children up to draw the straight hierarchy lines as it is presented, so they have a role in developing even the first hierarchical model. Do one hierarchy array and one linear array with the pre selected word with the children. Talk them through filling out (or helping the teacher to fill out) the array.

After the children have had their own successful experience with arrays, they can select the words from their independent texts or familiar, previously read favorites to study. They will also need to decide which type of array, hierarchical or linear, is appropriate. For 5th and 6th graders, this choice can and should be voiced using the now "owned" vocabulary words "hierarchical array" and "linear array."

This strategy is best used after reading, since it will help the children to expand their word banks.

Contextual Vocabulary Strategies

Vocabulary Self-Collection. This strategy is one in which children, even on the emergent level from grade 2 and up, take responsibility for their learning. It is also by definition, a student centered strategy, which demonstrates student ownership of their chosen vocabulary.

This strategy is one that can be introduced by the teacher early in the year, perhaps even the first day or week. The format for self-collection can then be started by the children. It may take the form of a journal with photocopied template pages. It can be continued throughout the year.

To start, ask the children to read a required text or story. Invite them to select one word for the class to study from this text or story. The children can work individually, in teams or in small groups. The teacher can also do the self-collecting so that this becomes the joint effort of the class community of literate readers. Tell the children that they should select words which particularly interest them or which are unique in some way.

After the children have had time to make their selections and to reflect on them, make certain that they have time to share them with their peers as a whole class. When each child shares the word which he or she has selected, have them provide a definition for the word. Each word that is given should be listed on a large experiential chart or even in a BIG BOOK format, if that is age and grade appropriate. The teacher should also share the word he or she selected and provide a definition. The teacher's definition and sharing should be somewhere in the middle of the children's recitations.

The dictionary should be used to verify the definitions. When all the definitions have been checked, a final list of child-selected (and single teacher-selected) words should be made.

Once this final list has been compiled, the children can record it in their word journals or they may opt to record only those words they find interesting in their individual journals. It is up to the teacher at the onset of the vocabulary self-collection activity to decide whether the children have to record all the words on the final list or can eliminate some. The decision made at the beginning by the teacher must be adhered to throughout the year.

To further enhance this strategy children, particularly those in grades 3 and beyond, can be encouraged to use their collected words as part of their writings or to record and clip the appearance of these words in newspaper stories or online. This type of additional recording demonstrates that the child has truly incorporated the word into his/her reading and writing. It also habituates children to be lifelong readers, writers, and researchers.

One of the nice things about this simple but versatile strategy is that it works equally well with either expository or narrative texts. It also provides children with an opportunity to use the dictionary.

Assessment is built into the strategy. As the children select the word for the list, they share how they used contextual clues and through the children's response to the definitions offered by their peers, their prior knowledge can be assessed.

What is most useful about this strategy is that it documents that children can learn to read and write by reading and writing. The children take ownership of the words in the self-collection journals and that can also be the beginning of writer observation journals as they include their own writings. They also use the word lists as a start for writers' commonplace books. These books are filled with newspaper, magazine, and functional document clippings using the journal words.

This activity is a good one for demonstrating the balanced literacy belief that vocabulary study works best when the words studied are chosen by the child.

The Relationship between Oral Vocabulary and the Process of Identifying and Understanding Written Words

One way to explore the relationship between oral vocabulary and the comprehension of written words is through the use of Oral Records (which are discussed at length in the appendix).

In *On Solid Ground: Strategies for Teaching Reading K-3*, Sharon Taberski (2000) discusses how oral reading records can be used by the K-3 teacher to assess how well children are using cueing systems. She notes that the running record format can also show visual depictions for the teacher of how the child "thinks" as the child reads. The notation of miscues in particular shows how a child "walks through" the reading process. They indicate if and in what ways the child may require "guided" support in understanding the words he or she reads aloud. Taberski notes that when children read they need to think about several things at once. First, they must consider whether what they are reading makes sense (semantic or meaning cues). Next, they must know whether their reading "sounds right" in terms of Standard English (syntactic and structural cues). Third, they have to weigh whether their oral language actually and accurately matches the letters the words represent (visual or graphophonic cues).

In taking the running record and having the opportunity first-hand to listen to the children talk about the text, the teacher can analyze the relationship between the child's oral language and word comprehension. Information from the running record provide the teacher with a road map for differentiated cueing system instruction.

For example, when a running record is taken, a child often makes a mistake but then self-corrects. The child may select from various cueing systems when he or she self-corrects. These include: "M" for meaning, "S" for syntax, and "V" for visual. The use of a visual cue means that the child is drawing on his or her knowledge of spelling patterns. Of course, Tabereski cautions that any relationship between oral language and comprehension that the teacher draws from an examination of the oral-reading records, must be drawn using a series of three or more of the child's oral reading records, taken over time, not just one.

A teacher can review children's running records over time to note their pattern of miscues and which cues they have the greatest tendency to use in their self-corrections. Whichever cueing system the children use to the greatest extent, it is necessary for the teacher to offer support in also using the other cueing systems to construct correct meaning. Taberski suggests that while assessing running records to determine the relationship between oral language and meaning, the children read from "just right" books.

Strategies for Promoting Oral Language Development and Language Comprehension

Read-Alouds (This is the corner piece of the balanced literacy approach for teaching reading. Therefore it is advised that the teacher candidate and new teacher read this material carefully. This may well appear as an essay topic in the Constructed Response section).

Comments:

Within the context of the Balanced Literacy Approach and the Literacy Block, the Read Aloud is part of the Whole Class Activities. The book selected should be one taken from the classroom library, which is appropriate for a read aloud. Before reading the book to the class, the teacher needs to be familiar with it. The teachers should also "plan" or at least "know" what nuances of content, style, rhythm, and vocabulary that will be emphasized in the reading.

In addition, specifically for the younger grades, the teacher should select a text which also enhances the development of phonemic awareness. This might include a text that can be used to teach rhyming, alliteration, or poetry.

Sometimes, read-aloud texts are selected for their tie-ins with the science, social studies and mathematics curriculum.

Generally teachers aim to teach one strategy during the read-aloud, which the children will practice in small groups or independently. Among these strategies for the first grader could be print strategies and talking about books.
As the teacher reads aloud, the teachers' voice quality should highlight his or her enjoyment of the read-aloud and involvement with its text. Often in a balanced literacy classroom, the teacher reads from a specially decorated Reader's Chair, as do the guest readers. This chair's decorativeness, complete with comfortable throwback pillows or rocking chair style frame, is meant to set an atmosphere that will promote the children's engagement in and love for lifelong reading.
The balanced literacy approach also advocates that teachers select books which children will enjoy reading aloud. Particularly accessible texts for the elementary school classroom read-alouds are collections of poetry.

Teachers must allow time for discussion during and after each Read Aloud period. After the children have made comments, the teacher should also talk about the reading.

Knowledge of Common Sayings, Proverbs and Idioms

Strategy: The Fortune Cookie Strategy (Reissman, 1994). Grades 3 and up

Distribute just before snack (fortune cookies) to the children. Have them eat the cookies and then draw their attention to the fortunes which are enclosed.

First, the teacher will model by reading aloud and sharing his/her own fortune. After reading the fortune aloud, the teacher will explain what the fortune means using its vocabulary as a guide. Finally the teacher can share whether or not the teacher agrees with the statement made in the fortune.

Children can either volunteer to share their fortunes or each can read the fortune aloud, explain the saying and tell whether he or she agrees with the proverb.

Next, children can be asked to go home and interview their parents or community members to get family proverbs and common sayings.

Once the children return with the sayings and proverbs, they can each share them and explain their meaning. The class as a whole can discuss to what extent these sayings are true for everyone. Proverbs and Sayings can become part of a word wall or be included in a special literacy center. The teacher can create fill in, put together, and writing activities to go with the proverbs. They tie in nicely with cultural study on the grade 3-6 level including Asian, Latin American, and African nations.

What makes proverbs particularly effective for vocabulary development are the limited number of words in their texts and the fact these short texts allow for guided and facilitated reading instruction.

This strategy also highlights in a positive way the uniqueness and commonality of the family proverbs which are contributed by children from ELL backgrounds. If possible their proverbs can also be posted in their native languages as well as in English.

See for further proverbs: http://www.serve.com/shea/germusa/prov1.htm

Write like a Babylonian:
http://www.upennmuseum.com/cuneiform.cgi

Write like an Egyptian:
http://www.upennmuseum.com/hieroglyphsreal.cgi

Knowledge of Foreign Words and Abbreviations Commonly Used in English (e.g. RSVP)

Strategy: RSVP your foreign language in English literacy

Of course, the English language is replete with abbreviations that are shortened forms of words from other languages. Not only can this be used for expanding children's vocabulary and writing variety; but also it can help to positively highlight the bilingual and sometimes trilingual abilities of ELL students.

The teacher should develop a word strip mix and match game with commonly found foreign words and abbreviations. These items should, if possible, be cut out of newspapers and flyers to highlight their authenticity as part of every day life objects. Among those common words and abbreviations might be: perfume, liqueur (chocolate, of course), latte, cappuccino, panni, brioche, latkes, etc. Food, local Starbucks, coffee houses, and bakeries are excellent sources of these abbreviations. To get sufficient material to cut out to start the game, just get an extra Sunday newspaper or pick up a few circulars from a large supermarket.

Model for the children how to play the game and find out the common words or abbreviations meaning and foreign derivation using the dictionary.

Next have the children as a whole class or in small groups, work to identify the derivations of the foreign words and even map them on a world map.

As part of additional, foreign word center activities, children can opt among a number of choices. These can include: maintaining a BIG BOOK OF FOREIGN WORDS or ABBREVIATIONS, to which many contribute, using the weekly food circulars and collecting labels with foreign words which can then be collaged with an accompanying product list, authoring stories and true accounts featuring as many foreign words as possible.

What is productive about this strategy is that it enhances vocabulary development while it also highlights the extent to which the English language as spoken, used and written in the United States currently, is embedded with foreign language words and terms. This of course, makes the native language talents of the ELL child positive and important ones.

Extending a Reader's Understanding of Familiar Words

Dictionary Use:

Dictionaries are useful for spelling, writing, and reading.
It is very important to initially expose and habituate students to enjoy using the dictionary.

Cooper (2004) suggests that the following be kept in mind as the teacher of grades K-6 introduces and then habituates children to a lifelong fascination with the dictionary and vocabulary acquisition.

Requesting or suggesting that children look up a word in the dictionary should be an invitation to a wonderful exploration, not a punishment or busy work that has no reference to their current reading assignment.

Model the correct way to use the dictionary for children even as late as the third – sixth grade. Many have never been taught proper dictionary skills. The teacher needs to demonstrate to the children that as an adult reader and writer, he or she routinely and happily uses the dictionary and learns new information that makes him or her better at reading and writing.

Cooper believes in beginning dictionary study as early as kindergarten and this is now very possible because of the proliferation of lush picture dictionaries which can be introduced at that grade level. He also suggests that children not only look at these picture dictionaries, but also begin to make dictionaries of their own at this grade level filled with pictures and beginning words. As children join the circle of lexicographers, they will begin to see themselves as compilers and users of dictionaries. Of course, this will support their ongoing vocabulary development.

In early grade levels, use of the dictionary can nicely complement the children's mastery of the alphabet. They should be given whole class and small group practice in locating words.

As the children progress with their phonetic skills, the dictionary can be used to show them phonetic re-spelling using the pronunciation key.

Older children in grades 3 and beyond need explicit teacher demonstrations and practice in the use of guide words. They also need to begin to learn about the hierarchies of various word meanings. In the upper grades, children should also explore using special content dictionaries and glossaries in the backs of their books.

Strategies for Promoting Comprehension Across the Curriculum by Expanding Knowledge of Content Area Vocabulary

Key Words

Cooper (2004) feels that it is up to the teacher to preview the content area text to identify the main ideas. Then the teacher should compile a list of terms related to the content thrust. These terms and words become part of the key concepts list. Next, the teacher sees which of the key concept words and terms are already defined in the text. These will not require direct teaching. Words for which children have sufficient skills to determine their meaning through base, root, prefixes or suffixes, also will not require direct teaching.

Instruction in the remaining key words, which should not be more than two or three in number, can be provided before, during or after reading. If students have previewed the content area and identified those words they need support on, the instruction should be provided before reading. Instruction can also easily be provided as part of guided reading support. After reading support is indicated, the text offers the children an opportunity to enrich their own vocabularies.

Having children work as a whole class or in small groups on a content specific dictionary for a topic regularly covered in their grade level social studies, science, or mathematics, curriculum offers an excellent collaborative opportunity for children to design a dictionary/word resource that can celebrate their own vocabulary learning. Such a resource can then be used with the next year's classes as well.

Development of Vocabulary Knowledge and Skills in Individual Students

Hierarchical and linear array vocabulary development strategies lend themselves well to support the struggling learners or second language learners. The use of the arrays allows these learners to use a visual format to "see" and diagram word relationships. Furthermore the diagrams are easy to make, and they can be illustrated. With sufficient support and modeling, many special needs children can do simple linear and hierarchical arrays on their own. The arrays can also be attractively displayed in resource rooms and in regular education classrooms as a demonstration of these individual students' ownership of their words.

English Language Learners should first capably demonstrate their capacity to fill out hierarchical and linear arrays in their native language and then can work with this same format to hone their English Language vocabulary development. Their native language hierarchical relationships and arrays can be displayed in their general education classrooms. Teachers may also want to encourage children grades 3 and beyond to make connections between some of the native, other than English, words and words derived from them in English. This could be a rich "buddy" (ELL child and native English Language speaker) investigation or it could be one for ELL children alone. At any rate, use of the array with the ELL child's native language makes that child a second language vocabulary owner which immediately includes the child positively in ongoing vocabulary development.

Cooper (2004) suggests that teachers who have children from different language backgrounds use any unscheduled or "extra" time that emerges for read-alouds.

Using the Semantic Feature Analysis Grid

Highly proficient readers can be asked to help same grade peers or better yet younger peers with their word analysis skills by having them work with these struggling readers on filling out teacher developed semantic analysis grids. Some 5th and 6th grade highly proficient readers may also evidence the aptitude and desire to create their own semantic analysis grids for their peer or younger peer tutees. In this way, highly proficient readers can gain insights into the field of teaching reading at an early age and younger struggling readers can have the edge taken off their struggles by working with a peer or an older student. For both individual students the experience is one that promotes and celebrates word analysis skills and nurtures the concept of a literate and caring community of readers.

ELL students can also add in deliberate items to the categories which reflect their cultures. For instance, Latino children can add in plantains and guava to the fruits their non-Latino peers might list. This provides the ELL learners with an opportunity to enrich the knowledge base of their peer's subject category inventory and puts them in a positive spotlight. The easy notations on the grid make it accessible for even ELL children with limited English language writing and speaking capacities.

Special Needs learners can benefit from the grid. It can be developed by teachers, paraprofessionals, and tutors. It can be notated by the children themselves. They can also illustrate it. It can be posted or kept in the word center. The grid provides these learners who are often spatial learners with a concrete demonstration of their word analysis achievement.

Biemiller's research indicates that the listening vocabulary for a 6th grader who tests at the 25 percentile in reading is equivalent to that attained by the 75th percentile 3rd grader. This deficit in vocabulary presents a formidable challenge for the 6th grader to succeed, not only on reading tests, but in various content subjects in elementary school and beyond.

Skill 16.3   Determine ways to help students use various aspects of text (e.g., genres, text structure, conventions of written English) to gain comprehension

Knowledge of Reading as a Process to Construct Meaning

If there were two words synonymous with reading comprehension as far as the balanced literacy approach is concerned, they would be "constructing meaning."

Cooper, Taberski, Strickland, and other key theorists and classroom teachers conceptualize the reader as interacting with the text and bringing his/her prior knowledge and experience to it. Writing is interlaced with reading and is a mutually integrative and supportive parallel process. Hence the division of literacy learning by the balanced literacy folks into reading workshop and writing workshop, with the same anchor "readings" or books being used for both.

Consider the sentence, "The test booklet was white with black print, but very scary looking."

According to the idea of constructing meaning as the reader read this sentence, the schemata (generic information stored in the mind) of tests the reader had experienced was activated by the author's notion that tests are scary. Therefore the ultimate meaning that the reader derives from the page is from the reader's own responses and experiences coupled with the ideas the author presents. The reader constructs a meaning that reflects the author's intent and also the reader's response to that intent.

It is also to be remembered that generally readings are fairly lengthy passages, composed of paragraphs which in turn are composed of more than one sentence. With each successive sentence, and every new paragraph, the reader refocuses. The schemata are reconsidered, and a new meaning is constructed.

Knowledge of levels of reading comprehension and strategies for promoting comprehension of imaginative literary texts at all levels

Sharon Taberski (2000) recommends that initially strategies for promoting comprehension of imaginative literary texts be done with the whole class.

Here are Taberski's four main strategies for promoting comprehension of imaginative literary texts. She feels that if repeated sufficiently during the K-3 years and even if introduced as late as grade 4, these strategies will even serve the adult lifelong reader in good stead.

Strategy One: "Stopping to Think" –reflecting on the text as a whole. x
As part of this strategy, the reader is challenged to come up with the answer to these three questions: What do I think is going to happen? (Inferential)
Why do I think this is going to happen? (Evaluative and inferential)
How can I prove that I am right by going back to the story? (inferential)

Taberski recommends that teachers introduce these key strategies with books that can be read in one sitting and recommends the use of picture books for these instructive strategies.

Taberski also suggests that books which are read aloud and used for this strategy also contain a strong storyline, some degree of predictability, a text that invites discussion and a narrative with obvious stopping points.

Strategy Two: story mapping, for promoting comprehension of imaginative/literary texts.

For stories to suit this strategy, they should have distinct episodes, few characters and clear-cut problems to solve. In particular, Taberski tries to use a story where a single, central problem or issue is introduced at the beginning of the story and then resolved or at least followed through by the close of the story. To make a story map of a particular story, Taberski divides the class into groups and asks one group of children to illustrate the "Characters" in the book. Another group of children are asked to draw the "Setting," while a third and fourth group of children tackle "Problem " and "Resolution." The story map may also help children hold together their ideas for writing in the writing workshop as they take their reading of an author's story to a new level.

Strategy Three: The Character Mapping strategy also used by Taberski focuses the children as readers on the ways in which the main character's personal traits can determine what will happen in the story. Character mapping works best when the character is a non-stereotypical individual, has been featured perhaps in other books by the same author, has a personality that is somewhat predictable, and is capable of changing behavior as a consequence of what happens.

Using writing to share, deepen, and expand understanding of literary texts is a cornerstone of the balanced literacy approach.

Strategy Four: Taberski advocates reading sections of stories aloud and then having the teacher pause to reflect on what's happened in the story and model writing down a response to it. The teacher can use a chart to record his/her response to the events or characters of a particular story being read and the children can contribute their comments as well. Later on, the children can start reflective reader's notebooks or journals recording their reactions to their readings independently.

The best types of texts for this type of response are those that relate to age appropriate issues for young children (i.e. homework, testing, bullies, and friendship), a plot that can be interpreted in different ways, a text that is filled with questions, and a text full of suspense or wonder.

Development of Literary Response Skills

Literary response skills are dependent on prior knowledge, schemata and background. Schemata (the plural of schema) are those structures which represent concepts stored in our memory.

Without schemata and experiences to call upon as they read, children have little ability to comprehend. Of course, the reader's schemata and prior knowledge have more influence on the comprehension of plot or character information that is implied rather than directly stated.

Prior Knowledge

Prior knowledge can be defined as all of an individual's prior experiences, learning, and development which precede his/her entering a specific learning situation or attempting to comprehend a specific text. Sometimes prior knowledge can be erroneous or incomplete. Obviously, if there are misconceptions in a child's prior knowledge, these must be corrected so that the child's overall comprehension skills can continue to progress. Prior knowledge of children includes their accumulated positive and negative experiences both in and out of school.

These might come from wonderful family travels, watching television, visiting museums and libraries, to visiting hospitals, prisons and surviving poverty.

Whatever the prior knowledge that the child brings to the school setting, the independent reading and writing the child does in school immeasurably expands his/her prior knowledge and hence broadens his/her reading comprehension capabilities.

The teacher must consider as he/she prepares to begin any imaginative/literary text the following about the students' level of prior knowledge:

1. What prior knowledge needs to be activated for the text, theme or for the writing to be done successfully?
2. How independent are the children in using strategies to activate their prior knowledge?

Holes and Roser (1987) have suggested five techniques for activating prior knowledge before starting an imaginative/literary text:
Free Recall: Tell us what you know about...

Unstructured Discussion: Let's talk about...

Structured Question: Who exactly was Jane Aviles in the life of the hero of the story?

Word Association: When you hear these words--hatch, elephant, who, think-- What author do you think of?

Recognition: Mulberry Street...What author comes to mind?

Previewing and predicting and story mapping are also excellent strategies for activating prior knowledge.

Development of Literary Analysis Skills

There are many exciting ways to sensitize and to teach children about the features and formats of different literary genres.

Strategy One: Genre Switch-Reader and Writer Transformation

This strategy should be introduced as a read aloud with young children or with children who are struggling readers. In a similar fashion, it would be introduced as a read-aloud for ELL learners. Older children in grades 3-6 might just be "started off" by a teacher prompt and do the required reading on their own.

To begin, the teacher selects a particular genre book. If it is close to Halloween, a goblin or suspense story will do well. The teacher begins to read the story with the open invitation to the students to determine as the story is being read, what type of story it is and what makes it that type of story.

Older children take notes in their reading journals, while younger children and those more in need of explicit teacher support contribute their ideas and responses as part of the discussion in class. Their responses are recorded on a chart.

As the reading continues, the story type components are listed on the chart (most of the responses are those which have been elicited from the children).

At some point in what is either an oral read aloud, guided reading or independent reading, the teacher directs the children's attention to the components which have emerged on the chart. They then use these components which are generally components of character - setting, plot, style, conflict, language – to identify the story genre.

The teacher provides the children with an opportunity to expound at length on why this story is an example of the genre which they have identified.
Once they have done so, the teacher challenges them to consider how this story with its set of given characters, plot, and setting would be changed if the genre were different. The teacher can challenge the class as a whole with the idea of changing the story to a radically different genre—i.e. from suspense to a fairy tale or a comedy or allow the children to come up another genre.

Then depending on the children's developed writing abilities, they might be given time to rewrite the story on their own or re-tell it in class prior to writing and illustrating it.

In the balanced literacy approach, this transformation of the story into another genre is done as part of the Writing Workshop component which uses the same reading material as the source for writing. The strategy results in the children having had the experience of an in-depth analysis of a particular genre as well as hands-on writing (or telling, if they can not yet write or can not yet write in English) experience of restyling that basic plot and characters into another genre. This authenticates the children's participation as readers and writers.

Strategy Two: Analyzing Story Elements

Story elements include plot (including conflict and resolution, setting (including time and place), characters (flat and round/static and dynamic), and theme (the main idea of the story). Students can use graphic organizers such as story maps, compare/contrast displays, and sequence boxes to display their understanding of these critical features of fiction.

Strategy Three: Analyzing Character Development

Characters in children's literature may be flat or round. A flat character is one-dimensional and is often defined by one characteristic. Rosie in *Rosie's Walk* is an example. A round character seems like someone you know, such as Jess in *Bridge to Terabithia*. Static characters do not change from the beginning to the end of the story, while dynamic ones do. Characters reveal themselves through their actions, their interactions, and through what they say.

Strategy Four: Interpreting Figurative Language

Similes are direct comparisons between two things using "like" or "as." "Her eyes were like stars" is a simile. Metaphors are indirect comparisons, such as "The earth is a big blue marble." Personification is giving human characteristics to non-animal beings. Frances, Shrek, or the animals in *Mr. Gumpy's Outing* are all examples of personification.

Strategy Five: Identifying Literary Allusions

Children can understand allusions best when they read a lot. A literary allusion when it appears in a story is also called *intertextuality*. That is when a reference, character, or symbol from one story appears or is alluded to in another. Recently, many popular children's books use literary allusions, from the Ahlbergs' *Each Peach Pear Plum* to Jon Scieszka's *The True Story of the Three Little Pigs*. Note that any character or plot element can become allusions, not just references from fairy tales.

Strategy Six: Analyzing the Author's Point of View

In fiction, point of view is the vantage point from which the narrator tells the story. We determine point of view by asking, where is the narrator standing in relation to the characters? Is the narrator inside or outside of the story? If inside, is the narrator one of the characters? This is *first person point of view.* If outside, can the narrator "see" into anyone else's mind besides his/her own? If the narrator cannot see into the mind and heart of other characters, then the point of view is *third person limited.* Narrators who can see what other characters are thinking and feeling are using *third person omniscient point of view.*

Use of Comprehension Strategies Before, During, and After Reading

Cooper (2004), Taberski (2000), Cox (2005) and other researchers recommend a broad array of comprehension strategies before, during, and after reading.

Cooper (2004) suggests a broad range of classroom posters on the walls plus explicit instruction to give children prompts to monitor their own reading. An example follows: My Strategic Reading Guide

I. Do I infer/predict important information, use what I know, think about what may happen or what I want to learn?
2. Can I identify important information about the story elements?
3. Do I generate questions and search for the answers?
4. Does this make sense to me? Does this help me meet my purpose in reading?
5. If lost, do I remember fix-ups?
   Re-read, read further ahead, look at the illustrations, ask for help, and think about the words, and evaluate what I have read.
6. Do I remember to think about how the parts of the stories that I was rereading came together?

Storyboard panels, which are used by comic strip artists and by those artists who do advertising campaigns as well as television and film directors, are perfect for engaging children K-6 in a variety of comprehension strategies before, during, and after reading. They can storyboard the beginning of a story, read aloud, and then storyboard its predicted middle or end. Of course, after they experience or read the actual middle or ending of the story, they can compare and contrast what they produced with its actual structure. They can play familiar literature identification games with a buddy or as part of a center by storyboarding one key scene or characters from a book and challenging a partner or peer to identify the book and characters correctly.

Use of Oral Language Activities to Promote Comprehension

Retelling

Retelling needs to be very clearly defined so that the child reader does not think that the teacher wants him or her to spill the WHOLE story back in the retelling. A child should be able to talk comfortably and fluently about the story he or she has just read. He or she should be able to tell the main things that have happened in the story.

When a child retells a story to a teacher, the teacher needs ways to help him or her assess the child's understanding. Ironically, the teacher can use some of the same strategies he or she suggests to the child to assess the child's understanding of a book which is not familiar to the teacher. These strategies include: back cover reading, scanning the table of contents, looking at the pictures, and reading the book jacket.

If the child can explain how the story turned out and provide examples to support these explanations, try not to interrupt him or her with too many questions. Children can use the text of the book to reinforce what they are saying and they can even read from it if they wish. It is also important to note that some children need to re-read the text twice and their re-reading of it is out of enjoyment.

When the teacher plans to use the retelling as a way of assessing the child, then the following ground rules have to be set and made clear to the child. The teacher explains the purpose of the retelling to determine how well the child is reading at the outset of the conference.

The teacher maintains in the child's assessment notebook or in his/her assessment record what the child is saying in phrases, not sentences. Just enough is recorded to indicate whether the child actually understood the story. The teacher also tries to analyze from the retelling why the child can not comprehend a given text. If the child's accuracy rate with the text is below 95 per cent, then the problem is at the word level, but if the accuracy rate for the text is above 95 per cent, the difficulty lies at the text level.

Development of the Reading Comprehension Skills and Strategies of Individual Students

ELL Learners bring to their classrooms different prior knowledge concerns than do their native English language speaking peers. Some of the ELL students have extensive prior knowledge in their native language and can read well on or above their chronological age level in their native language. Other ELL learners come to the United States from cultures where reading was not emphasized or circumstances did not give families native language literacy opportunities.

Rigg and Allen (l999) offer the following four principles regarding the literacy development and prior knowledge of ELL-second language learners:

1. In learning a language you learn to do the things you want to do with people who are speaking that language.
2. A second language, like the first, does not develop linearly, but rather globally.
3. Language can develop in rich context.
4. Literacy develops parallel to language, so as speaking and listening for the second language develop, so do writing and reading.

As far as retelling, it needs to be noted that English language learners have the problem of not bringing rich oral English vocabulary to the stories they are decoding. Therefore, often they "sound the stories out" well, but can not explain what they are about, because they do not know what the words mean.

Use of Oral Reading Fluency in Facilitating Comprehension

At some point it is crucial that just as the nervous, novice bike rider finally relaxes and speeds happily off, so too must the early reader integrate graphophonic cues with semantic and structural ones. Before this is done, the oral quality of early reader's has a stilted beat to it, which of course does not promote reading engagement and enjoyment.

The teacher needs to be at his/her most dramatic to model for children the beauties of voice and nuance that are contained in the texts whose print they are tracking so anxiously. Children love nothing more than to mimic their teacher and can do so legitimately and without hesitation, if the teacher takes time each day to recite a poem with them. The poem might be posted on chart paper and be up on the wall for a week.

First the teacher can model the fluent and expressive reading of this poem. Then with a pointer, the class can recite it with the teacher. As the week progresses, the class can recite it on their own.

Use of Writing Activities to Promote Literary Response and Analysis

In addition to the activities already mentioned, the activities below will promote literary response and analysis:

*   Have children take a particular passage from a story and retell it from another character's perspective.

- Challenge children to suggest a sequel or a prequel to any given story they have read.

- Ask the children to recast a story in which the key characters are male into one where the key characters are female (or vice versa). Have them explain how these changes alter the narrative, plot, or outcome.

- Encourage the children to transform a story or book into a Reader's Theater format and record it complete with sound effects for the audio-cassette center of the classroom.

- Have the children produce a newspaper as the characters of a given story would have reported the news in their community.

- Transform the story into a ballad poem or a picture book version for younger peers.

Give ELL children an opportunity to translate stories into their native language or to author in English with a buddy a favorite story that was originally published in their native language.

Knowledge of Levels of Reading Comprehension (Literal, Inferential, and Evaluative) and Strategies for Promoting Comprehension of Informational/expository Texts at All Three Levels

There are five key strategies for child reading of informational/expository texts.

1.   Inferencing is a process that involves the reader making a reasonable judgment based on the information given and engages children to literally construct meaning. In order to develop and enhance this key skill in children, they might have a mini lesson where the teacher demonstrates this by reading an expository book aloud (i.e. one on skyscrapers for young children) and then demonstrates for them the following reading habits: looking for clues, reflecting on what the reader already knows about the topic, and using the clues to figure out what the author means/intends.

2.   Identifying main ideas in an expository text can be improved when the children have an explicit strategy for identifying important information. They can make this strategy part of their everyday reading style, "walking" through the following exercises during guided reading sessions. The child should read the passage so that the topic is readily identifiable to him or her. It will be what most of the information is about.

Next the child should be asked to be on the lookout for a sentence within the expository passage that summarizes the key information in the paragraph. Then the child should read the rest of the passage or excerpt in light of this information and also note which information in the paragraph is less important. The important information the child has identified in the paragraph can be used to formulate the author's main idea. The child reader may even want to use some of the author's own language in stating that idea.

3.   Monitoring means self-clarifying: As one reads, the reader often realizes that what he or she is reading is not making sense. The reader then has to have a plan for making sensible meaning out of the excerpt. Cooper and other balanced literacy advocates have a stop and think strategy which they use with children. The child reflects, "Does this make sense to me?" When the child concludes that it does not, the child then either re-reads, reads ahead in the text, looks up unknown words or asks for help from the teacher.

What is important about monitoring is that some readers ask these questions and try these approaches without ever being explicitly taught them in school by a teacher. However, these strategies need to be explicitly modeled and practiced under the guidance of the teacher by most, if not all child readers.

4.   Summarizing engages the reader in pulling together into a cohesive whole the essential bits of information within a longer passage or excerpt of text. Children can be taught to summarize informational or expository text by following these guidelines. First they should look at the topic sentence of the paragraph or the text and ignore the trivia. Then they should search for information which has been mentioned more than once and make sure it is included only once in their summary. Find related ideas or items and group them under a unifying heading. Search for and identify a main idea sentence. Finally, put the summary together using all these guidelines.

Generating questions can motivate and enhance children's comprehension of reading in that they are actively involved. The following guidelines will help children generate meaningful questions that will trigger constructive reading of expository texts. First children should preview the text by reading the titles and subheadings. Then they should also look at the illustrations and the pictures. Finally they should read the first paragraph. These first previews should yield an impressive batch of specific questions.

Next, children should get into a Dr. Seuss mode and ask themselves a "THINK" question. Make certain that the children write down the question. Then have them read to find important information to answer their "think" question. Ask that they write down the answer they found and copy the sentence or sentences where they found the answer. Also have them consider whether, in light of their further reading through the text, their original question was a good one or not.

Ask them to be prepared to explain why their original question was a good one or not. Once the children have answered their original "think" question, have them generate additional ones and then find their answers and judge whether these questions were "good" ones in light of the text.

Strategies for Identifying Point of View, Distinguishing Facts from Opinions and Detecting Faulty Reasoning in Informational/expository Texts

Expository texts are full of information which may or may not be factual and which may reflect the bias of the editor or author. Children need to learn that expository texts are organized around main ideas. Expository content is commonly found in newspapers, magazines, content textbooks, and informational reference books (i.e. atlas, almanac, yearbook of an encyclopedia).

The five types of expository texts (also called "text structures") to which the children should be introduced through modeled reading and a teacher facilitated walk through are:

Description text: This usually gives the characteristics or qualities of a particular topic. It can be depended upon to be factual. Within this type of text, the child reader has to use all of his or her basic reading strategies, because these types of expository texts do not have explicit clue words.

Causation or Cause- Effect text: This text is one where faulty reasoning may come into play and the child reader has to use inferential and self-questioning skills to assess whether the stated cause-effect relationship is a valid one. Clue words to look for are: "therefore", "the reasons for", "as a result of", "because", "in consequence of", and "since." The reader must then decide whether the relationship is valid. For example, does the ventricle pump blood into the heart?

Comparison text: This is an expository text which gives contrasts and similarities between two or more objects and ideas. Many social studies, art, and science text books in class and non-fiction books include this contrast. Key words to look out for are: like, unlike, resemble, different, different from, similar to, in contrast with, in comparison to, and in a different vein. It is important that as children examine texts which are talking about illustrated or photographed entities can review the graphic representations for clues to support or contradict the text.

Collection text: This text presents ideas in a group. The writer presents a set of related points or ideas. This text structure is also called a listing or a sequence. The author frequently uses clue words such as first, second, third, finally, and next to alert the reader to the sequence. Based on how well the writer structures the sequence of points or ideas, the reader should be able to make connections. It is important the writer make clear in the expository text how the items are related and why they follow in that given sequence. Simple collection texts that can be literally modeled for young children include recipe making. A class of first graders, beginning readers and writers, were literally spellbound by a teacher's presentation of a widely known copyrighted collection text. The children were thrilled as the author followed the sequences of this collection text, and the children finally took turns stirring it until it was creamy and smooth. The children enjoyed eating their Cream Farina from a commercial cereal box which had cooking directions on it.

The children had constructed meaning from this five minute class demonstration and would now pay close attention to collection texts on other food and product instruction boxes because this text had become an authentic part of their lives.

Response structure expository texts present a question or response followed by an answer or a solution. Of course, entire mathematics text books and some science and social studies text books are filled with these types of structures. Again it is important to walk the child reader through the excerpt and to sensitize the child to the clue words which signal this type of structure. These words include, but are not limited to the problem is, the question is, you need to solve for, one probable solution would be, an intervention could be, the concern is, and another way to solve this would be.

Newspapers provide wonderful features which can be used by the teacher as read-alouds to introduce children grades 3-6 to point of view distinctions, specifically, editorials, editorial cartoons and key sports editorial cartoons. Children can also come to understand the distinction between fact and fiction, when they examine a newspaper advertisement or a supermarket circular for a product they commonly use, eat, drink or wear which includes exaggerated claims about what the product can actually do for the individual in question.

Finally the fact versus opinion distinction can be nicely explored if a teacher takes the children online to look at some star web sites and walks them through some exaggerated claims made about their particular movie star favorites. It is very important at some point, if the children have access to the internet, that the teacher show them how to examine web sites, look at who developed a particular web site and consider how credible the developers of the site are.

Use of Reading Strategies for Different Texts and Strategies

As children progress to the older grades (3-6), it is important for the teacher to model for them that in research on a social studies or science exploration, it may not be necessary to read every single word of a given expository information text. For instance, if the child is trying to find out about hieroglyphics, he or she might only read through those sections of a book on Egyptian or Sumerian civilization which dealt with picture writing. The teacher, assisted by a child, should model how to go through the table of contents and the index of the book to identify only those pages which deal with picture writing. In addition other children should come to the front of the room or to the center of the area where the reading group is meeting. They should then, with the support of the teacher, skim through the book for illustrations or diagrams of picture writing which is the focus of their need.

Children can practice the skills of skimming texts and scanning for particular topics that connect with their grade Social Studies, Science and Mathematics content area interests.

Use of Comprehension Skills Before, After, and During Reading

Cooper (2004) advocates that the child ask himself or herself what a text is about before he or she reads it and even during reading of the text, what the text is going to be about. The child should be continually questioning himself or herself as to whether the text confirmed the child's predictions. Of course after completing the text, the child can then review the predictions and verify whether they were correct.

Using another strategy, the child reader looks over the expository text subheadings, illustrations, captions and indices to get an idea about the book. Then the child, still before reading the text, decides whether he or she can find the answer to his or her question.

Use of Oral Language Activities to Promote Comprehension

Taberski advocates using the "Stopping to Think About" strategy with expository texts as well as fictional ones.

This strategy is centered on the reader's using three "steps" as he or she goes through the expository text. These steps may be expressed as questions.

I. What do I, the reader, think is going to happen?
2. What clues in the text or illustrations or graphics lead me to think that this is going to happen?
3. How can I prove that I am right by going back to the text to demonstrate that this does happen or is suggested by actual clues in the text?

Taberski (2000) deliberately uses expository texts that relate to her grade's social studies and science lessons to model for children how to "stop and think" about the way an expository text is organized. She sometimes deliberately reads a section of a text or a non-fiction book aloud until the end of its chapter, so that the children can consider what they have learned about the topic and how it is organized. Then together as a whole class or as a whole guided reading group, they make predictions about what is coming next.

Development of Reading Comprehension Skills and Strategies of Individual Students

While all child readers can benefit from explicit expository reading strategies, the English Language Learner can truly get a gateway for understanding second language materials by working with a native English language speaking buddy on the question generating strategy. Both the buddy (a peer) and the teacher should alert and walk through with the English Language Learner student how much of a resource illustrations and pictures can be for constructing meaning. If the teacher has time to work individually with the English Language Learner, the day's daily newspaper which is replete with graphics, photos and text is a wonderful tool for honing expository reading skills using these strategies.

The five strategies for enhancing expository reading skills are not beyond use with learners with special needs. However, rather than be offered in an array, these strategies would have to be presented one at a time probably one on one with explicit teacher modeling and then done as shared reading and shared writing with the specific child.

Highly proficient readers might enjoy sharing their skills with other peers and could serve as the newspaper reading buddies for special needs students. They might not only support special needs grade level or younger peers in reading through a designated newspaper section every day, but might also collaborate or oversee their peers or younger peers in designing a word search or crossword puzzle based on that particular section of the newspaper.

Use of editorial sports page cartoons is a good way to introduce special needs learners to opportunities for identifying point of view. They can also create their own takes on the topics of the editorial cartoons using an accessible, non-threatening storyboard format for their commentary.

The Role of Oral Language Fluency in Facilitating the Comprehension of Informational/expository Texts

Children on the middle and secondary levels of education, who are studying social studies content, have been exposed to what social studies educators call re-enactments. This is a Reader's Theater- version of history and cultural study based completely on fact and established historical texts and documents.

Even young children will enjoy and gain tremendous additional expository comprehension facility when they are asked to dramatize a well known historical document or song. They may act out the preamble to the Constitution or read aloud as a chorus the Declaration of Independence or dramatize the Battle Hymn of the Republic. This gives children an opportunity to examine in deep form the vocabulary, syntactic, and semantic clues of these texts. They then have to use their oral instruments (voices) to express the appropriate expression for the texts.

If the children are in grades 4 and above, they can also be asked to "explain" in writing how they used the word, syntactic and semantic clues to interpret their oral language recitation. Recitation and writing can be a powerful experience for children grades 4 and up as they build their expository reading and writing skills.

Use of Writing Activities to Promote Comprehension

K-W-L Strategy

This is a graphic organizer strategy which activates children's prior knowledge and also helps them to target their reading of expository texts. This focus is achieved through having the children reflect on three key questions.

Before the child read the expository passage:
"What do I *Know*?" and
"What do I or we *W*ant to find out?"

After the child has read the expository passage:
"What have I or we *L*earned from the passage?"

What is excellent about this strategy, which is broadly used and easily implemented in almost any classroom, is that it is almost totally student- centered and powerfully focuses the child's attention on the actual reading of expository passages. The K-W-L strategy also helps the child prepare for a potential writing task.

When the teacher first introduces the K-W-L strategy, the children should be allowed sufficient time to brainstorm what all of them in the class or small group actually know about the topic. The children should have a three-columned K-W-L worksheet template for their journals and there should be a chart up front to record the responses from class or group discussion. The children can write under each column in their own journal, and should also help the teacher with notations on the chart. This strategy involves the children actually gaining experience in note taking and having a concrete record of new data and information they have gleaned from the passage about the topic.

Depending on the grade level of the participating children, the teacher may also want to channel them into considering categories of information they hope to find out from the expository passage. For instance, they may be reading a book on animals to find out more about the animal's habitats during the winter or about the animal's mating habits.

When children are working on the middle- section (*Want*) strategy sheet, the teacher may give them a chance to share what they would like to learn further about the topic and help them to express it in question format.

K-W-L is useful and can even be introduced as early as grade 2 with extensive teacher support. It not only serves to support the child's comprehension of a particular expository text, but also models for children a format for note taking. Beyond note taking, when the teacher wants to introduce report writing, the K-W-L format provides excellent outlines and question introductions for at least three paragraphs of a report.

Cooper (2004) recommends this strategy for use with thematic units and with reading chapters in required science, social studies, or health text books. In addition to its usefulness with thematic unit study, K-W-L is wonderful for providing the teacher with a concrete format to assess how well children have absorbed pertinent new knowledge within the passage (by looking at the third *Learn* section). Ultimately it is hoped that students will learn to use this strategy, not only under explicit teacher direction with templates of K-W-L sheets, but also on their own by informally writing questions they want to find out about in their journals and then going back to their own questions and answering them after reading.

Use of Text Features (e.g. Index, Glossary) - Graphic Features (e.g. Charts, Maps) and Reference Materials

Traditionally, the aspects of expository text reading comprehension have been taught in a dry format using reference books from the school or public library, particularly, the Atlas, Almanac, and dusty large geography volumes, to teach these necessary and meaningful skills.

Although these worthy library and perhaps classroom library books can still be used, it is much easier to take a simple newspaper to introduce and provide children with daily ongoing, authentic experiences in learning these necessary skills as they also keep up with real world events that affect their daily lives.

They can go on a chronological hunt through the daily newspaper and discover the many formats of schedules contained therein. For instance, some newspapers include a calendar of the week with literary, sports, social, movie and other public events. Children can also go on scavenger hunts through various sections of the newspaper and on certain days find full blown timelines detailing famous individual's careers, business histories, and milestones in the political history of a nation or even key movies made by a famous movie director up for an Oscar.

The nature of the newspaper reportage and the public's need to know the why and wherefore behind the story of natural disasters, company takeovers, political downfalls and uprisings leads newspapers to represent events graphically and to use cause /effect diagramming and comparison/contrast wording. If the teacher specifically wants to make certain that the students come away with this material, he or she can pre-clip "teaching" stories from the news for the child and introduce them in a special NEWS center.

After children have been walked through these comparison/contrast news writings and cause/effect diagramming as it has appeared in the newspaper, they can be challenged to find additional examples of these text structures in the news or challenged to reframe or rewrite familiar stories using these text structures. They can even use desktop publishing to re-author the stories using the same text structures.

If a class participates in a local Newspaper in Education program, where the children receive a free newspaper two to three times a week within the classroom, the teacher can teach index skills using the index of the newspaper and having children compete or cooperate in small groups to find various features.

Map and chart skills take on much more relevance and excitement when the children work on these skills using sport charts detailing the batting averages and pass completions of their favorite players or perhaps the box scores of their older siblings' football and baseball games. Maps dealing with holiday weather become meaningful to children as they anticipate a holiday vacation.

Ability to Apply Reading Skills for Various Purposes

What is really intriguing about the use of newspapers as a model and an authentic platform for introducing children into recognizing and using expository text structures, features and references, is that the children can demonstrate their mastery of these structures by putting out their own newspapers detailing their school universe using some of these text structures.
They can also create their own timelines for projects or research papers they have done in class using newspaper models.

Application of Comprehension Strategies for Electronic Texts

If the class gets newspapers in the classroom as part of an ongoing Newspapers in Education program, it is natural and easy for the teacher to take the time to show children how their same news is covered online. All of the newspapers have e-news. Children can first do a K-W-L on what they know or think they know about e-news and then actually review their specific daily newspaper's site. With the support of the teacher or an older peer, they can examine the resource and perhaps note the following differences in electronic text:

- Use of moving pictures and video to document events
- Use of sound clips in addition to written text
- Use of music/sound effects not in printed text
- Links to other web resources and to other archived articles

Of course, this can lead to much rich discussion and to further detailed web versus print news resource analysis. For children in grades 5 and 6, this might even include a research investigation of a particular news story or event including broadcast media coverage.

Development of Reading Comprehension Skills and Strategies of Individual Students

Both English Language Learners and struggling readers can benefit from the structure and format of the K-W-L approach. It allows them to share their prior experiences and knowledge of the topics covered in the expository text through natural conversation. It provides them with a natural device for the teacher or tutor to customize and to scaffold instruction to meet their linguistic and experiential backgrounds. Through the discussion and sharing of other children's comments, struggling readers and children from ELL backgrounds have an opportunity to learn how to use questions to "walk through" and take notes on expository writing.

Highly proficient readers can do a comparative expository news event study between print accounts, e-news reportage, and broadcast media coverage. They can prepare charts and their own news mock-up to show the similarities and contrasts between what aspects of the event get covered in what media format. They may also want to write to actual reporters and editors from the different media to share their insights and see if these professionals are willing to respond.

"If we want children to become strategic readers, then we create classrooms that reinforce the strategies we've demonstrated and allow children to practice on books that match their needs."
Sharon Taberski

Skill 16.4 Understand how to help students use strategies for monitoring their own comprehension

Reading comprehension is not a passive process. When we read for understanding, we are consciously focused on obtaining meaning through a variety of methods. For instance, we might access background knowledge to help us understand new ideas. Or we might go back and re-read a few sentences to clarify a confusing concept.

When we apply various strategies to make sense of text, we first have to monitor our levels of comprehension. In other words, we need to know when comprehension is breaking down; we need to notice that we aren't actually understanding something. Furthermore, we need to know what it is that is causing our confusion. By understanding what we do not understand, as well as why we do not understand, we will be in a better position to pick the right strategy to fix our comprehension. There are various ways to teach students how to monitor their comprehension. Below is a brief description of two of the most common methods.

Think-alouds are deliberate explanations of comprehension strategies provided to students out-loud by the teacher. Basically, the teacher models to students his or her own comprehension strategies as he or she reads aloud some text. For example, the teacher might run across a confusing idea and mention to the class that an ideal strategy would be to go back and re-read a section of text. Or, the teacher might come across a difficult word and piece it apart to see if meaning can be derived from context. This strategy helps students in a few ways. First, students get to see that reading is not necessarily a continuous process, but rather one that takes multiple strategies to successfully understand what is written. Second, it actually gives students specific strategies they can use when they come across similar situations.

Another strategy to teach the monitoring of comprehension is by teaching students to use self-questioning strategies. Self-questioning strategies simply are active reading cues—essentially, reminders to students that they can keep comprehension visible as they read by asking themselves common questions about their text. For example, students can be trained to self-predict about the next section at the end of each section of a long story. They can also ask themselves continuously, "why?" In other words, as events unfold in a story, they can constantly ask themselves, "Why did this occur?" or "Why did the character do this or that?" These types of questions greatly assist in the comprehension of text simply because they force readers to be more aware of what is going on within the text. In essence, they cause readers to be less lazy as they read.

Skill 16.5 Describe the monitoring and fix-up strategies students can use to overcome difficulties when constructing and conveying meaning

Students are going to make mistakes when reading, it is inevitable. There will be words previously unknown, context that is difficult to interrupt, or other issues which will arise during reading. As the end result of reading, is to understand and have meaning from the text, it is important for readers to be able to recognize their errors and have a regular set of strategies to help them be able to achieve comprehension.

This idea of self-monitoring is one of the most crucial skills to master once a student has successfully completed the basics of learning to read. Self-monitoring itself is recognizing when what is being read does not make sense. This may be as basic as rereading a passage when it seems confusing. In this way, readers can use context clues or other whole passage information to gather information to help clarify the meaning of words, or the general idea behind a passage.

Another strategy of self-monitoring good readers use is to ask themselves questions as they are reading. These questions help to clarify the information and provide possible inferences for future reading. The self-questioning takes place silently and often is unrecorded and sometimes students aren't even aware of the questions they are asking themselves.

Summarizing is another strategy, which can be used to help students obtain meaning from reading, particularly when they have large bodies of information to take in themselves. Teaching students to periodically stop and summarize what has been read can be very productive for readers who are struggling with comprehension.

Making predictions is also helpful to achieving appropriate levels of comprehension. Students start off making predictions that are so off base and wild that they are impossible when considering the text and known information. Students, who are taught how to make predictions and base them on the known, have a better understanding of what was previously read. Thereby they have adequate if not better than adequate reading comprehension.

Incorporating these fix-up strategies when reading comes naturally to some students, but to others it requires specific time and teaching. Generalization is difficult for the students who struggle with reading skills and comprehension. Providing cues and graphic organizers may aid in the ability of these students to utilize the above-described strategies. Rereading text and passages multiple times is a good strategy for modeling how to use these fix-up strategies.

COMPETENCY 17.0 APPLY METHODS FOR ENHANCING STUDENTS' ORAL COMMUNICATION

Skill 17.1 Apply knowledge of methods used to teach students effective listening strategies and elements of effective speaking

Effective Listening Strategies:

Oral speech can be very difficult to follow. First, we have no written record in which to "re-read" things we didn't hear or understand. Second, oral speech can be much less structured and even than written language. Yet, aside from re-reading, many of the skills and strategies that help us in reading comprehension can help us in listening comprehension. For example, as soon as we start listening to something new, we should tap into our prior knowledge in order to attach new information to what we already know. This will not only help us understand the new information more quickly, it will also assist us in remembering the material.

We can also look for transitions between ideas. Sometimes, in oral speech, this is pretty simple when voice tone or body language changes. Of course, we don't have the luxury of looking at paragraphs in oral language, but we do have the animation that comes along with live speech. Human beings have to try very hard to be completely non-expressive in their speech. Listeners should take advantage of this and notice how the speaker changes character and voice in order to signal a transition of ideas.

Speaking of animation of voice and body language, listeners can also better comprehend the underlying intents of authors when they notice nonverbal cues. Simply looking to see expression on the face of a speaker can do more to signal irony, for example, than trying to extract irony from actual words. And often in oral speech, unlike written text, elements like irony are not indicated by the actual words, but rather by the tone and nonverbal cues.

One good way to follow oral speech is to take notes and outline major points. Because oral speech can be more circular (as opposed to linear) than written text, it can be of great assistance to keep track of an author's message. Students can learn this strategy in many ways in the classroom: by taking notes of the teacher's oral messages, as well as other students' presentations and speeches.

Other classroom methods can help students learn good listening skills. For example, teachers can have students practice following complex directions. They can also have students orally retell stories—or retell (in writing or in oral speech) oral presentations of stories or other materials. These activities give students direct practice in the very important skills of listening. They provide students with outlets in which they can slowly improve their abilities to comprehend oral language and take decisive action based on oral speech.

Effective Speaking Strategies:

Listening to oral presentations and speakers, as mentioned above requires a specific set of skills for the students to be taught and engage. It is the same for presenting material orally. The students must be made aware of ways to engage the listeners and focus their attention on the major points of the information.

First, it is important to teach the students how to make sure their presentation match their audience. Presenting technical information to an audience who has no background knowledge on the subject is not the best approach. If technical knowledge must be shared, the presenter should look for more common language or analogies that the presenter can draw to better engage the audience in the material.

Next, one must consider body language and all that encompasses. An effective speaker looks relaxed and composed, even if inside they are tied up in knots. Finding a way to present yourself as relaxed can be quite a challenge. It helps to make eye contact with members of the audience and to refrain from reading the speech to the audience from note cards. The more natural the presentation seems, the more likely the audience will be listening.

Finally, it is important to be prepared for questions and have a manner set forth to answer them. Traditionally, questions are kept for the end, however, it is sometimes necessary to clarify at a critical juncture otherwise, the audience may have misinterpretations throughout the remainder of the presentation.

Skill 17.2 Identify effective ways to help students select and use various methods of interpersonal, small-group, and public discourse to explore an idea

We will discuss listening in large and small group conversation. The difference here is that conversation requires more than just listening: It involves feedback and active involvement. This can be particularly challenging, as in our culture, we are trained to move conversations along, to discourage silence in a conversation, and to always get the last word in. This poses significant problems for the art of listening. In a discussion, for example, when we are instead preparing our next response—rather than listening to what others are saying—we do a large disservice to the entire discussion. Students need to learn how listening carefully to others in discussions actually promotes better responses on the part of subsequent speakers. One way teachers can encourage this in both large and small group discussions is to expect students to respond directly to the previous student's comments before moving ahead with their new comments. This will encourage them to pose their new comments in light of the comments that came just before them.

Cooperative Learning

Cooperative learning situations, as practiced in today's classrooms, grew out of searches conducted by several groups in the early 1970's. Cooperative learning situations can range from very formal applications such as STAD (Student Teams-Achievement Divisions) and CIRC (Cooperative Integrated Reading and Composition) to less formal groupings known variously as "group investigation," "learning together," "discovery groups." Cooperative learning as a general term is now firmly recognized and established as a teaching and learning technique in American schools.

Since cooperative learning techniques are so widely diffused in the schools, it is necessary to orient students in the skills by which cooperative learning groups can operate smoothly, and thereby enhance learning. Students who cannot interact constructively with other students will not be able to take advantage of the learning opportunities provided by the cooperative learning situations and will furthermore deprive their fellow students of the opportunity for cooperative learning.

These skills form the hierarchy of cooperation in which students first learn to work together as a group, so they may then proceed to levels at which they may engage in simulated conflict situations. This cooperative setting allows different points of view to be constructively entertained.

Learning centers

In a flexible classroom where students have some time when they can choose which activity they will participate in, learning centers are extremely important. They take out-of-class time for creating them, collecting the items that will make them up, and then setting up the center. In some classes, the students might participate in creating a learning center.

Small group work

In the diverse classrooms we are responsible for nowadays, small group work is vital. Children can be grouped according to their level of development or the small groups themselves can be diverse, giving the students who are struggling an opportunity to learn from a student who is already proficient. The better prepared student will learn from becoming a source for the weaker student, and the weaker student may be more likely to accept help from another student sometimes than from the teacher.

COMPETENCY 18.0 APPLY METHODS FOR ENHANCING STUDENTS' WRITTEN COMMUNICATION.

Skill 18.1 **Apply knowledge of teaching methods that help students use the writing process (i.e., prewriting, drafting, revising, editing, publishing) to construct texts for multiple purposes in a variety of genres**

There is no one specific method for teaching the writing process. Beginning teachers need to understand that this is a process that takes students a long time to master and that they need to continually model the steps in the writing process for the students. The prewriting stage is one that students prefer to skip and therefore is one that teachers need to constantly remind the students about. At first this part of the process will be teacher guided using such methodologies as helping the students discover what they want to say about a specific topic. Some of the ways students can become used to using this step before they start their actual draft include:

- Brainstorming
- Discussing
- Webbing
- Interviewing
- Surveying
- Listening
- Reading
- Writing jot notes
- Charting
- Mapping
- Outlining

Free writing is another way students can get their ideas down on paper before they start to refine their thoughts.

When teaching the drafting process, teachers should encourage the students to skip lines. This allows them space for revising and editing when they get to this stage. Quite often students will ask how to spell words when they are writing their first draft. In this process, since spelling is not as important as it is in later stages, teachers often tell them to write the words the way they think they are spelled. There will be plenty of time to make corrections later.

Revising and editing are the hardest stages of the writing process to teach. Exemplars provide the students with examples of what good and poor writing looks like. When students have a chance to study the exemplars and discuss the merits of each they have an idea of the improvements they need to make in their writing. In revising, students should read the writing out loud, either to themselves or to another student to pick up on what parts make sense and what parts need additions or deletions. Author's chair is a way of encouraging students to provide comments on writing, but they do need to be encouraged not to make disparaging remarks and to only provide constructive criticism.

Editing is a time consuming task and it would be unreasonable to expect students to pick up on all the mistakes in a piece of writing. Therefore, teachers should ask students to edit for specific purposes at one time, such as correct spelling, capitalization or punctuation. The easiest way to pick up on incorrect spelling is to read the writing backwards. This way the students are focusing on each word rather than the meaning of the piece. The use of a word processor helps students in finding words that are not spelled correctly.

Publication means getting the writing ready for others to read. For many students it means illustrating the work, creating an attractive cover or even using a word processor to produce the final draft.

Skill 18.2 Identify ways to guide students to refine their spelling knowledge through reading and writing

Spelling is of utmost importance in the writing process. At first young children will use invented spelling in which they write the words according to letter sounds. There are several factors that influence the development of spelling, such as:
- Surrounding students with an environment rich in print
- Understanding the developmental stages of spelling
- Understanding that learning to spell is problem solving
- Teaching of the rules of spelling
- Promoting an awareness about spelling

Spelling should be taught within the context of meaningful language experiences. Giving a child a list of words to learn to spell and then testing the child on the words every Friday will not aid in the development of spelling. The child must be able to use the words in context and they must have some meaning for the child. The assessment of how well a child can spell or where there are problems also has to be done within a meaningful environment.

The main reasons for assessing spelling are:
- To find out what the child knows about spelling patterns and strategies
- To determine what the teacher needs to teach
- To develop spelling growth over a period of time

In order for spelling assessment to be authentic, it must have meaning for the child. Taking a list of words that a child misspells from a piece of writing is one example of a spelling list that the teacher can use. If the teacher keeps a list of words the children ask to spell, this can also be the basis for a word list.

Since spelling is something that does happen over time, teachers may notice that the child keeps spelling the same words incorrectly again and again. Through explicit teaching of strategies and even tricks to help spell the words, eventually they will see success in spelling. Assessment is something that has to happen over the course of a grade. Correct spelling is not something that children learn and retain automatically.

When assessing spelling, there are behaviors that teachers should look for:
- Knowledge of sounds and symbols
- Development of visual memory
- Development of morphemic knowledge
- Mastery of high frequency words at specific grade levels
- Location and knowledge of how to use spelling resources
- Attempts at spelling unknown words
- Risk taking attempts in using invented spelling

Spelling Pattern Word Wall

One of the understandings emergent readers come to about a word is that if they know how to read, write, and spell one word, they can write, read, and spell many other words as well.

Create in your classroom a spelling pattern word wall. Wylie and Durrell have identified spelling patterns which are in their classic thirty-seven "dependable" rimes. The spelling word wall can be created by stapling a piece of 3" x 5" butcher block paper to the bulletin board. Then attach spelling pattern cards around the border with thumbtacks, so that the cards can be easily removed to use at the meeting area.

Once you decide on a spelling pattern for instruction, remove the corresponding card from the word wall. Then take a 1"x 3" piece of a contrasting color of butcher block paper and tape the card to the top end of a sheet the children will use for their investigation. Next read one of Wylie and Durrell's short rimes with the children and have them identify the pattern.

After the pattern is identified the children can try to come up with other words that have the same spelling pattern. The teacher can write these on the spelling pattern sheet, using a different color marker to highlight the spelling pattern within the word. The children have to add to the list until the sheet is full, which might take two days or more.

After the sheet is full, the completed spelling pattern is attached to the wall.

Some of the techniques teachers use to determine the words students need to spell include:

- Lists of misspelled words from student writing
- Lists of theme words
- Lists of words from the content areas
- Word banks
-

It is important for beginning writers to know that spelling is an important part of the writing process. However, insisting on correct spelling right from the beginning may actually hamper the efforts of beginning writers. In early spelling development, children should be allowed to experiment with words and use invented spelling. Spelling development is something that occurs over time as a developmental process. It does develop in clearly defined stages, which the teacher should take into consideration when planning lessons. Teachers should assess students' spelling knowledge and then plan mini-lessons to whole class and small groups as they are necessary.

Some of the ways teachers can provide spelling instruction in the context of meaningful reading and writing activities include:
- Shared reading
- Guided reading
- Shared writing
- Shared reading
- Poetry reading using rhyming words with the same spelling patterns
- Reading chants
- Writing lists
- Writing daily news in the classroom
- Writing letters
- Writing invitations

By planning spelling instruction teachers will help children recognize word patterns, help then discern spelling rules and help them develop their own tricks for remembering how to spell words. Direct instruction is necessary for students to develop the knowledge they need regarding the morphological structure of words and thus the relationships between words. Students also need to be taught graphophonic relationships to know the relationship between letters and sounds, the probability of letter sequences and the different letter patterns.

Developing visual methods of recognizing correct spelling is also an aid to helping students learn to spell when they can trace around the shape of a word. This helps them develop a visual memory as to whether or not the word looks as if it is spelled correctly. Memory aids (mnemonics) also aid in spelling development, such as in the word PAINT – Pat Added Ink Not Tar.

Along with direct teaching of spelling, teachers should model the process at all times. By talking about spelling and having students assist in class writing, they will help students develop the awareness that spelling is important. Some activities where teachers can use this approach include:

- Experience charts
- Writing notes to parents
- Writing class poems and stories
- Editing writing with students

- Students also need to be encouraged to take risks with spelling. Rather than have students constantly asking how words are spelled, the teacher can use "Have a Go Sheets. These sheets consist of three columns in which the student writes the word as he/she thinks it is spelled. Then the student asks the teacher or another student if it spelled correctly. If it is incorrect the student will tell the student which letters are in the correct place and the student will try again. After the third try, the teacher can either tell the student how to spell the word and add
this to the list of words the student has to learn or work on the necessary spelling strategy

COMPETENCY 19.0 APPLY METHODS FOR PROMOTING VOCABULARY DEVELOPMENT

Skill 19.1   **Determine how to help students use graphophonemic, syntactic, and semantic relationships (e.g., letter/sound correspondence, phonemic awareness, structural analysis, context) to identify unfamiliar words**

See skill 13.1

Use of Semantic and Syntactic Cues to Help Decode Words

Semantic Cues

Students will need use their base knowledge of word meanings, semantics, to help them decipher unknown words or text as well as to clarify reading when it does not seem to make sense. Some prompts the teacher can use which will alert the children to semantic cues include:
- Does that sentence make sense?
- Which word in that sentence does not seem to fit?
- Why doesn't it fit?
- What word might make sense in that sentence?

Syntactic Cues

The first strategy good readers use from their own knowledge base to help determine misreading, is syntactic cues. Syntactic cues use the order of words and the student's knowledge of the oral English language to help determine if what was read could be accurate. Some prompts the teacher can use to encourage and develop syntactic cues in reading include:
- You read (child's incorrect attempt). Does that sound right?
- You read (child's incorrect attempt). When we talk, do we talk that way?
- How would we say it?
- Recheck that sentence. Does it sound right the way you read it?

Specific Terminology Associated With Phonics

It is important to have a clear understanding of the terms associated with phonics. Here are some definitions, which are helpful in having a clear understanding of phonic development in children.

Phoneme – a phoneme is the smallest unit of sound in the English language. In print phonemes are represented by the letter and a slash. So, /b/ represents the sound the letter b would make.

Morpheme- a morpheme is the smallest unit of grammar in the English language. In other words, it is the smallest unit of meaning, not just sounds.

Consonant Digraph – a consonant digraph are two consonants of the English language who when placed together in a word make a unique sound, neither makes when alone. Examples: ch, th, sh, and wh.

Consonant Blend- a consonant blend is when two consonants are put together, but each retains their individual sound. The two sounds go together in a seamless manner to produce a blended sound. Examples: st, br, cl, etc.

Schwa sound- schwa sound is a vowel sound which is neutral. It typically occurs in the unaccented syllable of a word. An example would be the sound of the a at the end of the word sofa. It is represented in print by an upside down e

Development of Phonics Skills with Individual Students

In *ON SOLID GROUND* (2000), researcher and educator Sharon Taberski said that it is much harder for children from ELL backgrounds and children from homes where other English dialects are spoken to use syntactic cues to attempt to self-correct.

These children, through no fault of their own, do not have sufficient experience hearing Standard English spoken to use this cueing system as they read. The teacher should sensitively guide them through by modeling the use of syntactic and semantic cues.

Highly proficient readers can be paired as buddy tutors for ELL or special needs classroom members or to assist the resource room teacher during their reading time. They can use the CVC Game developed by Jacki Montrieth to support their peers and can even modify the game to meet the needs of classroom peers. Of course, this also offers the highly proficient reader the opportunity to do a service learning project, while still in elementary school. It also introduces the learner to another dimension of reading, the role of the reader as trainer and recruiter of other peers into the circle of readers and writers!.

If the highly proficient readers are so motivated or if their teachers so desire, the peer tutors can also maintain an ongoing reading progress journal for their tutees. This will be a wonderful way to realize the goals of the reading and writing workshop.

There are many different strategies to help children who are struggling with their phonics skill development. A beginning step is to identify the area of difficulty within phonics. A simple assessment to help determine the exact area of difficulty is the CORE Phonics Survey which can be downloaded free. Once the area of deficit has been identified, small group instruction can be developed around these areas to increase specific skills.

When working on specific phonics skills, it is important to utilize decodable texts. There are numerous publishers who have available a variety of different skills and texts for use within the classroom. If students continue to struggle, it may be necessary to utilize a more specific systematic and explicit phonics program. Some examples of these include: Wilson Reading, Early Intervention Reading, and Open Court.

Development of Word Analysis Skills and Strategies, Including Structural Analysis

Structural analysis is a process of examining the words in the text for meaningful word units (affixes, base words, inflected endings). There are six types of word types which are formed and therefore can be analyzed using structural analysis strategies. They include:

1. Common prefixes or suffixes added to a known word ending with a consonant
2. Adding the suffix –ed to words that end with consonants
3. Compound words
4. Adding endings to words that end with the letter e
5. Adding endings to words that end with the letter y
6. Adding affixes to multisyllabic words

When teaching and using structural analysis procedures in the primary grades, teachers should remember to make sound decisions on which to introduce and teach. Keeping in mind the number of primary words in which each affix appears and how similar they are will help the teacher make the instructional process smoother and more valuable to the students.

Adding affixes to words can be started when students are able to read a list of one-syllable words by sight at a rate of approximately twenty words correct per minute. At the primary level, there is a recommended sequence for introducing affixes. The steps in this process are:
- Start by introducing the affix in the letter-sound correspondence format
- Practice the affix in isolation for a few days
- Provide words for practice which contain the affix (word lists, flash cards, etc.)
- Move from word lists to including passage reading, which include words with the affix (and some from the word lists/flash cards).

1. Word Study Group

This involves the teacher taking time to meet with children from grades 3-6 in a small group of no more than 6 children for a word study session. Taberski (2000) suggests that this meeting take place next to the Word Wall. The children selected for this group are those who need to focus more on the relationship between spelling patterns and consonant sounds.

It is important that this not be a formalized traditional reading group that meets at a set time each week or biweekly. Rather the group should be spontaneously formed by the teacher based on the teacher's quick inventory of the selected children's needs at the start of the week. Taberski has templates in her book of *Guided Reading Planning Sheets.* These sheets are essentially targeted word and other skills sheets with her written dated observations of children who are in need of support to develop a given skill.

The teacher should try to meet with this group for at least two consecutive twenty minute periods daily. Over those two meetings, the teacher can model a Making Words Activity. Once the teacher has modeled making words the first day, the children would then make their own words. On the second day, the children would "sort" their words.

Other topics for a word study group within the framework of the Balanced Literacy Approach that Taberski advocates are: inflectional endings, prefixes and suffixes, and/or common spelling patterns. These are covered later in this chapter.

It should be noted that this activity would be classified by theorists as a structural analysis activity because the structural components (i.e. prefixes, suffixes, and spelling patterns) of the words are being studied.

2. *Discussion Circles*

Cooper (2004) believes that children should not be "taught" vocabulary and structural analysis skills. Flesch and E.D. Hirsch , who are key theorists of the phonics approach and advocates of Cultural Literacy (a term coined and associated with E. D. Hirsch), believe that specific vocabulary words at various grade and age levels need to be mastered and must be explicitly taught in schools. As far as J. David Cooper is concerned, all the necessary and meaningful (for the child and ultimately adult reader) vocabulary can't possibly be taught in schools (no apologies to Hirsch). To Cooper it is far more important that the children be made aware of and become interested in learning words by themselves. Cooper feels that through the child's reading and writing, he or she develops a love for and a sense of "ownership" of words. All of Cooper's suggested structural analysis word strategies are therefore designed to foster the child's love of words and a desire to "own" more of them through reading and writing.

Discussion Circles is an activity which fits nicely into the balanced literacy lesson format. After the children conclude a particular text, Cooper suggests that respond to the book in discussion circles. Among the prompts, the teacher-coach might suggest that the children focus on words of interest they encountered in the text. These can also be words that they heard if the text was read aloud. Children can be asked to share something funny or upsetting or unusual about the words they have read. Through this focus on children's response to words as the center of the discussion circle, peers become more interested in word study.

3. Banking, Booking, and Filing It: Making Words My Own

Children can literally realize the goal of making words their own and exploring word structures through creating concrete objects or displays that demonstrate the words they own. Children can create and maintain their own files of words they have learned or are interested in learning.

The files can be categorized by the children according to their own interests. They should be encouraged to develop files using science, history, physical education, fine arts, dance, and technology content. Newspapers and web resources, which the teacher has approved, are excellent sources for such words. In addition, this provides the teacher with the opportunity to instruct the child in appropriate age and grade-level research skills. Even children in grades 2 and 3 can begin simplified bibliographies and webliographies for their "found" words. Children can learn how to annotate and note the page of a newspaper, book, or URL for a particular word.

They can also copy down the word as it appears in the text (print or electronic). If appropriate, the child can place the particular words found for a given topic or content in an actual bank of the child's own making. The words can be printed on cards. This allows for differentiated word study and appeals to those children who are kinesthetic and spatial learners. Of course, children can also choose to create their own word books which include their specialized vocabulary and descriptions of how they identified or hunted down their words. Richard Scarry, watch out! Scarry books can be anchor books to inspire this structural analysis activity.

ELL learners can share their accounts in their native language first and then translate (with the help of the teacher) these accounts into English with both the native language and the English language versions of the word exploration posted.

4. Write out your Words, Write with your words

Ownership of words can be demonstrated by having the children use them as part of their writings. The children can author a procedural narrative (a step by step description) of how they went about their word searches to compile the words they found for any of the activities. If the children are in grades K-1, or if the children are struggling readers and writers, their procedural narratives can be dictated. Then they can be posted by the teacher.

ELL students can share their accounts in their native language first and then translate (with the help of the teacher) these accounts into English with both the native language and the English language versions of the word exploration posted.

Children with special needs may model a word box on a specific holiday theme, genre or science/social studies topic with the teacher. Initially this can be done as a whole class. As the children become more confident, they can work with peers or with a paraprofessional to create their own individual or small team/pair word boxes.

Special needs children can create a storyboard with the support of a paraprofessional, their teacher or a resource specialist. They can also narrate their story of how they all found the words, using a tape recorder.

5.- Word Study Museum Within the Classroom

This strategy has been presented in detail so it can be used by the teachers within their own classrooms. In addition, the way the activity is described and the mention at the end of the description of how the activity can address family literacy, ELL, and special needs children's talents, provides an example of other audiences a teacher should consider in curriculum design.
Almost every general education teacher and reading specialist will have to differentiate instruction to address the needs of special education and ELL learners. Family or shared literacy is a major component of all literacy instruction.

Children can create either a single or multiple exhibits, museum style, within their classrooms celebrating their word study. They can build actual representations of the type of study they have done including word trees (made out of cardboard or foam board), elaborate word boxes and games, word history timelines or murals, and word study maps. They can develop online animations, Kids Spiration graphic organizers, quick movies, digital photo essays, and PowerPoint presentations to share the word they have identified. The classroom or the gym or cafeteria can be transformed into a gallery space. Children can author brochure descriptions for their individual, team or class exhibits. Some children can volunteer to be tour guides or docents for the experience. Other children can work to create a banner for the Museum. The children can name the Museum themselves and send out invitations to its opening. Invitations can be sent to parents, community, staff members and peer or younger classes.

Depending on their age and grade level, children can also develop interactive games and quizzes focused on particular exhibits. An artist or a team of class artists can design a poster for the exhibit, while other children choose to build the exhibits. Another small group can work on signage and a catalogue or register of objects within the exhibit. Greeters who will welcome parents and peers to the exhibit can be trained and can develop their own scripts.

If the children are in grades 4-6, they can also develop their own visitor feedback forms and design word-themed souvenirs. The whole museum within the school or classroom can be captured digitally or with a regular camera. The record of this event can be hung near the word walls. Of course, the children can use many of their newly recognized and owned words to describe the event.

The Word Study Museum activity can be used with either a phonics-based or a balanced literacy approach. It promotes additional writing, researching, discussing, and reading about words.

It is also an excellent family literacy strategy in that families can develop their own Word Exhibits at home. This activity can also support and celebrate learners with disabilities. It can be presented in dual languages by children who are ELL learners and fluent in more than a single language.)

Relationship Between Word Analysis Skills and Reading Comprehension

The explicit teaching of word analysis requires that the teacher pre-select words from a given text for vocabulary learning. These words should be chosen based on the storyline and main ideas of the text. The educator may even want to create a story map for a narrative text or develop a graphic organizer for an expository text. Once the story mapping and/or graphic organizing have been done, the educator can compile a list of words which relate to the storyline and/or main ideas.

The number of words that require explicit teaching should only be two or three. If the number is higher than that, the children need guided reading and the text needs to be broken down into smaller sections for teaching. When broken down into smaller sections, each text section should only have two to three words which need explicit teaching.

Some researchers, including Tierney and Cunningham, believe that a few words should be taught as a means of improving comprehension.

It is up to the educator whether the vocabulary selected for teaching needs review before reading, during reading, or after reading.

Strategies, to support word analysis and enhance reading comprehension, include:

- Use of a graphic organizer such as a word map
- Semantic mapping
- Semantic feature analysis
- Hierarchical and linear arrays
- Preview in context
- Contextual redefinition
- Vocabulary self-collection
- (Note that these terms are in the Glossary.)

See Skill 2.2 for more information.

Skill 19.2 Apply methods for helping students use multiple strategies to determine the meaning of unfamiliar words and concepts

Identification of Common Morphemes, Prefixes, and Suffixes

This aspect of vocabulary development is to help children look for structural elements within words which they can use independently to help them determine meaning.

Some teachers choose to directly teach structural analysis. In particular, those who teach by following the phonics-centered approach for reading do this. Other teachers, who follow the balanced literacy approach, introduce the structural components as part of mini lessons that are focused on the students' reading and writing.

Structural analysis of words as defined by J. David Cooper (2004) involves the study of significant word parts. This analysis can help the child with pronunciation and constructing meaning.

The term list below is generally recognized as the key structural analysis components.

Root Words

This is a word from which another word is developed. The second word can be said to have its "root" in the first, such as *vis, to see,* in visor or vision. This structural component can be illustrated by a tree with roots to display the meaning for children. Children may also want to literally construct root words using cardboard trees to create word family models.

ELL learners can construct these models for their native language root word families, as well for the English language words they are learning. ELL learners in the 5th and 6th grade may even appreciate analyzing the different root structures for contrasts and similarities between their native language and English.

Learners with special needs can focus in small groups or individually with a paraprofessional on building root word models.

Base Words
These are stand-alone linguistic units which cannot be deconstructed or broken down into smaller words. For example, in the word *re-tell*, the base word is "tell."

Contractions

These are shortened forms of two words in which a letter or letters have been deleted. These deleted letters have been replaced by an apostrophe.

Prefixes

These are beginning units of meaning which can be added (the vocabulary word for this type of structural adding is "affixed") to a base word or root word. They can not stand alone. They are also sometimes known as "bound morphemes" meaning that they can not stand alone as a base word. Examples are *re-, un-,* and *mis-.*

Suffixes

These are ending units of meaning which can be "affixed" or added on to the ends of root or base words. Suffixes transform the original meanings of base and root words. Like prefixes, they are also known as "bound morphemes," because they can not stand alone as words. Examples are *-less, -ful*, and *-tion.*

Compound Words

These occur when two or more base words are connected to form a new word. The meaning of the new word is in some way connected with that of the base word. Examples are *firefighter, newspaper*, and *pigtail.*

Inflectional Endings

These are types of suffixes that impart a new meaning to the base or root word. These endings in particular change the gender, number, tense, or form of the base or root words. Just like other suffixes, these are also termed "bound morphemes." Examples are *–s* or *-ed.*

Comments

Definitions are included because the structural analysis components are explicitly taught in schools which advocate the phonics-centered approach and are also incorporated into the word work component of the schools which advocate the balanced literacy approach for instruction.

Definition questions, that is multiple choice questions which have only a single right answer, test whether the teacher candidate has memorized the appropriate terminology. They constitute for no less than 15% of the multiple choice question on the test. Therefore by taking the time to memorize these easy definitions, scores are likely to improve.

Some of these activities are presented in detail to help answer the constructed response questions of the test.

Knowledge of Greek and Latin Roots That Form English Words

Knowledge of Greek and Latin roots which comprise English words can measurably enhance children's reading skills and can also enrich their writing.

Word Webs

Sharon Taberski (2000) does not advocate teaching Greek and Latin derivatives in the abstract to young children. However, when she comes across (as is common and natural) specific Greek and Latin roots while reading to children, she uses that opportunity to introduce children to these rich resources.

For example, during readings on rodents (a favorite of first and second graders), Taberski draws her class's attention to the fact that beavers, gnaw at things with their teeth. She then connects the "dent" root or derivative to the children's lives, other words they are familiar with or experiences. The children then volunteer *"dentist," "dental," "denture."* Taberski begins to place these in a graphic organizer, or word web.

When she has tapped the extent of the children's prior knowledge of "dent" words, she shares with them the fact that *dens/dentis* is the Latin word for teeth. Then she introduces the word "indent," which she has already previewed with them as part of their conventions of print study. She helps them to see that the "indenting" of the first line of a paragraph can even be related to the "teeth" Latin root in that it looks like a "print" bite was taken out of the paragraph.

Taberski displays the word web in the Word Wall Chart section of her room. The class is encouraged throughout, say, a week's time to look for other words to add to the web. Taberski stresses that for her, as an elementary teacher of reading and writing, the key element of the Greek and Latin word root web activity is the children's coming to understand that if they know what a Greek or Latin word root means, they can use that knowledge to figure out what other words mean.

She feels the key concept is to model and demonstrate for children how fun and fascinating Greek and Latin root study can be.

Greek and Latin Roots Word Webs With an Assist From the World Wide Web

Older children in grades 3-6 can build on this initial print activity by searching online for additional words with a particular Greek or Latin root which has been introduced in class.

They can easily do this in a way that authentically ties in with their own interests and experiences by reading reviews for a book which has been a read-aloud online or by just reading the summaries of the day's news and printing out those words which appear in the stories online that share the root discussed.

The children can be encouraged to circle these instances of their Latin or Greek root and also to document the exact date and URL for the citation. These can be posted as part of their own online web in the word wall section study area. If the school or class has a website or webpage, the children can post this data there as a special Greek and Latin root word page.

Expanding the concept of the Greek and Latin word web from the printed page to the world wide web, nicely inculcates the child in the habits of lifelong reading and researching online. This beginning expository research will serve them well in intermediate level content area work and beyond.

Use of Syllabification as a Word Identification Strategy

Strategy: Clap Hands, Count those Syllables as They Come!! (Taberski, 2000)

The objective of this activity is for children to understand that there are every syllable in a polysyllabic word can be studied for its spelling patterns in the same way that monosyllabic words are studied for their spelling patterns.

The easiest way for the K-3 teacher to introduce this activity to the children is to share a familiar poem from the poetry chart (or to write out a familiar poem on a large experiential chart).

First the teacher reads the poem with the children. As they are reading it aloud, the children clap the beats of the poem and the teacher uses a colored marker to place a tic (/) above each syllable.

Next, the teacher takes letter cards and selects one of the polysyllabic words from the poem which the children have already "clapped" out.

The children use letter cards to spell that word on the sentence strip holder or it can be placed on a felt board or up against a window on display. Together the children and teacher divide the letters into syllables and place blank letter cards between the syllables. The children identify spelling patterns they know.

Finally and as part of continued small group syllabification study, the children identify other polysyllabic words they clapped out from the poem. They make up the letter combinations of these words. Then they separate them into syllables with blank letter cards between the syllables.

Children who require special support in syllabification can be encouraged to use many letter cards to create a large butcher paper syllabic (in letter cards with spaces) representation of the poem or at least a few lines of the poem. They can be told that this is for use as a teaching tool for others. In this way, they authenticate their study of syllabification with a real product that can actually be referenced by peers.

Techniques for Identifying Compound Words

The teaching of compound words should utilize structural analysis techniques. (See above section on structural analysis).
Here are some other strategies for helping students to identify and read compound words.

- Use songs and actions to help children understand the concept that compound words are two smaller words joined together to make one bigger word
- Use games like concentration, memory and go fish for students to practice reading compound words
- Use word sorts to have students distinguish between compound words and nonexamples of compound words

Identification of Homographs

Homographs are words that are spelled the same but have different meanings. A subgroup within this area includes words that are spelled the same, have different meanings, and are pronounced differently. Some examples of homographs include:

- Lie
- Tear
- Bow
- Fair
- Bass

Teaching homographs can be interesting and fun for the students. Incorporating them into passages where the students can use the context clues to decipher the different meanings of the homographs.   Games are also a good strategy for using to help students understand multiple meaning words. Jokes and riddles are usually based on homographs, and students love to make collections or books of these.

Semantic Feature Analysis: This technique for enhancing vocabulary skills by using semantic cues is based on the research of Johnson and Pearson (1984) and Anders and Bos (1986). It involves young children in setting up a feature analysis grid of various subject content words which is an outgrowth of their discussion about these words.

For instance, Cooper (2004) includes a sample of a Semantic Features Analysis Grid for Vegetables. .

Vegetables	Green	Have Peels	Eat Raw	Seeds
Carrots	-	+	+	-
Cabbage	+	-	+	-

Note: that the use of the + for yes, - for no, and possible use for + and - if a vegetable like squash could be both green and yellow.

Teachers of children in grade one and beyond can design their own semantic analysis grids to meet their students' needs and to align with the topics the kids are learning. Select a category or class of words (could be planets, rodent family members, winter words, weather words).

Use the left side of the grid to list at least three if not more items that fit this category. The number of actual items listed will depend on the age and grade level of the children with three or four items fine for K-1 and up to 10-15 for grades 5 and 6. Brainstorm with the children or if better suited to the class, the teacher may list on his/her own features that the items have in common. As can be noted from the example excerpted from *Cooper's Literacy -Helping Children Construct Meaning (*2004), these common features such as vegetables' green color, peels, and seeds are usually fairly easy to identify.

Show the children how to insert the notations +, -, and even ?, (If they are not certain) on the grid. The teacher might also explore with the children the possibility that an item could get both a + and a -. For example, a vegetable like broccoli might be eaten cooked or raw depending on taste and squash can be green or yellow.

Whatever the length of the grid when first presented to the children (perhaps as a semantic cue lesson in and of itself tied in to a text being read in class), make certain that the grid as presented and fillied out is not the end of the activity.

Children can use it as a model for developing their own semantic features grids and share them with the whole class. Child-developed grids can become part of a Word Work center in the classroom or even be published in a Word Study Games book by the class as a whole. Such a publication can be shared with parents during open school week and evening visits and with peer classes.

Contextual Redefinition

This strategy encourages children to use the context more effectively by presenting them with sufficient context BEFORE they begin reading. It models for the children the use of contextual clues to make informed guesses about word meanings.

To apply this strategy, the teacher should first select unfamiliar words for teaching. No more than two or three words should be selected for direct teaching. The teacher should then write a sentence in which there are sufficient clues supplied for the child to successfully figure out the meaning. Among the types of context clues the teacher can use are: compare/contrast, synonyms, and direct definition.

Then the teacher should present the words only on the experiential chart or as letter cards. Have the children pronounce the words. As they pronounce them, challenge them to come up with a definition for each word. After more than one definition is offered, encourage the children to decide as a whole group what the definition is. Write down their agreed upon definition with no comment as to its accurate meaning.

T

hen share with the children the contexts (sentences the teacher wrote with the words and explicit context clues). Ask that the children to read the sentences aloud. Then have them come up with a definition for each word. Make certain that as they present their definitions, the teacher does not comment. Ask that they justify their definitions by making specific references to the context clues in the sentences. As the discussion continues, direct the children's attention to their previously agreed upon definition of the word. Facilitate their discussing the differences between their guesses about the word when they saw only the word itself and their guesses about the word when they read it in context. Finally have the children check their use of context skills to correctly define the word by using a dictionary.

Development of Word Analysis Skills by Individual Students

This type of direct teaching of word definitions is useful when the children have dictionary skills and the teacher is aware of the fact that there are not sufficient clues about the words in the context to help the students define it. In addition, struggling readers and students from ELL backgrounds may benefit tremendously from being walked through this process that highly proficient and successful readers apply automatically

By using this strategy, the teacher can also "kid watch" and note the students' prior knowledge as they guess the word in isolation. The teacher can also actually witness and hear how various students use context skills.

Through their involvement in this strategy, struggling readers gain a feeling of community as they experience the ways in which their struggles and guesses resonate with other peers' responses to the text.

Skill 19.3   Assess the effectiveness of techniques for promoting students' independent vocabulary acquisition

See skills 19.1 and 19.2

COMPETENCY 20.0 APPLY METHODS FOR ESTABLISHING A LEARNING ENVIRONMENT THAT SUPPORTS THE LITERACY DEVELOPMENT OF ALL STUDENTS

Skill 20.1 Identify ways to empower learners who have a range of capacities, abilities, multiple intelligences, first languages, and learning styles

The physical set up of your classroom is exceedingly important to support the effective development of all children.

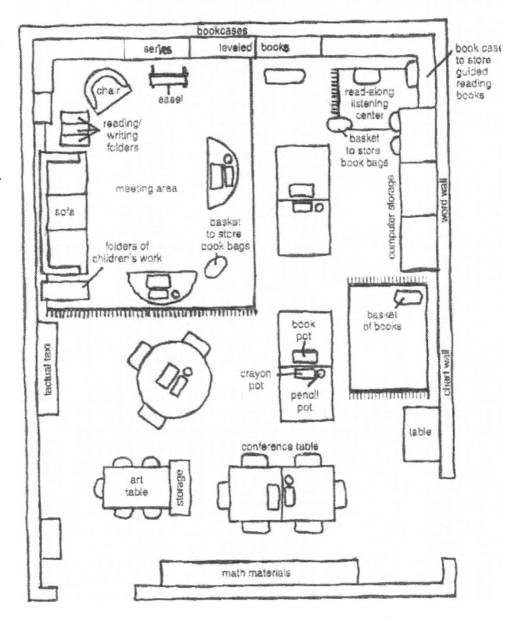

Understanding Our Role and Goals

The homey look of the classroom belies its deliberate design as a space where children can experience, practice, share and learn. Some teachers have done away with the large desk and use smaller tables instead. Sharon Taberski advocates for young children K-3 adjusting the height of the table legs so the children can use the tables as writing spaces and sit on the floor. Sharon gives each of her children a personal 12"x 9"x 2" tray on which they place their home possessions, books, homework, folder, etc. This is kept in a small storage unit near the coat closet during the day.

Children put their completed homework in a wire basket and notes from parents or the office in a second wire basket. Supplies such as pencils, markers, crayons, scissors, and erasers are not brought from home, but rather available for all in the class from "community" containers at the center of each of the children's tables.

All the children's reading, writing, and individual math folders are stored together in plastic bins in the meeting area. Every child has an individual book bag which is kept in one of two large wicker baskets set in different areas of the room.

This storing of materials away from children decreases their "fiddling with" their belongings during class, makes the room look much neater, and frees the children to focus on their learning experiences, rather than where their belongings are at any given time of day.

As you can see on the accompanying diagram the 10'x10' meeting area is the center of classroom learning. This is where the whole class is gathered at the beginning of the reading and the writing workshop and for sharing sessions. It is also the demonstration and modeling center for both the teacher and for children.

Generally, the presenter sits on the adult chair (in some balanced literacy classrooms, this is a rocking chair) near the easel with the chart. Generally, this chair and the easel are strategically positioned so that the teacher can see the door and any visitors or urgent messages from the office. Rearranging furniture during the day takes away from instruction time and is disruptive. Have a designated comfortable section of the room that can be a gathering place for a literacy community and then organize the rest of the classroom activities around that center.

The conference table which is at the back of the room (see diagram) is another key piece of classroom space furniture. It is the place where the four or five children and the teacher confer, wait and do their work. Having children come to a set conference table, rather than the teacher's going to them (although some teachers do advocate going to the children) saves time as far as Taberski is concerned. It serves to keep her and the children on task.

Taberski keeps two separate trays of supplies: a small magnetic board, letters, chalkboard, chalk, sentence strips, index cards, and blank books for her demonstrations during her conferences. She believes that teachers should store materials close to where they are used, so the teacher does not have to take time from the child to get up and get the materials.

The Classroom Library

On the tables, Taberski generally has book crates with books that are not leveled. Children choose from these books during the first independent reading session of her day which is from 8:40-9:00. During the second reading session from 9:30-10:20 the children select books from the leveled reading bins which are stored on the bookcase shelves.

Beyond the leveled books, which have already been discussed, Taberski also maintains a non-leveled, non fiction library which includes dictionaries, atlases, almanacs and informational books related to the themes, projects and investigations that the children will undertake throughout the year.

Beyond the leveled books and non-fiction books in the classroom, Taberski and other balanced literacy advocates generally include at least 10-15 big books which they routinely use to engage children with the text.

Since Guided Reading with groups of 6 children is a major part of the balanced literacy approach, Taberski and other disciplined and dedicated teacher educators "bundle" up six copies of selected books so that they can distribute them to their guided reading groups whenever they choose to do them. Taberski models the concept of a home library collection for the children by keeping books which she particularly likes in a bookcase behind her chair. She sometimes places "her" books on the easel so that they can be shared by the children and returned to her.

Wall Works

Much of creating a family atmosphere lies in the use of the room walls to document the children's learning experiences, skills work, and readings.

Generally at least one wall in a reading classroom is the Chart Wall. Charts with various spelling patterns discussed in class can be posted. If a child later has issues or concerns with that particular pattern, he or she should be directed to look at and to review the chart.

One of the centerpieces of the K-2 classroom is the High Frequency Word Chart. This is a growing list of commonly used words which the teacher tapes under the appropriate beginning letter according to the children's directions. At the end of each month, the newest high frequency words go into the children's folders and become part of their spelling words. Therefore reading, writing, and spelling are all intricately connected.

Supplies for children K-3 and beyond can include:

A red plastic double pocket reading folder
A blue plastic double pocket reading folder
A four sectioned pressed board spelling/poetry folder
A 4" x 6" assessment notebook for reading
A 4" x 6" assessment notebook for writing
A reading response notebook (loose-leaf- 60 pages)
A handwriting notebook

The Reading Folder contains the assessment notebooks, the reading response notebooks, a Weekly Reading Log, and the strategy sheets the child may be using that particular week.

The Assessment Notebook is a key evaluative tool and a recording document for the conscientious balanced literacy specialist. The teacher uses the notebook to record the child's running record, the retellings of stories shared by the child, and summarizing talks about leveled books read. Within the assessment books, the teacher also has notes about the child's progress, the strategies the child has learned to use well, the books he or she has read and those strategies the child still needs to practice. These assessment notebooks must be kept accessible so that the teacher can use them to confer with the child, parents, and administrator as needed.

The reading response notebook becomes a compilation of reading strategy sheets and children's writings and art in response to literature.

The Weekly Reading Log allows the child to maintain for himself or herself the titles of books they have read and written a bit about the narrative, style, and genre of that given book.

Book Bags: These are 10" x 12" heavy duty freezer bags which keep 3-10 books a child is "working on" during his/her free time. The teacher generally matches the children to the books and changes these books as needed by the children.

Writing Folders

Children keep several pieces of writing in their folders at a time. Within the writing folder is also a handwriting notebook and a beginning word book as well. The Spelling/Poetry Folder is one which helps children focus on the sequence of letters in words and learn more how words work.

The balanced literacy advocates have a definite schedule for the teaching of reading and writing workshop from which they generally do not deviate. A sample follows.

8:40-9:00- FIRST INDEPENDENT READING/WORD STUDY GROUP

9:00-9:30- MEETING-WHOLE GROUP SESSION in the meeting area
Read Aloud, Shared Reading, or Shared Writing

9:30-10:30- READING WORKSHOP
Reading Conferences or Guided Reading
Second Independent Reading
Reading Share 10:20-10:30

10:30-10:40- Writing Mini Lesson or Writing Share

10:40-11:20- Writing Workshop Writing Conferences, Guided Writing, Modeled Writing, Independent Writing

(11:10-11:20)-Writing Share

Skill 20.2 Analyze strategies for promoting the literacy skills of students who are gifted

Teaching students who are gifted require significantly different types of reading skills than struggling or even average readers. Breaking the code generally comes quite easily to the gifted. They are usually reading several grade levels above their age prescribed grade level.

Curriculum compacting generally is encouraged throughout the education of the gifted. In this way, the student, who requires many fewer repetitions than the average student to master skills, can move forward in their learning without having to wait for the children who require more time to reach proficiency. This strategy allows the gifted students to be exposed to and master the same required curriculum as all other students, simply at a different pace.

Comprehension is often the focus for literacy instruction for the students who are also gifted. Literature circles are a strategy where the students themselves are taught to build a discussion and dialogue about the book read. There are generally roles assigned within the group of students who will be discussing a piece of literature. The teacher takes a back seat and perhaps provides periodic questions for discussion if the conversation lags. Otherwise, the topics, questions and discussion is generated from the students. They generally discuss higher-level questions and not simple recall. Additionally, often times the questions have no solid right or wrong answer, instead they are designed to promote conversation.

Content area reading is another way to encourage and develop literacy skills in the gifted. Often times, there are numerous topics of which the students are very curious and would like to learn more and explore. Setting up independent learning projects revolving around these self selected topics and providing appropriate reading materials encourages the students to learn more and more about the topics. Periodic meetings and conversations with the teacher ensure adequate comprehension and provides the necessary accountability.

There are identified students who are gifted for whom reading is not enjoyable. There are also students who are gifted but also have a learning disability. It is important to keep these things in mind as well. These students would benefit from similar incentive and strategies that work for other students who may be struggling with reading. However, remember that these particular students may find it even more of a frustrating experience than other struggling readers due to their higher level of acquiring and processing information.

Skill 20.3 Evaluate methods for addressing the strengths and needs of students with learning disabilities

There is no reason identified by scientist to explain why some children learn to read with no problems and other struggle to be successful. Doctors and researchers use fMRI's and other brain scanning techniques to pinpoint the parts of the brain being used when completing reading activities and in these scans, they can see definite differences between better and slower readers. However the underlying cause still remains a mystery.

There are some identified factors, which may contribute to reading difficulties:
- Language Development
- Birth Defects
- Genetic History
- Language Exposure
- Hearing Difficulties, including intermittent losses from infections
- Life experiences, especially as related to prior knowledge

This is not a complete list, but simply a few suggestions of identified reasons reading problems may occur. No matter the cause, children who experience problems need to have adaptations and/or modifications developed in order to help their skills develop.

Providing instruction to meet the individual needs of learners can be a daunting experience as no two readers are exactly the same. Their own personal life experience allow them to bring to text unique and personal information another student may not have. In this way, planning instruction can be a challenge. However, it is important for students to have instruction designed to meet their needs.

The reading specialist can tap into the student with more prior knowledge to help support those with less. Those with stronger phonics skills can provide support to those who struggle. It is a complex balancing act for the teacher, but one that is essential. Other strategies include:

- Providing texts on the student's reading level
- Using individual assessment data to complete plans
- Providing different assignments based on the same reading to help students develop the skills they are lacking
- Small group or individual instruction
- Differentiated instruction

Oftentimes, students absorb the culture and social environment around them without deciphering contextual meaning of the experiences. When provided with a diversity of cultural contexts, students are able to adapt and incorporate multiple meanings from cultural cues vastly different from their own socioeconomic backgrounds. Socio-cultural factors provide a definitive impact on a students' psychological, emotional, affective, and physiological development, along with a students' academic learning and future opportunities.

The educational experience for most students is a complicated and complex experience with a diversity of interlocking meanings and inferences. If one aspect of the complexity is altered, it affects other aspects, which may impact how a student or teacher views an instructional or learning experience. With the current demographic profile of today's school communities, the complexity of understanding, interpreting, synthesizing the nuances from the diversity of cultural lineages can provide many communication and learning blockages that could impede the acquisition of learning for students.

Teachers must create personalized learning communities where every student is a valued member and contributor of the classroom experiences. In classrooms where socio-cultural attributes of the student population are incorporated into the fabric of the learning process, dynamic interrelationships are created that enhance the learning experience and the personalization of learning. When students are provided with numerous academic and social opportunities to share cultural incorporations into the learning, everyone in the classroom benefits from bonding through shared experiences and having an expanded viewpoint of a world experience and culture that vastly differs from their own.

Researchers continue to show that personalized learning environments increase the learning affect for students; decrease drop-out rates among marginalized students; and decrease unproductive student behavior which can result from constant cultural misunderstandings or miscues between students. Promoting diversity of learning and cultural competency in the classroom for students and teachers creates a world of multicultural opportunities and learning. When students are able to step outside their comfort zones and share the world of a homeless student or empathize with an English Language Learner (ELL) student who has just immigrated to the United States and is learning English for the first time and is still trying to keep up with the academic learning in an unfamiliar language; then students grow exponentially in social understanding and cultural connectedness.

Personalized learning communities provide supportive learning environments that address the academic and emotional needs of students. As socio-cultural knowledge is conveyed continuously in the interrelated experiences shared cooperatively and collaboratively in student groupings and individualized learning, the current and future benefits will continue to present the case and importance of understanding the "whole" child, inclusive of the social and the cultural context.

The student's capacity and potential for academic success within the overall educational experience are products of her or his total environment: classroom and school system; home and family; neighborhood and community in general. All of these segments are interrelated and can be supportive, one of the other, or divisive, one against the other. As a matter of course, the teacher will become familiar with all aspects of the system, the school and the classroom pertinent to the students' educational experience. This would include not only process and protocols but also the availability of resources provided to meet the academic, health and welfare needs of students. But it is incumbent upon the teacher to look beyond the boundaries of the school system to identify additional resources as well as issues and situations which will effect (directly or indirectly) a student's ability to succeed in the classroom.

Examples of Resources
- Libraries, museums, zoos, planetariums, etc.
- Clubs, societies and civic organizations, community outreach programs of private businesses and corporations and of government agencies
These can provide a variety of materials and media as well as possible speakers and presenters
- Departments of social services operating within the local community

These can provide background and program information relevant to social issues which may be impacting individual students. And this can be a resource for classroom instruction regarding life skills, at-risk behaviors, etc.

Initial contacts for resources outside of the school system will usually come from within the system itself: from administration; teacher organizations; department heads; and other colleagues.

Examples of Issues/Situations
- Students from multicultural backgrounds: Curriculum objectives and instructional strategies may be inappropriate and unsuccessful when presented in a single format which relies on the student's understanding and acceptance of the values and common attributes of a specific culture which is not his or her own.

- Parental/family influences: Attitude, resources and encouragement available in the home environment may be attributes for success or failure. Families with higher incomes are able to provide increased opportunities for students. Students from lower income families will need to depend on the resources available from the school system and the community. This should be orchestrated by the classroom teacher in cooperation with school administrators and educational advocates in the community.

Family members with higher levels of education often serve as models for students, and have high expectations for academic success. And families with specific aspirations for children (often, regardless of their own educational background) encourage students to achieve academic success, and are most often active participants in the process.

A family in crisis (caused by economic difficulties, divorce, substance abuse, physical abuse, etc.) creates a negative environment which may profoundly impact all aspects of a student's life, and particularly his or her ability to function academically. The situation may require professional intervention. It is often the classroom teacher who will recognize a family in crisis situation and instigate an intervention by reporting on this to school or civil authorities.

Regardless of the positive or negative impacts on the students' education from outside sources, it is the teacher's responsibility to ensure that all students in the classroom have an equal opportunity for academic success. This begins with the teacher's statement of high expectations for every student, and develops through planning, delivery and evaluation of instruction which provides for inclusion and ensures that all students have equal access to the resources necessary for successful acquisition of the academic skills being taught and measured in the classroom.

Students with Exceptionalities

The term "students with disabilities" never implies one particular type of disability. First, there is significant disagreement over the term "disability," itself. Many people argue that it suggests a defect in a person's character. Regardless, disabilities are often physical; however, many learning disabilities relate to an individual's ability to learn or communicate, for example. While common characteristics cannot easily be applied to all students with disabilities, it is assumed that most disabilities will hamper an individual's ability to perform a specific action. For example, deaf or "hard of hearing" individuals have a difficult time with auditory listening; people with multiple sclerosis may have trouble with muscle function and cannot walk; people with Attention Deficit Hyperactivity Disorder (ADHD) may have trouble concentrating on academic studies. It is important to remember that just because a student has a disability, not all human functions work improperly. In fact, even students with specific disabilities may not be inflicted by all possible symptoms of that particular disability.

How can teachers identify students with disabilities? Well, first remember that students have a right to privacy; often, students who know of a particular disability will not want peers or even teachers to know. Some disabilities necessitate special school care, while others require that parents (and/or doctors) notify school nurses or administrators of specific disabilities. In such cases, teachers often will be notified, yet the teacher should be very cautious about letting that information get out of his/her hands.

Many disabilities may be obvious, particularly those that are physical. In such cases, teachers will notice physical or behavioral abnormalities. Chances are, all of the student's peers have noticed, as well, and it is important to pay attention to teasing or bullying. Quite often, teachers will be informed about a student's disability because of involvement of an Individual Education Plan (IEP). This is brought about as the parent or previous teacher has requested that a student be tested for a particular disability; usually in this case, it is a learning disability.

Increasingly, educators have noticed that learning disabilities must be attended to. Such disabilities may include auditory processing disabilities, attention deficit hyperactivity disorder, visual processing disabilities (including varying degrees of blindness), autism, etc. (By the way, autism is a disorder that usually shows up within the few three years of a child's life; it hinders normal communication and social interactive behavior.)

Students Acquiring English

Teaching students who are learning English as a second language poses some unique challenges, particularly in a standards-based environment. The key is realizing that no matter how little English a student knows, the teacher should teach with the student's developmental level in mind. This means that instruction should not be "dumbed-down" for ESOL students. Different approaches should be used, however, to ensure that these students (a) get multiple opportunities to learn and practice English and (b) still learn content.

Many ESOL approaches are based on social learning methods. By being placed in mixed level groups or by being paired with a student of another ability level, students will get a chance to practice English in a natural, non-threatening environment. Students should not be pushed in these groups to use complex language or to experiment with words that are too difficult. They should simply get a chance to practice with simple words and phrases.

In teacher-directed instructional situations, visual aids, such as pictures, objects, and video are particularly effective at helping students make connections between words and items they are already familiar with

ESOL students may need additional accommodations with assessments, assignments, and projects. For example, teachers may find that written tests provide little to no information about a student's understanding of the content. Therefore, an oral test may be better suited for ESOL students. When students are somewhat comfortable and capable with written tests, a shortened test may actually be preferable; take note that they will need extra time to translate.

Adapting Instruction

A positive environment, where open, discussion-oriented, non-threatening communication among all students can occur, is a critical factor in creating an effective learning culture. The teacher must take the lead and model appropriate actions and speech, and intervene quickly when a student makes a misstep and offends (often inadvertently) another.

Communication issues that the teacher in a diverse classroom should be aware of include:

- Be sensitive to terminology and language patterns that may exclude or demean students. Regularly switch between the use of "he" and "she" in speech and writing. Know and use the current terms that ethnic and cultural groups use to identify themselves (e.g., "Latinos" (favored) vs. "Hispanics").
- Be aware of body language that is intimidating or offensive to some cultures, such as direct eye contact, and adjust accordingly.
- Monitor your own reactions to students to ensure equal responses to males and females, as well as differently-performing students.
- Don't "protect" students from criticism because of their ethnicity or gender. Likewise, acknowledge and praise all meritorious work without singling out any one student. Both actions can make all students hyper-aware of ethnic and gender differences and cause anxiety or resentment throughout the class.
- Emphasize the importance of discussing and considering different viewpoints and opinions. Demonstrate and express value for all opinions and comments and lead students to do the same

When teaching in diverse classrooms, teachers must also expect to be working and communicating with all kinds of students. The first obvious difference among students is gender. Interactions with male students are often different than those with female students. Depending on the lesson, female students are more likely to be interested in working with partners or perhaps even individually. On the other hand, male students may enjoy a more collaborative or hands-on activity. The gender of the teacher will also come into play when working with male and female students. Of course, every student is different and may not fit into a stereotypical role, and getting to know their students' preferences for learning will help teachers to truly enhance learning in the classroom.

Most class rosters will consist of students from a variety of cultures, as well. Teachers should get to know their students (of all cultures) so that they may incorporate elements of their cultures into classroom activities and planning. Also, getting to know about a student's background/cultural traditions helps to build a rapport with each student, as well as further educate the teacher about the world in which he or she teaches. See Skill 3.5 for more information about a culturally diverse classroom.

For students still learning English, teachers must make every attempt to communicate with that student daily. Whether it's with another student who speaks the same language, word cards, computer programs, drawings or other methods, teachers must find ways to encourage each student's participation. Of course, the teacher must also be sure the appropriate language services begin for the student in a timely manner, as well.

Teachers must also consider students from various socioeconomic backgrounds. These students are just as likely as anyone else to work well in a classroom; unfortunately, sometimes difficulties occur with these children when it comes to completing homework consistently. These students may need help deriving a homework system or perhaps need more attention on study or test-taking skills. Teachers should encourage these students as much as possible and offer positive reinforcements when they meet or exceed classroom expectations. Teachers should also watch these students carefully for signs of malnutrition, fatigue and possibly learning disorders.

Individuals with Disabilities

Collaborative teams play a crucial role in meeting the needs of all students, and they are important step to identifying students with special needs. Under the Individuals with Disabilities Act (IDEA), which federally mandates special education services in every state, it is the responsibility of public schools to ensure consultative, evaluative and if necessary, prescriptive services to children with special needs. In most school districts, this responsibility is handled by a collaborative group of called the Child Study Team (CST). If a teacher or parent suspects a child to have academic, social or emotional problems are referred to the CST where a team consisting of educational professionals (including teachers, specialists, the school psychologist, guidance, and other support staff) review the student's case and situation through meetings with the teacher and/or parents/guardians. The CST will determine what evaluations or tests are necessary, if any, and will also assess the results. Based on these results, the CST will suggest a plan of action if one is felt necessary.

Inclusion, mainstreaming, and least restrictive environment

Inclusion, mainstreaming and least restrictive environment are interrelated policies under the IDEA, with varying degrees of statutory imperatives.

- Inclusion is the right of students with disabilities to be placed in the regular classroom
- Lease restrictive environment is the mandate that children be educated to the maximum extent appropriate with their non-disabled peers
- Mainstreaming is a policy where disabled students can be placed in the regular classroom, as long as such placement does not interfere with the student's educational plan

One plan of action is an Academic Intervention Plan (AIP). An AIP consists of additional instructional services that are provided to the student in order to help them better achieve academically if the student has met certain criteria (such as scoring below the state reference point on standardized tests or performing more than two levels below grade-level).

Another plan of action is a 504 plan. A 504 plan is a legal document based on the provisions of the Rehabilitation Act of 1973 (which preceded IDEA). A 504 plan is a plan for instructional services to assist students with special needs in a regular education classroom setting. When a students' with physical, emotional, or other impairments (such as Attention Deficit Disorder) impact his or her ability to learn in a regular education classroom setting, that student can be referred for a 504 meeting. Typically, the CST and perhaps even the student's physician or therapist will participate in the 504 meeting and review to determine in a 504 plan will be written.

Finally, a child referred to CST may qualify for an Individualized Education Plan (IEP). An IEP is a legal document which delineates the specific, adapted services a student with disabilities will receive. An IEP differs from a 504 plan in that the child must be identified for special education services to qualify for an IEP, and ALL students who receive special education services must have an IEP. Each IEP must contain statements pertaining to the student's present performance level, annual goals, related services and supplementary aids, testing modifications, a projected date of services, and assessment methods for monitoring progress. Each year, the CST and guardians must meet to review and update a student's IEP.

Skill 20.4   Identify methods for creating an inclusionary environment

The physical set up of your classroom is exceedingly important to support the effective development of all your children. (Of course your room must "coordinate" with the other classrooms in what ever school you are currently working or hope to work in—so if the "home decoration" below piece won't fly, copy the room layout and style of a veteran teacher on your floor who has a parallel grade and skip the rest of this, except to review it for a possible constructed response question.)

See Skills 5.5 and 3.4

DOMAIN V. **ASSESSMENT**

COMPETENCY 21.0 APPLY KNOWLEDGE OF CURRENT PRINCIPLES OF READING ASSESSMENT

Skill 21.1 Demonstrate an understanding of basic characteristics of assessment methods and instruments

Characteristics and Uses of Criterion-referenced and Norm-referenced Tests to Assess Reading Development and Identify Reading Difficulties

Criterion-referenced – tests where the children are measured against criteria or guidelines which are uniform for all the test takers. Therefore by definition, no special questions, formats or considerations are made for the test taker who is either from a different linguistic/cultural background or is already identified as a struggling reader/writer. On a criterion-referenced test, it is possible that a child test taker can score 100% because the child may have actually been exposed to all of the concepts taught and mastered them. A child's score on such a test would indicate which of the concepts have already been taught and what he or she needs additional review or support to master.

Two criterion-referenced tests that are commonly used to assess children's reading achievement are the Diagnostic Indicators of Basic Early Literacy Skills (DIBELS) and the Stanford Achievement Test. DIBELS measures progress in literacy from kindergarten to grade three. It can be downloaded from the Internet free at dibels.uoregon.edu. The Stanford is designed to measure individual children's achievement in key school subjects. Subtests covering various reading skills are part of this test. Both DIBELS and the Stanford Achievement Test are group-administered.

DEGREES OF READING POWER (DRP) –This test is targeted to assess how well children understand the meaning of written text in real life situations. This test is supposed to measure the process of children's reading, not the products of reading such as identifying the main idea and author's purpose.

CTPIII- This is a criterion-referenced test which measures verbal and quantitative ability in grades 3-12. It is targeted to help differentiate among the most capable students, i.e., those who rank above the 80th percentile on other standardized tests. This is a test that emphasizes higher order thinking skills and process-related reading comprehension questions.

Norm-referenced –test in which the children are measured against one another. Scores on this test are reported in percentiles. Each percentile indicates the percent of the testing population whose scores were lower than or the same as a particular child's score. Percentile is defined as a score on a scale of 100 showing the percentage of a distribution that is equal to it or below it. This type of state standardized norm-referenced test is being used in most districts today in response to the No Child Left Behind Act. While this type of test does not help tract the individual reader's progress in his/her ongoing reading development, it does permit comparisons across groups.

There are many more standardized norm-referenced tests to assess children's reading than there are criterion-referenced. In these tests, scores are based on how well a child does compared to others, usually on the local, state and national level. IF the norming groups on the tests are reflective of the children being tested (e.g. same spread of minority, low income, gifted students), the results are more trustworthy.

One of the best known norm-referenced test is the Iowa Test of Basic Skills. It assesses student achievement in various school subjects and has several subtests in reading. Other examples of norm-referenced tests used around the country are the Metropolitan Achievement Tests, the Terra Nova-2, and the Stanford Diagnostic Reading Test-4. These are all group tests. An individual test that reading specialists use with students is the Woodcock Reading Mastery Test.

Concepts of Validity, Reliability, and Bias in Testing

Validity is how well a test measures what it is supposed to measure. Teacher made tests are therefore not generally extremely valid, although they may be an appropriate measure for the validity of the concept the teacher wants to assess for his/her own children's achievement.

Reliability is the consistency of the test. This is measured by whether the test will indicate the same score for the child who takes it more than once.

Bias in testing occurs when the information within the test or the information required to respond to a multiple choice question or constructed response (essay question on the test) is information that is not available to some test takers who come from a different cultural, ethnic, linguistic or socio-economic background than do the majority of the test takers. Since they have not had the same prior linguistic, social or cultural experiences that the majority of test takers have had, these test takers are at a disadvantage in taking the test and no matter what their actual mastery of the material taught by the teacher, can not address the "biased" questions. Generally other "non-biased" questions are given to them and eventually the biased questions are removed from the examination.

To solidify what might be abstract to the reader, on a recent reading test in my school system, the grade four reading comprehension multiple choice had some questions about the well known fairy tale of the gingerbread boy. These questions were simple and accessible for most of the children in the class. But two children who were recent new arrivals from the Dominican Republic had learned English there. They were reading on grade four level, but in their Dominican grade school, the story of the Gingerbread Boy was not a major one. Therefore a question about this story on the standardized reading test did demonstrate examiner bias and was not fair to these test takers.

Skill 21.2   Articulate assessment practices based on learning theories and research in literacy

The Use of Data and Ongoing Reading Assessment to Adjust Instruction to Meet Students' Reading Needs

Assessment is the practice of collecting information about children's progress, and evaluation is the process of judging the children's responses to determine how well they are achieving particular goals or demonstrating reading skills.

Assessment and evaluation are intricately connected in the literacy classroom. Assessment is necessary because teachers need ways to determine what students are learning and how they are progressing. In addition, assessment can be a tool which can also help students take ownership of their own learning and become partners in their ongoing development as readers and writers. In this day of public accountability, clear, definite and reliable assessment creates confidence in public education.

There are two broad categories of assessment

Informal assessment utilizes observations and other non-standardized procedures to compile anecdotal and observation data/evidence of children's progress. It includes but is not limited to checklists, observations, and performance tasks. Formal assessment is composed of standardized tests and procedures carried out under circumscribed conditions. Formal Assessments include: state tests, standardized achievement tests, NAEP tests, and the like.

To be effective, assessment should have the following characteristics:

I. It should be an ongoing process with the teacher making informal or formal assessments on an ongoing basis. The assessment should be a natural part of the instruction and not intrusive.

2. The most effective assessment is integrated into ongoing instruction. Throughout the teaching and learning day, the child's written, spoken and reading contributions to the class or lack thereof, need to and can be continually noted.

3. Assessment should reflect the child's actual reading and writing experiences. The child should be able to show that he or she can read and explain or react to a similar literary or expository work.

4. Assessment needs to be a collaborative and reflective process. Teachers can learn from what the children reveal about their own individual assessments. Children, even as early as grade two, should be supported by their teacher to continually and routinely ask themselves questions assessing their reading. They might ask: "Am I understanding what the author wanted to say?," " What can I do to improve my reading?" and "How can I use what I have read to learn more about this topic?"

Teachers need to be informed by their own professional observation AND by children's comments as they assess and customize instruction for children.

5. Quality assessment is multidimensional and may include but not be limited to samples of writings, student retellings, running records, anecdotal teacher observations, self-evaluations, and records of independent reading. From this multidimensional data, the teacher can derive a consistent level of performance and design additional instruction that will enhance the child's reading performance.

6. Assessment must take into account children's age and ethnic/cultural patterns of learning.

7. Assess to teach children from their strengths, not their weaknesses. Find out what reading behaviors children demonstrate well and then design instruction to support those behaviors.

8. Assessment should be part of children's learning process and not done TO them, but rather done WITH them.

Skill 21.3 Describe ways to align assessment practices with literacy goals and curriculum

Characteristics and uses of Group versus Individual Reading Assessments

In assessment, tests are used for different purposes. They have different dimensions or characteristics whether they are given individually or in a group and whether they are standardized or teacher-made.

The chart below shows the relationships of these elements.

	Standardized	**Teacher-made**
Individual	*Characteristics* • is uniformly administered *Uses* • is best for younger children • helps with placement for special services	*Characteristics* • has more flexibility *Uses* • assists teaching decisions • used for diagnostic purposes
Group	*Characteristics* • is uniformly administered • is time efficient *Uses* • permits comparisons across groups • used for policy decisions by administrators	*Characteristics* • has high face validity • is time efficient *Uses* • informs teach-reteach & enrichment decisions • documents students' learning

Techniques for Assessing Particular Reading Skills

Sharon Taberski recommends that the teacher build in one-on-one time for supporting individual children as needed in considering what makes sense, sounds right and matches the letters.

She has noted that emergent and early readers tend to focus on meaning without adequate attention to graphophonic cues. She suggests using the following prompts for children who are having problems with graphophonic cues:

Does what you said match the letters?

If the word were what you said ___, what would it have to start with?

READING   183

Look carefully at the first letters... then look at the middle letters. . then look at the last letters. What could it be?

If it were _____, what would it end with?
Oral retellings can be used to test children's comprehension.

Children who are retelling a story to be tested for comprehension should be told that that is the purpose when they sit down with the teacher.
It is a good idea to let the child start the retelling on his or her own, because then the teacher can see whether he or she needs prompts to retell the story. Many times more experienced readers summarize what they have read. This summary usually flows out along with the characters, the problem of the story and other details.
Other signs that children understand what they are reading when they give an oral retelling include their use of illustrations to support the retelling, references to the exact text in the retelling, emotional reaction to the text, making connections between the text and other stories or experiences they the readers have had, and giving information about the text without the teacher's asking for it.

Skill 21.4   Analyze how students' reading can be evaluated based on results from a balance of formal and informal assessments

The Characteristics and Uses of Formal and Informal Assessments

Informal Assessments

A running record of children's oral reading progress in the early grades K-3 is a pivotal informal assessment. It supports the teacher in deciding whether a book a child is reading is matched to his/her stage of reading development. In addition this assessment allows the teacher to analyze a child's miscues to see which cueing systems and strategies the child uses and to determine which other systems the child might use more effectively. Finally the running record offers a graphic account of a child's oral reading.

Generally, a teacher should maintain an annotated class notebook with pages set aside for all the children or individual notebooks for each child. One of the benefits of using running records as an informal assessment is that they can be used with any text and can serve as a tool for teaching, rather than an instrument to report on children's status in class.

Another good point about using running records is that they can be taken repeatedly and frequently by the teacher, so that the educator can truly observe a pattern of errors. This in turn provides the educator with sufficient information to analyze the child's reading over time. As any mathematician or scientist knows, the more samples of a process you gather over time, the more likely the teacher is to get an accurate picture of the child's reading needs.

Using the notations which Marie Clay developed and shared in her *An Observation Study of Early Literacy Achievement*, Sharon Taberski offers in her book, *On Solid Ground*, a lengthy walk through keeping a running record of children's reading. She writes in the child's miscue on the top line of her running record above the text word. Indeed she records all of the child's miscue attempts on the line above the text word. Sharon advises the teacher to make all the miscue notations as the child reads, since this allows the teacher to get additional information about how and why the child makes miscue choices. Additionally, the teacher should note, self corrections (coded SC) when the child is monitoring his/her own reading, crosschecks information, and uses additional information.

As part of the informal assessment of primary grade reading, it is important to record the child's word insertions, omissions, requests for help, and attempts to get the word. In informal assessment the rate of accuracy can be estimated by dividing the child's errors by the total words read.

Results of a running record assessment can be used to select the best setting for the child's reading. If a child reads from 95%-100% correct, the child is ready for independent reading. If the child reads from 92% to 97% right, the child is ready for guided reading. Below 92% the child needs a read-aloud or shared reading activity. Note that these percentages are slightly different from those one would use to match books to readers.

One of the increasingly popular and meaningful forms of informal assessment is the compilation of the literacy portfolio. What is particularly compelling about this type of informal portfolio is that artists, television directors, authors, architects and photographers use portfolios in their careers and jobs. This is a most authentic format for documenting children's literacy growth over time. The portfolio is not only a significant professional informal assessment tool for the teacher, but a vehicle and format for the child reader to take ownership of his or her progress over time. It models a way of compiling one's reading and writing products as a lifelong learner, which is the ultimate goal of reading instruction.

Portfolios can include the following six categories of materials:

Work samples: These can include children's story maps, webs, K-W-L charts, pictures, illustrations, storyboards, and writings about the stories which they have read.

Records of independent Reading and Writing: These can include the children's journals, notebooks or logs of books read with the names of the authors, titles of the books, date completed, and pieces related to books completed or in progress.

Checklists and Surveys: These include checklists designed by the teacher for reading development, writing development, ownership checklists, and general interest surveys.

Self Evaluation Forms: These are the children's own evaluations of their reading and writing process framed in their own words. They can be simple templates with starting sentences such as: "I am really proud of the way I ...

I feel one of my strengths as a reader is _____
To improve the way I read aloud I need to _____
To improve my reading I should _____

Generally at the beginning of a child's portfolio in grade 3 or above there is a letter to the reader explaining the work that will be found in the portfolio and from fourth grade level up, children write a brief reflection detailing their feelings and judgments about their growth as readers and writers.

When teachers are maintaining the portfolios for mandated school administrative review, district review, or even for their own research, they often prepare portfolio summary sheets. These provide identifying data on the children and then a timeline of their review of the portfolio contents plus professional comments on the extent to which the portfolio documents satisfactory and ongoing growth in reading.

Portfolios can be used beneficially for child-teacher and of course, parent/teacher conversations to review the child's progress, discuss areas of strength, set future goals, make plans for future learning activities and evaluate what should remain in the portfolio and what needs to be cleared out for new materials.

Rubrics
Holistic scoring involves assessing a child's ability to construct meaning through writing. It uses a scale called a RUBRIC which can range from 0 to 4.

O- This indicates the piece can not be scored. It does not respond to the topic or is illegible.

1- The writing does respond to the topic, but does not cover it accurately.

2- This piece of writing does respond to the topic but lacks sufficient details or elaboration.

3- This piece fulfills the purpose of the writing assignment and has sufficient development (which refers to details, examples, and elaboration of ideas).

4- This response has the most details, best organization, and presents a well expressed reaction to the original writer's piece.

MISCUE ANALYSIS

This is a procedure that allows the teacher a look at the reading process. By definition, the miscue is an oral response different from the text being read. Sometimes miscues are also called unexpected responses or errors. By studying a student's miscues from an oral reading sample, the teacher can determine which cues and strategies the student is correctly using or not using in constructing meaning. Of course, the teacher can customize instruction to meet the needs of this particular student.

INFORMAL READING INVENTORIES (IRI)

These are a series of samples of texts prearranged in stages of increasing difficulty. Listening to children read through these inventories, the teacher can pinpoint their skill level and the additional concepts they need to work on.

COMPETENCY 22.0 ANALYZE WAYS TO IMPLEMENT LITERACY ASSESSMENT

Skill 22.1   Specify ways to evaluate students' ability to read with accuracy and fluency

See skill 6.1

Skill 22.2   Determine the meaning of unfamiliar words and concepts

See skill 16.2

Skill 22.3   Construct meaning from a variety of texts

See Skills 1.1 and 1.2

Skill 22.4   Describe ways to assess students' use of monitoring and fix-up strategies to construct and convey meaning

See Skills 1.1 and 1.2

Skill 22.5   Identify methods for evaluating students' print and nonprint texts using appropriate assessments

Technological advances have brought computers into classrooms across the country. It is to the benefit of the reading specialist to become familiar and competent in the use of these technological advances. They can be time saving devices and provide additional incentive for students. In the area of reading there are several ways the reading specialist can use computers to generate assessment information on students to plan effective instruction.

In the case of formal assessments, most major test manufacturers provide for a small fee, the ability to enter the raw scores into software to obtain the more standardized results. This saves hours of scoring time on the part of the reading specialist and also limits the number of errors that might be made. Sometimes these software packages then also provide a list of skills the teacher can use to plan the instruction.

There are also independent Internet and CD based software that provides lessons for the students to complete right at the computer. Periodically, the student completes an assessment. The teacher to chart the student's progress as they complete the predesigned lessons can then access this information. Many of these programs have a placement test as well, which allows the lesson order to be structured to meet the deficits for students on the individual level.

Informal assessments are less likely to have premade technology available, as the assessments are often teacher created. There are some, such as the Qualitative Reading Inventory IV (QRI-IV). This provides the Individual Reading Inventory passages, comprehension questions and word lists on a CD to help the teacher manage the information better.

As teachers familiarize themselves with more general programs, such as Microsoft's Office Suite©. These products allow the teacher to create their own methods for tracking the assessment data and then plan appropriate instruction. Teachers can also manage their lessons plans using the same software.

There are other programs available to determine the readability of books and passages, tell trade books which provide skills a teacher may need to teach their students and a myriad of other pieces of information invaluable to the reading specialist.

If we have learned anything in education over the last few decades, it is that students do not all learn in the same way. Furthermore, we have learned that a steady diet of lecture and textbook reading is an extremely ineffective method of instruction. While students definitely should be exposed to lecture and textbooks, they will greatly benefit with the creativity and ingenuity of teachers who find outside resources to assist in the presentation of new knowledge.

Let's first discuss some possibilities: textual and media references, hands-on materials, and technology. Lately, some people have referred to the concept of "multiple texts" as a method of bringing into the classroom multiple types of texts. For example, a social studies teacher might ask students to read an historical novel to complement a unit of study.

In addition to texts, appropriately selected video or audio recordings may be useful. For example, a science teacher may wish to show a short clip of a video that demonstrates how to conduct a particular experiment before students do it on his or her own. Or, a Language Arts teacher may bring in an audio recording of a book to present a uniquely dramatized reading of the book.

Hands-on materials are very important to student learning. For example, math teachers may introduce geometric principles with quilt blocks. The very idea of a science experiment is that hands-on materials and activities more quickly convey scientific ideas to students than do lectures and textbooks.

Finally, technologies, such as personal computers, are very important for student learning. First, it is extremely important that students learn new technologies so that they can easily adapt to the myriad of uses found in business and industry. Second, technology can provide knowledge resources that go beyond what a school library, for example, may be able to offer. Students will need increasingly to learn how to search for, evaluate, and utilize appropriate information in the Internet. Third, using technology is highly motivating for students and can provide that necessary incentive to encourage reading for students who are struggling.

Choosing an appropriate reference, text, material, or technology depends on many factors. First, realize that whatever is brought into the class should be done so based on the knowledge that the item will assist students in learning academic standards. There is no reason for any teacher, for example, to show a movie to his or her students that is not for the explicit purpose of helping students reach specific academic objectives, tied to the curriculum. Second, consider the developmental level of the students you are working with. You would not want to introduce complex experiments to second graders; likewise, you would not want to assume that twelfth graders have no knowledge of the Internet.

In choosing materials, teachers should also keep in mind that not only do students learn at different rates, but also they bring a variety of cognitive styles to the learning process. Prior experiences influence the individual's cognitive style, or method of accepting, processing, and retaining information. According to Marshall Rosenberg, students can be categorized as:

a) rigid-inhibited
b) undisciplined
c) acceptance-anxious
d) creative

"The creative learner is an independent thinker, one who maximizes his/her abilities, can work by his/herself, enjoys learning, and is self-critical." This last category constitutes the ideal, but teachers should make every effort to use materials that will stimulate and hold the attention of learners of all types.

Aside from textbooks, there is a wide variety of materials available to today's teachers. Microcomputers are now commonplace, and some schools can now afford laser discs to bring alive the content of a reference book in text, motion, and sound. Hand-held calculators eliminate the need for drill and practice in number facts, while they also support a problem solving and process to mathematics. Videocassettes (VCR's) are common and permit the use of home-produced or commercially produced tapes. Textbook publishers often provide films, recordings, and software to accompany the text, as well as maps, graphics, and colorful posters to help students visualize what is being taught. Teachers can usually scan the educational publishers' brochures that arrive at their principal's or department head's office on a frequent basis. Another way to stay current in the field is by attending workshops or conferences. Teachers will be enthusiastically welcomed on those occasions when educational publishers are asked to display their latest productions and revised editions of materials.

In addition, yesterday's libraries are today's media centers. Teachers can usually have opaque projectors delivered to the classroom to project print or pictorial images (including student work) onto a screen for classroom viewing. Some teachers have chosen to replace chalkboards with projectors that reproduce the print or images present on the plastic sheets known as transparencies, which the teacher can write on during a presentation or have machine-printed in advance. In either case, the transparency can easily be stored for later use. In an art or photography class, or any class in which it is helpful to display visual materials, slides can easily be projected onto a wall or a screen.

Cameras are inexpensive enough to enable students to photograph and display their own work, as well as keep a record of their achievements in teacher files or student portfolios.

Studies have shown that students learn best when what is taught in lecture and textbook reading is presented more than once in various formats. This also allows for different learning styles or modalities to be explored and tapped. In some instances, students themselves may be asked to reinforce what they have learned by completing some original production—for example, by drawing pictures to explain some scientific process, by writing a monologue or dialogue to express what some historical figure might have said on some occasion, by devising a board game to challenge the players' mathematical skills, or by acting out (and perhaps filming) episodes from a classroom reading selection. Students usually enjoy having their work displayed or presented to an audience of peers. Thus, their productions may supplement and personalize the learning experiences that the teacher has planned for them.

Skill 22.6   Include state assessments, that represent the Michigan English Language Arts Content Standards and Benchmarks

The testing process for the state of Michigan is decided by the state department of education and is part of the No Child Left Behind requirements. This is part of the accountability protocol to determine which districts are meeting the requirements of NCLB.

The Michigan Educational Assessment Program (MEAP) is constantly undergoing revisions and changes. MEAP puts out English Language Arts (ELA) Content documents at various assessed grade levels, which provide the teacher with invaluable insight into the expectations and organizational structure of the assessment.

These expectations are broken into the various components of an Integrated Language Arts curriculum including: reading, writing, listening, speaking, and viewing. Using these broad areas the MEAP assesses all of the ELA standards and benchmarks for the appropriate grade levels.

There are MEAP ELA assessments are at grades three through eight and then again in grade twelve. A new second grade test has just been released as well, but is not part of the current testing schedule, however, it is likely to be started in the 2007-2008 school year. It is important to understand also; there are allowable accommodations for students with identified special needs in the administration of these assessments. Information about the MEAP process can be found at: http://www.michigan.gov/mde/0,1607,7-140-22709_31168---,00.html .

COMPETENCY 23.0 UNDERSTAND THE APPROPRIATE USES OF ASSESSMENT

Skill 23.1   Evaluate uses of classroom assessment techniques (e.g., rubrics, checklists, portfolios) to plan for and support instruction

See Skill 21.1

Skill 23.2   Analyze ways to select, create, and correctly interpret results of developmentally appropriate tools and various measurements used for assessment and evaluation

The information contained within student records, teacher observations and diagnostic tests are only as valuable as the teacher's ability to understand it. Although the student's cumulative record will contain this information, it is the responsibility of each teacher to read and interpret the information. Diagnostic test results are somewhat uniform and easy to interpret. They usually include a scoring guide that tells the teacher what the numbers actually mean. Teachers also need to realize that these number scores leave room for uncontrollable factor and are not the ultimate indicator of a child's ability or learning needs. Many factors influence these scores including the rapport the child had with the tester, how the child was feeling when the test was administered, and how the child regarded the value or importance of the test. Therefore, the teacher should regard these scores as a "ball park" figure.

When a teacher reads another teacher's observations, it is important to keep in mind that each person brings to an observation certain biases. The reader may also influence the information contained within an observation with his/her own interpretation. When using teacher observations as a basis for designing learning programs, it is necessary to be aware of these shortcomings.

Student records may provide the most assistance in guiding instruction. These records contain information that was gathered over a period of time and may show student growth and progress. They also contain information provided by several people including teachers, parents, and other educational professionals. By reading this compilation of information the teacher may get a more accurate "feel for" a student's needs. All of this information is only a stepping-stone in determining how a child learns, what a child knows, and what a child needs to know to further his/her education.

Once the general student records are reviewed or if you are lacking in records, it is sometimes helpful to use a universal screening tool to gather general information to drive instruction. There are many different broad spectrum screening tools available some such as the Dynamic Indicators of Basic Early Literacy Skills (DIBELS), even are free on the internet. These broad tools can provide the teacher with a quick and easy overview of the student across curriculum areas.

From this point, the teacher can then use more specific skill based assessments to determine exact teaching points. The broad screening quickly provides general areas of strength or deficit, which can be further whittled down to exact holes in the student's learning by the administration of more specific assessments. An example might work in the following manner:

The DIBELS screening suggests deficits in Phonological Awareness. The teacher then gives a specialized test such as the Comprehensive Test of Phonological Processing and determines that the student specifically has difficulty with phonemic memory. This teacher can then plan instruction to remediate this specific deficit and not spend time teaching skills with which the student is already successful. The key to this circle of assessment is to be familiar with first the broad screeners and then to have available and know how to use a variety of more specific tools.

Skill 23.3 Describe the use of state and classroom assessments for formative and summative evaluation purposes

The teaching, learning, and assessing process is as follows:
1. Teachers know what is in the standards.
2. Teachers develop a plan for the school year to ensure that all the standards are covered.
3. Teachers develop objectives for specific lessons within the school year.
4. Teachers provide various assessments throughout the year to ensure that students are progressing adequately.
5. Teachers use the data from those assessments to make modifications to instruction (or to repeat certain topics).
6. Students are assessed on the MEAP.
7. Schools and teachers can analyze the data from the MEAP to determine how to plan for instruction in the next year.

Notice that all elements funnel back to instruction. All assessments, in fact, are designed in part to give teachers information about how they need to enhance or modify their instruction.

Now, each year, teachers can use assessment data from the MEAP tests to determine how well their students have done each year. But many people make the analogy that analyzing year-end test data provides as much information as the score of a basketball or baseball game gives people about the specific things that were done well and poorly throughout the game. When we just focus on the data from year-end tests, we see what areas students mastered and what areas they did not master. However, to really see how instruction can be modified, teachers need to focus on providing multiple opportunities for assessment throughout the year to get as much information within the year on what could be improved. A simple and short assessment at the end of a lesson tells a teacher, for example, if students mastered the material from the lesson. Or, a reading inventory kept throughout the year tells how much a student has progressed in reading skill, rather than just giving us a "score" at the end of the year which will not show the ups and downs throughout the year.

When we say that common statistical methods should be used to identify students' strengths and weaknesses, we mean that different statistical methods should not used to compare outcomes. Here's a good example: A teacher gives a student a 10 question quiz. A student gets 8 questions correct, and the teacher identifies performance as 80% correct. Yet, when the test scores from the state come back, and the teacher sees that the student is in the 60th %ile ("percentile"), what this means is that 60% of students taking the test scored LOWER than the student, not that the student only answered 60% correct. The point here is knowing what the scores mean and not to compare one type of score to another type, as the numbers will not relate.

Assessment is observing an event and making a judgment about its status of success. There are seven purposes of assessment:

- To assist student learning
- To identify students' strengths and weaknesses
- To asses the effectiveness of a particular instructional strategy
- To assess and improve the effectiveness of curriculum programs
- To assess and improve teaching effectiveness
- To provide data that assists in decision making
- To communicate with and involve parents

There are mainly four kinds of assessment:

1. Observation: noticing someone and judging their action.
2. Informal continuous assessment - less structured. Informal continuous assessment is informal because it is informal - not formal like a test or exam. It is continuous because it occurs periodically - on a daily or weekly basis.
3. Informal continuous assessment: more structured means setting up assessment situations periodically. An assessment situation is an activity you organize so that the learners could be assessed. It could be a quiz. It could also be a group activity, where the participants will be assessed.
4. Formal assessment is a structured infrequent measure of learner achievement. It involves the use of test and exam. Exams are used to measure the learner's progress.

The purpose of informal assessment is to help our learners learn better. This form of assessment helps the teacher to how well the learners are learning and progressing. Informal assessment can be applied to home work assignments, field journals, daily class work, which are good indicators of student progress and comprehension.

Formal assessment on the other hand is highly structured keeping the learner in mind. It must be done at regular intervals and if the progress is not satisfactory, parent involvement is absolutely essential. A test or exam is a good example of formal assessment. A science project is also is a formal assessment.

The purpose for testing the students is to determine the extent to which the instructional objectives have been met. Therefore, the test items must be constructed to achieve the desired outcome from the students. Gronlund and Linn advise that effective tests begin with a test plan that includes the instructional objectives and subject matter to be tested, as well as the emphasis each item should have. Having a test plan will result in valid interpretation of student achievement.

After determining the content of the test, a teacher selects appropriate test items. The test items used in typical classroom tests are either objective questions or essay questions. In an objective question, the student must either supply the answer or select the answer from a number of choices. In the supply answer type of objective question, the student typically writes a short answer. For example, "_____is the author of Moby Dick" or "Who is the author of Moby Dick?" is a short answer question. The drawback to this test item is the possible ambiguity of student-supplied answers.

Another common form of objective question is the true/false test item. Gronlund and Linn point out some limitations to this test item is its susceptibility to guessing, the difficulty involved in constructing a true/false item that is valid, and the limited specific learning outcomes it can measure. However, they also point out its usefulness in identifying cause and effect relationships as well as distinguishing fact and opinion.

A third form of test item is the matching exercise. An advantage of this type of test item is its ability to test large blocks of material in a short time. The major problem with this type of test item is its emphasis on memorization. Kenneth H. Hoover does not favor this type of test item, but points out that it can be appropriate when the exercise contains at least five, but not more than twelve items, uses only homogeneous items, and contains at least three extra answers to choose from.

The most commonly used objective question where the student chooses an answer is the multiple-choice question. The multiple-choice test item consists of a stem and a list of responses, of which only one is the best answer. The responses, which are not the answer, are called distracters. Gronlund and Linn point out that multiple-choice test items are most useful for specific learning outcomes that utilize the student's ability to understand or interpret factual information. Since the multiple-choice test item can be adopted to most subject matter, and because of its versatile nature, it is the most commonly used item on standardized tests. However, as Gronlund and Linn point out, the multiple-choice test item cannot test the ability to organize and present ideas.

The best way to test the student's ability to organize and present ideas is with the essay test item. This type of test item also utilizes the student's ability to think and problem solve. However, the main drawbacks to this type of question are the unreliability of scoring and the amount of time necessary to score the item. Nevertheless, it is valuable when the specific learning outcomes cannot be measured any other way.

Therefore, it is true that all test items have useful purposes as well as drawbacks. It is important to keep the specific learning outcome and the subject matter covered in mind when constructing each item. The effective teacher evaluates and re-evaluates each test item with each test presentation.

Validity and Reliability

A desirable assessment is both reliable and valid. Without adequate reliability and validity, an assessment provides unusable results. A reliable assessment provides accurate and consistent results; there is little error from one time to the next. A valid assessment is one which test what it intends to test.

Reliability is directly related to correlation. A perfect positive correlation equals + 1.00 and a perfect negative correlation equals -1.00. The reliability of an assessment tool is generally expressed as a decimal to two places (eg. 0.85). This decimal number describes the correlation that would be expected between two scores if the same student took the test two times.

Actually, there are several ways to estimate the reliability of an instrument. The method which is conceptually the most clear is the test-retested method. When the same test is administered again to the same students, if the test is perfectly reliable, each student will receive the same score each time. Even as the scores of individual students vary some from one time to the next, it is desirable for the rank order of the students to remain unchanged. Other methods of estimating reliability operate off of the same conceptual framework. Split-half methods divide a single test into two parts and compare them. Equivalent forms methods use two versions of the same test and compare test. With some types of assessment, such as essays and observation reports, reliability concerns also deal with the procedures and criteria used for scoring. The inter-rater reliability ask the question: How much will the results vary depending on who is scoring or rating the assessment data?

There are three commonly described types of validity: Content validity, criterion validity, and construct validity. Content validity describes the degree to which a test actually tests, say, arithmetic. Story problems on an arithmetic test will lower is validity as a measure of arithmetic since reading ability will also be reflected in the results. However, note that it remains a valid test of the ability to solve story problems. Criterion validity is so named because of the concern with the test's ability to predict performance on another measure or test. For example, a college admissions test is highly valid if it predicts very accurately those students who will attain high GPAs at that college. The criterion in this case is college GPA. Construct validity is concerned with describing the usefulness or reality of what is being tested. The recent interest in multiple intelligences, instead of a single IQ score, is an example of the older construct of intelligence being reexamined as potentially several distinct constructs.

A student's readiness for a specific subject is not an absolute concept, but is determined by the relationship between the subject matter or topic and the student's prior knowledge, interest, motivation, attitude, experience and other similar factors.

Thus, the student's readiness to learn about the water cycle depends on whether the student already knows related concepts such as evaporation, condensation, and filtration. Readiness, then, implies that there is not a "gap" between what the student knows and the prerequisite knowledge base for learning.

A pretest designed to assess significant and related prerequisite skill and abilities is the most common method of identifying the student's readiness. This assessment should focus, not on the content to be introduced, but on prior knowledge judged to be necessary for understanding the new content. A pretest, which focuses on the new content, may identify students who do not need the new instruction (who have already mastered the material), but it will not identify students with readiness gaps.

The most common areas of readiness concerns fall in the basic academic skill areas. Mastery of the basic skill areas is a prerequisite for almost all subject area learning. Arithmetic skills and some higher level mathematics skills are generally necessary for science learning or for understanding history and related time concepts. Reading skills are necessary throughout the school years and beyond. A student with poor reading skills is at a disadvantage when asked to read a textbook chapter independently. Writing skills, especially handwriting, spelling, punctuation, and mechanics, are directly related to success in any writing-based activity. A weakness in any of these basic skill areas may at first glance appear to be a difficulty in understanding the subject area. A teacher who attempts to help the student master the subject matter through additional emphasis on the content will be misusing instructional time and frustrating the student. An awareness of readiness issues helps the teacher to focus on treating the underlying deficiency instead of focusing on the overt symptoms.

Once a readiness gap has been identified, then the teacher can provide activities designed to close the gap. Specific activities may be of almost any form. Since most learning builds upon previous learning, there are few activities or segments of learning that can be viewed solely as readiness or non-readiness activities. In a very direct very few types of learning can be identified as solely readiness activities without legitimacy in their own right.

While growth and maturation rates vary greatly from individual to individual, there are some generalizations that can be made concerning development characteristics of children. Most children appear to go through identifiable, sequential stages of growth and maturation, although not at the same rate. For the curriculum developers, it is often necessary to make some generalizations about the development level of the students of a particular age group or grade level. These generalizations, then, provide a framework for establishing the expectations of the children's performance. Textbooks, scope and sequence charts, school curriculum planners, and more, translate these generalizations into plans and expectations for the students. The curriculum plan that emerges identifies general goals and expectations for the average student.

One of the teacher's responsibilities in this situation is to realize the nature of the initial rough estimate of what is appropriate for a given group of students. The teacher should expect to modify and adjust the instructional program based on the needs and abilities of the students. A teacher may do this by grouping students for alternative instruction, adjusting or varying the materials (textbooks), varying the teaching methods, or varying the learning tasks.

Bias

Bias exists in assessment when, after getting the results, it is obvious that demographic variables account for score variation. In other words, test bias would exist if a test question assumes that the test taker understands some of the contextual information in the question. For example, let's say a test question is trying to assess a student's understanding of a science concept that has been taught in class. However, the teacher uses an example to set up the question that assumes all students have the same cultural background. This test question would be assumed to be biased.

There are a few ways to systematically notice potential bias. First, when test questions are developed, they should focus on assessing discrete skills or areas of knowledge that have been taught. With teacher-created test materials, teachers should not include elements on the test that might require students to access information that they may not have. While some students possibly could know that additional information, not all students will, and it will instead look like those other students did not know the material the teacher really intended for the student to know. So, test questions should be simply written, contain basic vocabulary, and not include elements that pertain to any one culture or religion.

On a wider level, teachers may notice that an entire demographic group has performed worse compared to other demographic groups on a particular question. This might be a clue to possible bias.

How can teachers eliminate bias on their own assessments that they create? They can work ensure that everything tested has been taught. This is an important task. Teachers should carefully examine their tests for material that students would have no way of knowing. Teachers should also be very sensitive to the things that they take for granted. Something as simple as forgetting that different religions celebrate different holidays can lead to bias.

Skill 23.4 **Describe methods for communicating effectively with parents, guardians, surrogates, colleagues, and students about the learners' progress and development**

The most common method of communicating with caregivers and parents has been through the traditional report card or parent teacher interviews. Many teachers today have a much more informal relationship with parents and welcome parents into the classroom on a regular basis. Student learning is not just a matter of recording the results of testing. It includes the following:

- Work samples to show growth over time
- Journals
- Anecdotal notes
- Peer and self-evaluation
- Portfolios
- Student led conferences
- Rubrics and exemplars
- Goal setting

Just as there are various methods of showing parents how their children are doing in school, there are many ways by which schools can provide parents with the opportunity to see how their children are doing. These include such occasions as:

- Curriculum nights
- Newsletters from school on a weekly basis
- Homework communication journal
- Agendas
- Reading logs
- Monthly assemblies
- Phone calls to report good and bad behavior
- Letters and notes to parents

COMPETENCY 24.0 APPLY KNOWLEDGE OF THE USES OF SELF-ASSESSMENT.

Skill 24.1 Describe ways to help students document and evaluate the development of their communication abilities

Self-assessment for students can take the form of:
- Writing conferences
- Small and large group discussions
- Learning logs
- Response journals
- Checklists, inventories and questionnaires
- Teacher-student conferences

The self-assessments teachers use for students should require them to reflect on their learning and ask them to make suggestions as to how they can improve. Students should have enough time to make thoughtful reflections.

When students have exemplars to use for comparison with their own work, it is very likely that they will meet the criteria of these samples over time. The key is to make sure that students understand what the criteria for good work are before they start. They may need help clarifying these criteria so that they make sense and they can work with them.

It takes practice for anyone to develop meaningful reflection about their work. Students do need instruction in how to assess their own work and time in which to develop. The teacher can give them specific questions to answer, such as:

- What did I do today?
- What did I do well?
- What do I need help with?
- Is there something I am confused about?
- What do I want to know more about?

Time for reflection can be given at the end of an assignment or at the end of a day. Rubrics should be presented to the students before they start so they have a clear idea of how they will be assessed.

Skill 24.2 Apply strategies to evaluate students' abilities to perform these tasks at their developmental levels

Assessment of the Reading Development of Individual Students

For young readers who are from ELL backgrounds, even if they have been born in the United States, the use of pictures validates their story authoring and story telling skills and provides them with access and equity to the literary discussion and book talk of their native English speaking peers. These children can also demonstrate their storytelling abilities by drawing sequels or prequels to the story detailed in the illustrations alone. They might even be given the opportunity to share the story aloud in their native language or to comment on the illustrations in their native language.

Since many stories today are recorded in two or even three languages at once, discussing story events or analyzing pictures in a different native language is a beneficial practice which can be accomplished in the 21st century marketplace.

Use of pictures and illustrations can also help the K-3 educator assess the capabilities of children who are struggling readers if the children's learning strength is spatial. Through targeted questions about how the pictures would change if different plot twists occurred or how the child might transform the story through changing the illustrations, the teacher can begin to assess struggling reader's deficits and strengths.

Children from ELL backgrounds can benefit from listening to a recorded version of a particular story which they can read along with the tape. This gives them another opportunity to "hear" the story correctly pronounced and presented and to begin to internalize its language structures. In the absence of taped versions of some key stories or texts, the teacher may want to make sound recordings her or himself.

Highly proficient readers can also be involved in creating these literature recordings for use with ELL peers or younger peers. This of course develops oral language proficiency and also introduces these skilled readers into the intricacies of supporting ELL reading instruction. When they actually see their tapes being used by children, they will be tremendously gratified.

Adjustment of Reading Instruction Based on Ongoing Assessment

The running records taken of children help the teacher learn about the cueing systems that children use. It is important for the teacher to adjust reading instruction based on the pattern of miscues gathered from several successive reading records. When the teacher carefully reviews a given student's substitutions and self corrections, certain patterns begin to surface. A child may use visual cues as he or she reads and adds meaning to self correct. To the alert teacher, the reliance on visual miscues indicates that the reader doesn't make sense of what she is reading. This means that the teacher needs to check to see what cueing system the child uses when he or she is reading "just right" books. Children, who use meaning and structure but not visual/graphophonic cues, need to be reminded and facilitated to understand the importance of getting and reconstructing the author's message. They have to be able to share the author's story, not their own.

Not only can and should the teacher use the material in the children's ongoing assessment notebook to adjust the child's current instruction but the material also serves to document for the child his/her growth as a successful reader over time. In addition, if the same concerns surface over the use of a particular cueing system or high frequency word, the teacher can adjust the class wall chart and even devote a whole class lesson to the particular element.

Instructional Reading Strategies for Promoting the Development of Particular Reading Skills

Phonemic awareness can be developed through using leveled books that deal with rhyming words and segmenting phonemes into words. Children can also work with word or letter strips to continue the poems from the books and create their own "sequels" to the phoneme-filled story. They can also create an in-style rhyming story using some of the same phonemes from the leveled story they have heard.

Word Identification- Selective Cue Stage. Sometimes children have not yet experienced an awareness of the conventions of print and labeling in their own home environments. The teacher or an aide may have to go on a label adventure and support children in recognizing or affixing labels to parts of the classroom, halls and school building. A neighborhood walk with a digital or hand held camera may be required to help children identify uses and functions of print in society. A classroom photo essay or bulletin board could be the outgrowth of such an activity.

Sight Vocabulary- Beginning readers may enjoy outdoing Dolch (1936), who compiled the best known sight vocabulary word list. They can create their own class version of this list with illustrations and even some comments about why they have nominated certain words for the list.

Uses of Large Group, Small Group, and Individualized Reading Instruction

The framework for organizing the balanced literacy classroom is referred to as the one book-whole class mode. What this means is that everyone in the class has experiences with the same book. Everyone in the class discusses the literature. The teacher starts by activating prior knowledge and developing the context or background for the piece of literature. Some of the children within the class may have less prior knowledge or context with which to frame the book. The teacher will need to provide a preview of the book or develop key concepts to provide a stronger base for what the class will read together.

Some children will have to work with a paraprofessional or with a reading tutor before the class studies the book. Different modes of reading are accommodated within the class, by the books being read as a read-aloud, as part of shared reading or as guided reading. Student reader choices can also include: cooperative reading, reading with a partner, or independent reading.

Following the reading, the children respond to it which can be done through a literature circle and/or the whole class or in writing.

Skill 24.3 Identify methods for evaluating students' collections of personal work and the critical standards they use to judge the merit and aesthetic qualities of each selection

Grading student work is a time consuming task, especially when it involves grading writing. When teacher set goals for grading assignments, it makes the work much easier. When students have guidelines to follow or checklists that they must pass in along with the assignment, teachers can determine how well students can self-assess and where they need extra help.

The state standards must be at the forefront in grading, just as they are in instruction. By working backwards when planning instruction, teachers will have a clear idea of the work they expect students to be able to do at the end of the unit. The standards will determine what you expect the student to be able to do to show that learning has taken place. The steps to follow in determining the merit and aesthetic qualities of students work are:

1. What are the learning goals for this assignment?
2. Did the students follow the directions set out in the assignment?
3. What qualities of a written assignment would show that the student has achieved the objectives of the lesson?
4. What does an paper with the grade of "A" look like? "B"? "C"?

Students should know the answers to these questions before they start the unit so that they are clear on what the assignment is asking of them. Students should also have a choice in how they demonstrate their learning

DOMAIN VI. PROFESSIONAL, PROGRAM, AND CURRICULUM DEVELOPMENT

COMPETENCY 25.0 ANALYZE METHODS FOR ASSISTING STUDENTS WITH READING DIFFICULTIES.

Skill 25.1   Distinguish the nature and causes of reading disabilities; articulate principles for remediating reading difficulties

See Skill 15.2.

Skill 25.2   Analyze the instructional implications of research dealing with students with learning/reading disabilities

Awareness of Strategies and Resources for Supporting Individual Students

Children who come from family backgrounds where English is not spoken lack a solid understanding of its syntactic structure. Therefore as they are being assessed using the oral running record, they may need additional support from their teacher in examining the structure and meaning of English. A child from a non-native English Language speaking background may often pronounce words that make no sense to him or her and just go on reading. They have to learn to stop to construct meaning. This child may have to be prompted to self-correct.

Children from non-native English Language speaking backgrounds can benefit from independent reading opportunities to listen to a familiar story on tape and read along. This also gives them practice in listening to standard English oral reading. Often these children can begin to internalize the language structures by listening to the book on tape several times.

Highly proficient readers can sometimes support early readers through a partner relationship. Some children, particularly the emergent and beginning early readers, benefit from reading books with partners. The partners sit side by side and each one takes turns reading the entire text.

Use of talking book and author web resources provides special needs learners with visual or auditory handicapping conditions immediate contact with authors. This can lead to direct sharing in the joy of oral language story telling. In addition to the accessibility of the keyboard, children's responses to literature can be shared with a broad network of other readers, including close and distance peers. Technology literally invites special needs learners into the circle of connected readers and writers.

Skill 25.3   Recognize appropriate ways to assist with the development of individualized education plans for students with severe learning problems related to literacy

See skill 20.3

COMPETENCY 26.0 APPLY KNOWLEDGE OF PROFESSIONAL PRACTICES RELATED TO STUDENTS AND OTHERS

Skill 26.1 Specify ways to demonstrate respect for the contributions, abilities, and languages of all learners; describe how to help students understand their own and others' cultures and languages; identify appropriate strategies for engaging parents, guardians, and surrogates as collaborators in promoting and sustaining literacy development; describe effective approaches to communicating with administrators, staff, and the community concerning practices, assessment, and data; and identify effective methods for working with the community to achieve literacy goals

See Skill 5.1

COMPETENCY 27.0 UNDERSTAND METHODS FOR PROMOTING PROFESSIONAL GROWTH

Skill 27.1   Identify and assess the benefits of engaging in reflective practice emphasizing inquiry-based teaching; describe purposes for reading professional journals and publications; identify benefits of participating in professional organizations that promote literacy (e.g., International Reading Association [IRA], National Council of Teachers of English [NCTE]); analyze ways to participate in professional discourse; and describe the benefits of taking informed stands on literacy issues, making presentations at meetings and conferences, and writing for publication

Educational journals are full of literacy research. These are often available at the school if the district has a subscription. As the reading specialist you should have a subscription to these, which include:

- The Reading Teacher
- Educational Leadership
- Adolescent Learning

In addition, experts are writing about the findings of research into literacy and there are many published books on the subject. Consider the writings of:

- Marie Clay
- Donald Graves
- Regi Routman
- Susan Taberski

Participating in professional organizations that promote literacy will put teachers in touch with experts in the field and give them resources that they can draw upon to help them in their classrooms. Such participation offers teachers the opportunities to work with these professionals and to hear speakers on all aspects of literacy. They can gain valuable information and tips for dealing with the various issues that arise in their classrooms and provide them with a sounding board for ideas they would like to try out.

Many of the methods teachers try in the classroom turn out to be exceptional ways of promoting literacy. By writing about them, they can get a chance to give advice to other teachers and often they are invited to speak at conventions about their findings.

It is imperative one keeps up on the current research validated methods for working in the field of reading. This can be best done through membership to professional organizations such as International Reading Association (IRA) or the National Reading Conference (NRC). Joining these or other similar organizations will help the professional stay current with methodologies and provide appropriate literature and other publications for review.

Technology and the availability of the Internet also provide staff with materials and strategies to help keep abreast of the issues and current literature in the field of reading. Online journals, search engines, study groups and chat groups can be integral to ongoing professional development. Coursework at the graduate level will also help educators continue to build their understandings, as does mentoring and collaborative teaching. In fact, finding an experienced mentor in the same field can provide more information as to roles, issues and current topics in the field of reading than a variety of other sources.

Other specific skills in reading, such as Reading Recovery[©], require additional training specifically in their program. These types of programs usually have a rigorous ongoing professional development plan that require numerous hours over years.

It is important to seek out conferences and workshops specifically designed for reading specialists because districts typically provide inservices to the majority of their populations, which would be regular education teachers, they often overlook the lower incidence employees. Sometimes therefore the standard professional development of the district will not pertain to this area of expertise. Other times, reading specialists may be asked to provide inserivces to groups of **teachers.**

Having a professional development plan can be an integral component of staying current. In this plan, the reading teacher looks ahead down the road at what skills she would like to attain and then develops a plan over the years to help achieve these goals. Looking into the future as an educator and having a set plan for what goals and objectives the teacher hopes to achieve herself helps tremendously in implementing the current research.

As with any educational profession thinking of yourself as an appropriate role model for your students is paramount. Appropriate ethics and demonstration regularly of those ethics is a key component to professionalism.

COMPETENCY 28.0 APPLY KNOWLEDGE OF METHODS FOR CREATING PROFESSIONAL DEVELOPMENT PROGRAMS FOR READING TEACHERS AND PARAPROFESSIONALS.

Skill 28.1 Identify methods for implementing professional development programs that emphasize the interaction of prior knowledge, experience, and the school context; analyze methods for promoting collegiality with literacy professionals in discussions and consultations about learners; describe approaches to supervising, observing, and supporting reading teachers and paraprofessionals; identify appropriate methods for evaluating reading teachers' and paraprofessionals' interactions with students and providing feedback on their performance; and analyze the use of multiple indicators to evaluate professional growth

When administrators provide time for teachers to get together to plan instructional activities geared towards reading, a spirit of collaboration will exist in the school. One way to accomplish this is to provide the teachers with time to visit other schools and observe what is happening in another classroom in the district. Teachers within the same division (primary, Elementary, eg.) or teachers of one grade in the school can get together on a regular basis to discuss how they are teaching various concepts and to discuss how to best help students that are struggling with reading. The Reading Specialist should be part of this team as well as the teacher giving support to the struggling readers. It may mean after school time or shut down days for the school. Administrators can also schedule the timetable in such a way that these teachers have time off during the school day for this purpose.

Reading specialists, administrators and teachers are always on the lookout for professional development opportunities that will help them in teaching reading. Many school districts offer professional development in many areas and provide an outline of this to the schools at the beginning of the year. However, this often involves travel and for schools that manage their own budgets, this is something that has to be looked at carefully.

With the many demands placed on teachers, it is often not feasible to hold PD sessions after school hours on a regular basis. Teachers do not mind if this is scheduled into the timetable at the beginning of the year and the sessions are only for short periods of time. Using the PD time allowable by the school district to shut down schools for a half or full day is one way of bringing appropriate professional development to the staff. Schools within close proximity to one another can work together to share the cost of bringing in guest speakers and experts in the field of reading.

Another method that has seen success is to add 15 minutes to the school day from Monday to Thursday and give teachers Friday afternoons for professional development. When this becomes a district wide policy, teachers know exactly what is expected of them on Friday. Some of these sessions can be school PD where the teachers get time to plan together, discussing how best to teach the children and how to make sure they are teaching the state-mandated outcomes. Some of these Fridays can be a chance for teachers to get together with those from other schools. For example, there could be a PD for Grade 1 teachers, those in middle literacy, high school English teachers etc. When small groups are formed in this way, you have professional learning communities within the school district.

Professional development opportunities for teacher performance improvement or enhancement in instructional practices are essential for creating comprehensive learning communities. In order to promote the vision, mission and action plans of school communities, teachers must be given the toolkits to maximize instructional performances. The development of student-centered learning communities that foster the academic capacities and learning synthesis for all students should be the fundamental goal of professional development for teachers.

The level of professional development may include traditional district workshops that enhance instructional expectations for teachers or the more complicated multiple day workshops given by national and state educational organizations to enhance the federal accountability of skill and professional development for teachers. Most workshops on the national and state level provide clock hours that can be used to renew certifications for teachers every five years. Typically, 150 clock hours is the standard certification number needed to provide a five year certification renewal, so teachers must attend and complete paperwork for a diversity of workshops that range from 1-50 clock hours according to the timeframe of the workshops.

Florida requires districts and schools to provide in-service professional development opportunities for teachers during the school year dealing with district objectives/expectations and relevant workshops or classes that can enhance the teaching practices for teachers. Clock hours are provided with each class or workshop and the type of professional development being offered to teachers determines clock hours. Each year, schools are required to report the number of workshops, along with the participants attending the workshops to the Superintendent's office for filing. Teachers collecting clock hour forms are required to file the forms to maintain certification eligibility and job eligibility.

The research by the National Association of Secondary Principals,' "Breaking Ranks II: Strategies for Leading High School Reform" created the following multiple listing of educational practices needed for expanding the professional development opportunities for teachers:

- Interdisciplinary instruction between subject areas
- Identification of individual learning styles to maximize student academic performance

Training teachers in understanding and applying multiple assessment formats and implementations in curriculum and instruction.

- Looking at multiple methods of classroom management strategies
- Providing teachers with national, federal, state and district curriculum expectations and performance outcomes
- Identifying the school communities' action plan of student learning objectives and teacher instructional practices
- Helping teachers understand how to use data to impact student learning goals and objectives
- Teaching teachers on how to disaggregate student data in improving instruction and curriculum implementation for student academic equity and access
- Develop leadership opportunities for teachers to become school and district trainers to promote effective learning communities for student achievement and success

In promoting professional development opportunities for teachers that enhance student achievement, the bottom line is that teachers must be given the time to complete workshops at no or minimal costs. School and district budgets must include financial resources to support and encourage teachers to engage in mandatory and optional professional development opportunities that create a "win-win" learning experience for students.

As a teacher of any sort you will experience many forms of evaluations. Through student teaching to formal evaluations completed by supervisors, ongoing critical looks at your performance will be a part of the regular process. One area that is often under utilized but perhaps more valuable than outside evaluations is the self-assessment.

Examining with a critical eye one's own performance is the highest level of reflection. There are several forms that self-assessments can undertake. One format is to videotape yourself completing a lesson with the students. Then replaying the tape for yourself at a later time. Before watching the tape, you should have specific questions or areas in mind. Simply watching the tape itself is much less valuable than when you watch it with a purpose. The questions might include things like: Did I keep the students engaged throughout the lesson? Was I clear in explaining the content I wanted them to understand? What could I do to improve the understanding of this concept for the students?

Another method of self-assessment might include providing your students with surveys to complete. When compiling the data from the questions, you will have a better understanding of how you are perceived by your students and what skills you can work on to improve the weak areas. Carefully written questions focused on the items you are interested in learning about is necessary.

Sometimes a self-assessment could be as simple as keeping a reflection journal. With this strategy, the teacher simply keeps a regular notebook and after each day or week or even lesson takes a few minutes to write down her thoughts and feelings. Writing down what went well, what did not go well, what could have been done differently, or what was a surprise can provide valuable insight into teaching style and improvement. The drawback to this strategy is finding the time to use this method. Self reflection has been found to provide the most immediate and effective changes to instructional practice. If used authentically and kept confidential, it can be one of the best tools for improvement available to an educator.

Regular use of self-evaluation tools allows the teacher to understand what goals and objectives to include in the personal improvement plan. These ideas then become a part of the professional development plan. Remembering to review the state standards and using them, as a guide for the self-evaluation will provide further guidance and a place to start for the development of such plans.

COMPETENCY 29.0 ANALYZE THE ROLE OF READING SPECIALISTS IN CURRICULUM DEVELOPMENT

Skill 29.1   **Articulate the process and benefits of participating in curriculum development, alignment, and evaluation; recognize the importance of being sensitive to school factors (e.g., class size, resources, community concerns); apply strategies for coordinating and supporting all services associated with reading programs (e.g., budgeting, needs assessment, grant writing); identify programs with federal, state, and local support that are designed to help students with reading difficulties; and analyze the use of multiple indicators to determine curriculum effectiveness**

As a specialist of any kind within a school building, it is imperative that collaboration among all staff be of top priority. It is not enough to simply service the students who are assigned through whatever means the district or building uses. Current educational trends have collaboration of the utmost priority.

In some cases reading specialists are becoming literacy coaches and then become responsible for working closely with regular educators to increase the reading skills of the students across the building. This collaborative model has the reading specialist working in the classroom beside the teacher in a team teaching model. At times, lessons may be modeled to demonstrate new or innovative ideas or different ways to structure lessons. Still other times, the two professionals would work together to provide instruction to groups of students.

This coaching model also provides out of the classroom time where professional development activities may occur. These may take the form of study groups, individual discussion sessions, or workshop offerings for different strategies. For this to be a successful implementation, it is important for all parties to realize this is a learning session for everyone and one party is not evaluating another.

Another less formal collaboration model simply involves regular meetings where children and their needs are discussed. These meetings may be formal or informal. Usually they revolve around the assessment data gathered on the students, but may not. As the data and needs of the students are reviewed, the teachers present will discuss items indicating various needs. This allows for the most appropriate professional development to occur.

As it is directly related to an immediate need for the teacher with his current students, the skills learned are more likely to be implemented. In an informal setting, anyone with knowledge can share his or her ideas, suggestions, strategies or skills. It is in this format that all parties feel less threatened and comfortable sharing.

As the reading specialist, it is vital to collaborate with other reading specialists as much as possible. Today's use of technology and the availability of email can make this a much less cumbersome task. Collaboration is a vital part of growth for all teachers and should not be seen as a negative. It should instead be viewed as a team. A team of professionals working together to ensure that all students receive the most appropriate educational experience possible.

Reading specialists have traditionally been responsible for working with students who are struggling in small groups or individually. This allows for a more focused approach to meet the needs of the students.

Promoting growth in reading is also a fundamental responsibility. The specialist of course encourages growth in the students with whom she directly works; however, she may also encourage growth in other students through other methods. They might include: a reading incentive program, a student run bookstore, small literature discussion groups, or other creative methods.

COMPETENCY 30.0 APPLY KNOWLEDGE OF LITERACY RESEARCH

Skill 30.1 **Analyze literacy research methodologies (e.g., ethnographic, descriptive, experimental); analyzing the findings of literacy research; describe methods and benefits of sharing interpretations of research findings with colleagues and the community; and identify appropriate applications of literacy research in a variety of contexts**

Over the years, theories regarding language development have been very vocal and disagreed in many levels. The major disagreement can be tracked back to the 1950's where two predominant theories emerged.

Behaviorism developed and believed that language was the direct result of the situations surrounding the child. Behaviorists believed that the environment controlled all language and solely these outside forces influenced its development.

On the other hand, nativism theorists believed that all language was similar to genetic traits. They believed that language was determined before birth and developed in a similar manner to other innate characteristics. They ruled out that any outside factors could influence the development process.

Currently, these two opposing viewpoints have been combined to form the interactionist theories. This term indicates that children's language skills are a direct result of inherent predetermined skills and the surrounding environment.

It is this combination approach that is most accepted in today's society. In relation to reading, it is important to understand the fact that reading is language based. Children who struggle in language developmental will almost certainly have difficulty obtaining a solid foundation in reading skills.

As language develops, students begin to understand how sounds blend together to form words, how words go together to form sentences, and how sentences go together to form stories. It is through these stories and sentences that meaning is conveyed from one party to another.

If a student is unable to convey that meaning or draw conclusions from the message that someone else is sending, they miss a key component of language development. With this skill missing, the natural progression that text conveys meaning is also missed. Since the ultimate goal of reading is comprehension or understanding, one can see the significant deficit these children experience.

Speech pathologists who specialize in language development can therefore be an essential component to preventing and helping children with language disorders. In this way, these trained specialists can also help in preventing and remediating language issues, which will help reading skills.

In summary, language development is crucial to the progress students will experience in reading. Language and reading go hand in hand and this fact should be remembered when bringing in professionals with expertise to help work with children who are struggling.

Various subject areas have added to philosophical debates of teaching. For example, reading teachers have long debated whether phonics or whole language was more appropriate as an instructional methodology. Language Arts teachers have debated the importance of the canon (famous works of literature); some teachers feel that the canon is irrelevant and that the only reason to teach literature is to teach thinking skills and an appreciation of good literature. Math teachers have debated the extent to which application is necessary in math instruction; some feel that it is more important to teach structure and process, while others feel it is only important to teach math skills in context.

In reading, there has been no greater debate than the approach to teaching reading. Educators speak of the great pendulum in education where strategies and methods seem to swing from side to side like a giant pendulum. In reading instruction, this great swing has swung between three major philosophies: literature-based, phonics, and whole language.

Literature-Based- In this method, teachers incorporate all reading instruction through true literature pieces. Using trade books, poetry or other forms of literature, the students are exposed and taught all of the necessary skills to be successful readers.

Phonics- Phonics instructional approach involves teaching very explicitly and sequentially the phonics skills children need to be readers. In this way, the children read controlled texts, which revolve around the current phonics skill being introduced and practiced. These controlled texts provide numerous repetitions of the skills.

Whole Language- Whole language instruction revolves around a readers' workshop approach. In this manner, the students have assigned tasks to complete that take them through reading skills. The teacher works with the children to guide them through the necessary tasks, but does not explicitly teach skills. It is though through the process of reading many different texts students will learn the necessary skills to become readers.

There is not one approach that is right or wrong. All of these methods have great value and should not be discounted. It is important to understand clearly the different philosophies involved in reading to be able to work with many different teachers. Understanding the approaches helps the reading specialist to be able to provide curricular suggestions to help students make the necessary progress.

GLOSSARY

These definitions are critical for success on all multiple choice questions on the examinations. Proper use of these terms, is crucial for success in tackling a constructed response involving balanced literacy.

ABILITY GROUPING- grouping of children with similar needs for instructional purposes. Ability groups do not remain constant throughout the year, but change as the children's needs within them change.

ALLITERATION- occurs when words begin with the same consonant sound, as in *Peter Piper picked a pair of pickled peppers.*

ALPHABETIC PRINCIPLE- the idea that written spellings represent spoken words.

ANCHOR BOOK- a balanced literacy term for a book that is purposely read repeatedly and used as part of both the reading and writing workshop.

It is a good idea to use certain books that become the children's familiar and cherished favorites for both reading and then to inspire children's writing.

ASSONANCE- Occurs when words begin with the same vowel sound.

AUTHENTIC ASSESSMENT- assessment activities which reflect the actual workplace, family community and school curriculum.

BALANCED LITERACY LESSON FORMAT- The Balanced Literacy Approach has its own specific format for the delivery of the literacy lesson, whether it is a reading or writing workshop lesson. The format begins with a 10-15 minute mini-lesson which the teacher delivers to the whole class. This mini-lesson is then followed by a thirty-minute small group (when the children break into small groups to work) lesson. It concludes with a 10-minute share during which the whole class reconvenes to share what they have done in the small groups.

One can refer to this format as the whole-small-whole group approach.

BENCHMARKS- school state, or nationally mandated statements of the expectations for student learning and achievement in various content areas.

BICS-BASIC INTERPERSONAL COMMUNICATION SKILLS (ELL term-Bilingual Education)- learning second language skills and becoming proficient in a second language through face to face interaction-translation through speaking, listening, and viewing.

BLENDING- the process of hearing separate phonemes and being able to merge them together to read the word.

BOOK FEATURES- children need to be familiar with the following book features: front and back cover, title and half- title page, dedication page, table of contents, prologue and epilogue, and foreword and after notes. For factual books, children need to be familiar with: labels, captions, glossary, index, headings and subheadings of chapters, charts and diagrams, and sidebars.

CHECKLIST- an assessment form which lists targeted learning and social behaviors as indicators of achievement, knowledge or skill. They can be professionally- or teacher-prepared.

CINQUAIN- a five line poem that can be read and then used as a model for writing. Generally line 1 of this format is a single word, line 2 has 2 words, which describe the title of line 1, line 3 is comprised of 3 words which are movement words, line 4 has 4 words which express feeling and line 5 has a single word which is a synonym for line 1's single word.

COMPREHENSION- this occurs when the reader correctly interprets the print on the page and constructs meaning from it. Comprehension depends on activating prior knowledge, cultural and social background of the reader, and the reader's ability to use comprehension monitoring strategies.

CONCEPTS ABOUT PRINT- include: how to handle a books, how to look at print, directionality, sequencing, locating skills, punctuation, and concepts of letters and words.

CONSONANT DIAGRAPHS- two consecutive consonants that represent one new speech sound. In the word "digraph" the *ph* which sounds like /f/ is a digraph.

CONTEXTS- sentences deliberately prepared by the teacher which include sufficient contextual clues for the children to decipher meaning.

CONTEXTUAL REDEFINITION- using context to determine word meaning.

COOPERATIVE READING- Children read with a partner or buddy. It can be silent or oral reading.

CRISSCROSSERS- an ELL term for second language learners who have a positive attitude toward both first language and second language learning. These second language learners, children from ELL backgrounds, are comfortable navigating back and forth between the two languages as they learn.

CUES- as they self monitor their reading comprehensions, readers have to integrate various sources of information or cues to help them construct meaning from text and graphic illustrations.

DECODING-"sounding out" a printed sequence of letters based on knowledge of letter sound correspondences.

DIPHTHONGS- two vowels in one syllable where the two sounds are heard. For instance in the word *house* both the "o" and the "u" are heard.

DIRECTIONALITY-children use their fingers to indicate left to right direction and return sweep to the next line.

DIFFERENTIATED INSTRUCTION- The need for the teacher, based on observation of individual student's work, progress, test results, fluency, and other reading/literacy behaviors, to provide modified instruction and alternative strategies or activities. These activities are specifically developed by the teacher to address the individual student's different needs.

EARLY READERS- recognize most high frequency words and many simple words. They use pictures to confirm meaning. Using meaning, syntax, and phonics, they can figure out most simple words. They use spelling patterns to figure out new words. They are gaining control of reading strategies. They use their own experiences and background knowledge to predict meanings. They occasionally use story language in their writing. This stage follows emergent reading.

EMERGENT READERS- the stage of reading in which the reader understands that print contains a consistent message. The reader can recognize some high frequency words, names, and simple words in context. Pictures can be used to predict meaning. The emergent reader begins to attend to left to right directionality and features of print and may identify some initial sounds and ending sounds in words.

ENCODE- to change a message into symbols. For example, readers encode oral language into writing.

ENGLISH as a SECOND LANGUAGE- a way of teaching English to speakers of other languages using English as the language of instruction.

EXPOSITORY TEXT-. is non-fiction that provides information and facts. This text type is what newspapers, science, mathematics and history texts use. Currently there is much focus, even in elementary schools, on teaching children how to comprehend and author expository texts. They must produce brochures, guides, recipes, and procedural accounts on most elementary grade levels. The teaching of reading of expository texts requires working with a particular vocabulary and concept structure that is very different from that of the narrative text. Therefore time must be taken to teach the reading of expository texts and contrast it with the reading of narrative texts.

FIRST LANGUAGE- an ELL term for the language any child acquires in the first few years of life. It is through this acquired language that the child acquires phonological and phonemic awareness.

FLUENT READERS- identify most words automatically. They can read chapter books with good comprehension. They consistently monitor, cross-check, and self-correct reading. They can offer their own interpretations of text based on personal experiences and prior reading experiences. Fluent readers are capable of reading a variety of genres independently. Furthermore, they can respond to texts or stories by sharing pertinent examples from their lives. They can also readily make connections to other books which they have read. Finally, they are capable of beginning to create spoken and written writings which are in the style of a particular author.

FORMAL ASSESSMENT- a test or an observation of a performance task which is done under controlled and regulated conditions.

FUNCTIONAL READING- the reading of instructions, recipes, coupons, classified ads, notices, signs, and other documents which we have to read and correctly interpret in school and in society.

GRADE EQUIVALENT/GRADE SCORE- a score transformed from a raw score on a standardized test into the equivalent score earned by an average student in the norming group.

GRAPHIC ORGANIZERS- graphic organizers express relationships among various ideas in visual form including: sequence, timelines, character traits, fact and opinion, main idea and details, differences and likenesses. Graphic organizers are particularly helpful for visual learners.

GUIDED READING- one of the key modes of instruction in the balanced literacy theory approach. During guided reading, the teacher "guides" the child through silent reading of a text by giving them prompts, target questions, and even helping the child start an answer to a specific prompt or question. At the end of each guided reading section or excerpt of the text, the child stops to talk with the teacher about the text. By definition, guided reading is an interactive discussion between the child and the teacher. This mode of reading instruction is generally used when children need extra support in constructing meaning because the text is complex or because their current independent reading capacities are still limited.

HIGH FREQUENCY- frequently used words. These words appear many more times than do other words in ordinary reading material. Examples of such words include: *as, in, of*, and *the*. These words are also sometimes called service words. These words are also part of sight vocabulary words. A classic best-known high frequency word list was generated by Dolch (l936).

INDEPENDENT READING- a set period of time within the daily literacy block when children read books with 95%-100% accuracy on their own. This reading of books by themselves which they can understand without teacher support promotes lifelong literacy and love of learning, which enhances reading mileage, builds fluency, and helps children orchestrate integrated cue strategies.

INFORMAL ASSESSMENT- observations of children made under informal conditions; these can include kid watching, checklists, and individual child/teacher conversations.

INFORMAL READING INVENTORY (IRI) - a series of reading excerpts that can be used to determine a child's reading strengths and needs in comprehension and decoding. Many published reading series have an IRI to go with their series.

JUSTIFIED PRINT- the positioning of print on the page so that each line ends either a sentence or a phrase.

KID WATCHING- term used within the balanced literacy approach for the teacher's deliberate, detailed, and recorded observations of individual student and class literacy behaviors., often done during small group work. The teacher then reconfigures lessons on experiences to meet the students' individual and group needs.

KINESTHETIC- learning is tactile; as contrasted with an activity where the learner sits still or attempts to sit still in one place. Cutting and moving syllable or word strips or using sandpaper letters are kinesthetic activities.

LANGUAGE EXPERIENCE- Children giving dictation to the teacher who writes their words on a chart or their drawings. This shows children that words can be written down.

LEARNING LOGS- daily records of what students have learned.

LISTENING POST- sets of headphones attached to a single tape player. Children can go to centers where they listen to audiotapes of books while reading the print book. These posts are in many libraries as well.

LITERATURE CIRCLES- a group discussion involving four to six children who have read the same work of literature (narrative or expository text). They talk about key parts of the work, relate it to their own experience, listen to the responses of others, and discuss how parts of the text relate to the whole.

MANIPULATION- moving around or switching sounds within a word or words within a phrase or sentence.

MEANING VOCABULARY- words whose meanings children understand and can use.

MISCUE- an oral reading error made by a child which differs from the actual printed text.
MISCUE ANALYSIS- the teacher keeps a detailed recording of the errors or inaccurate attempts of a child reader during a reading assessment. These are recorded within a running record. This helps the teacher see whether the cues-syntactic, semantic, or graphophonemic-the child is using are accurate.

MONITORING READING- various strategies that children use to monitor their readings. A sample are maintaining fluency by bringing prior knowledge to the story to make predictions, using these predictions to do further checking, searching, and self-correcting as the story progresses, and using problem-solving word study skills to make links from known words to unknown words.

MORPHEMES- the smallest units of meaning in words. There are two types of morphemes; free morphemes, which can stand alone such as *love,* and bound morphemes, which must be attached to another morpheme to carry meaning such as *ed* in *loved.*

NARRATIVE TEXT- one of the two basic text structures. The narrative text tells or communicates a story. Narrative texts are novels, short stories and plays. Some poems are narratives as well. The narrative text needs to be taught differently than the expository text because of its structure.

ONE TO ONE MATCHING- matching one spoken word with one written word.

ONSET-RIME BLENDING –ONSET-Everything before the vowel and RIME (the vowel and everything after it). For example, the word "sleep" can be broken into /sl/ and /eep/. Word families are build using rimes. The /eep/ word family would include *jeep, keep* and *weep.*

ORTHOGRAPHY- a method of representing spoken language through letters and diacritics.

PERCENTILE- if a child scores at the 56th percentile for his/grade level, his/her score is equal to or above that of 56 percent of the children taking that standardized test and below that of 46 percent of the children on whose scores the test was normed.

PERFORMANCE ASSESSMENT- having children do a task that demonstrates their knowledge, skills and competency. Having children author their own alphabet book on a particular topic would be a performance assessment for knowledge of the alphabet.

PHONEME- The speech sound units that make a difference in meaning. The word "rope" has three phonemes /r/, /o/, and /p/. Change one phoneme, say /r/ to /n/, and you have a different word *nope.*

PHONEMIC AWARENESS- the understanding that words are composed of sounds. Phonemic awareness is a specific type of phonological awareness dealing only with phonemes in a spoken word.

PHONICS- the study of relationships between phonemes (speech sounds) and graphemes (letters) that represent the phonemes. It is also decoding or the sounding out of unknown words. that are written.

PHONOLOGICAL AWARENESS- the ability to recognize the sounds of spoken language and how they can be blended together, segmented, and switched/manipulated to form new combinations and words.

PHONOLOGICAL CUES- readers use their knowledge of letter/sound and sound/letter relationships to predict and confirm reading.

PHONOLOGY- the study of speech structure in language that includes both the patterns of basic speech units (phonemes) and the tacit rules of pronunciation.

PORTFOLIOS- collections of a child's work over time. They include a cover letter, reflections from the child and teacher, and other supportive documents including standards, performance task examples, prompts and sometimes peer comments.

PRIMARY LANGUAGE- (ELL term)- the language an individual is the most fluent in and at ease with. This is usually, but not always the individual's first language.

PROMPTS- when the teacher intervenes in the child's independent reading to help the child pronounce or comprehend a specific word or prompt. On a reading record, the teacher notes the prompt. When the teacher wants to match a child with a particular book or determine the child's stage of reading/level, the teacher does not use prompts.

QUESTION GENERATING STRATEGY FOR AN EXPOSITORY TEXT- first the child previews the text by reading titles, subheads, looking at pictures or illustrations, and reading the first paragraph. Next the child asks a "think" question which he or she records. Then the child reads to find information that might answer the "think" question. The child may write down the information found or think about another question that is answered by what the child is reading. The child continues to read using this strategy.

READING FOR INFORMATION- Reading with the purpose of extracting facts and expert opinion from the text. Children should be introduced to the following information reading resources: web resources that are age and grade appropriate for children, the concept of the table of contents, chapter headings, glossaries, pictures, maps, charts, diagrams and text structures in an information text. They should be taught to use notes, graphs, organizers, and mind maps to share information extracted from a text.

RECODE- To change information from one code into another, as recoding writing into oral speech.

RECOGNITION VOCABULARY- the group of words which children are able to correctly pronounce, read orally and understand on sight.

RECORD OF READING BEHAVIOR – (running record) an objective observation during which the teacher records, using a standard set of symbols, everything the child reader says as the child reads a book selected by the teacher.
REFLECTION- to analyze, discuss, and react to one's learning on any grade or age level.

RETELLING- retelling can be written or oral. Children are expected and encouraged to tell as much of a story as they can remember. Re-telling is far more extensive than just summarizing. Children should include the beginning, middle and end plot lines and should be able to tell about the book's characters.

RUBRIC- a set of guidelines or acceptable responses for the completion of any task. Usually a rubric ranges from 0 to 4 with 4 being the most detailed response and 0 indicating a response to the task which lacked detail or was in other ways insufficient.

SCAFFOLDING- refers to the teacher support necessary for the child to accomplish a task or to achieve a goal which the child could not accomplish on his/her own. Vygotsky termed this window of opportunity the "zone of proximal development." Ultimately as the child becomes more proficient or capable, the scaffold is withdrawn. The goal of scaffolding is to help the child to perform the reading task independently and internalize the behavior. During SHARED READING, the task is scaffolded by the teacher's reading to the children aloud. As the teacher reads, the teacher scaffolds the initial decoding and helps with the meaning making/construction.

SEARCHING- children pause to search in the picture, print, or their memory for known information. This can happen as the child tackles an unknown word or after an error.

SECOND LANGUAGE-(ELL term)-A language acquired or learned simultaneously with or after a child's acquisition of a first language.

SEGMENTING- the process of hearing a spoken word and identifying its separate phonemes or syllables.

SELF-CORRECTION- children begin to correct some of their own reading errors. Generally this behavior is accompanied by the re-reading of the previous phrase or sentence.

SEMANTIC CUES- children use their prior knowledge, sense of the story, and pictures to support their predicting and confirming the meaning of the text.

SEMANTIC WEB- a visual graphic organizer that the teacher can use to introduce a reading on a specific topic. It visually represents many other words associated with a target word. The web can help activate the children's prior knowledge and extend or clarify it. It can also serve to check new learning after guided or independent reading.

SPATIAL LEARNING- Using images, color, or layout to help readers whose learning style is spatial.

STANDARD SCORE- how far a child's grade on a standardized test is from the average score (mean) on the test in terms of the standard deviation. If a child scores 70 on a standardized test and the standard deviation is 5 and the average (mean) score is 65, the child is one standard deviation above the average.

STANDARDIZED TEST- a test given under specified conditions allowing comparisons to be made. A set of norms or average scores on this test will be used for comparisons.

STOP AND THINK STRATEGY- a balanced literacy strategy for constructing meaning. As the text is being read, the child asks himself or herself, does this make sense to me? If it does not make sense to me, I should then try to re-read it or read ahead. I can also look up words that I don't know or ask for help. Generally the teacher models this strategy with the whole class as a mini lesson and then it is posted prominently in the classroom for continued reference by the children.

STRATEGIC READERS- as defined by researchers Marie Clay and Sharon Taberski, strategic readers are self improving and do the following as they read:

(A lengthy glossary explanation of this term has been provided because it can appear in a variety of multiple choice questions on the examination as well as part of a constructed response question).

- Monitor their reading to see if it makes sense semantically, syntactically, and visually.
- Look for and use semantic, syntactic, and visual clues.
- Uncover and identify new things about the text.
  Cross check and use one cueing system against another.
- Self-correct their reading when what they first read does not match the semantic, syntactic and visual clues
- Solve for and identify new words using multiple cueing systems

Beyond these behaviors, a strategic or self-improving reader uses many strategies to construct meaning. When their reading experience is going well- they know the words and understand the text or story-they are working continuously (even if they are not conscious of it) at maintaining meaning. If and when the strategic or self-improving reader runs into an unfamiliar word, then the reader has many strategies to identify that word. Becoming a successful strategic reader is a goal that can and should be shared with children as early as the middle of the first grade, although the term "self-improving reader" might be used at that point.

TEXT FEATURES- children need to be alerted to the following text features which may initially appear strange to them. The features of text include: a period which marks the end of a "telling sentence;" a question mark that is at the end of a sentence that asks a question, an exclamation mark used to express surprise or excitement at the end of a sentence, capital letters which begin a sentence and the names of persons, places, and things; bold italicized or underlined text to highlight key ideas; quotation marks which show dialogue, a hyphen used to break a long word up into its syllables, a dash used to show a break in an idea, or to indicate a parenthetical element or an omission; an ellipse, which shows an omission or break in the text; and a paragraph in nonfiction which shows a new point being made.

TRANSITIONAL READERS- recognize an increasing number of "hard" words that are content related. They can provide summaries of the stories that they read. They are more at ease with handling longer, more complex, connected text with short chapters. Transitional readers can read independent level texts with correct phrasing, expression, and fluency. When they encounter unfamiliar words, they have a variety of strategies to figure out the unfamiliar words. Their reading demonstrates that they are able to integrate meaning, syntax and phonics in a consistent manner so that they can understand the texts they are reading.

VENN DIAGRAM- a diagram consisting of two or three intersecting circles to visually represent similarities and differences for texts, characters and topics. No author study is complete without VENN DIAGRAMS comparing different author's works. This is the most commonly used graphic organizer in elementary schools today. It can be used effectively as part of an answer to a constructed response question.

VISUAL CUES- readers use their knowledge of graphemes to predict and confirm text. The graphemes may be words, syllables or letters.

WORD ANALYSIS- the analysis of words employing letters, phonic structures, contextual clues, or dictionary skills.

WORD IDENTIFICATION- how the reader determines the pronunciation, and the meaning of an unknown word.

WORD RECOGNITION- The process of determining the pronunciation and some degree of the meaning of an unknown word.

WORD WORK- the term that the balanced literacy approach uses for the study of vocabulary.

BIBLIOGRAPHY OF PRINT RESOURCES

PROFESSIONAL BOOKS:

Adams, M. (1990). *Beginning to read: Thinking and Learning about Print.* Cambridge, MA: MIT Press.

Anders, P., & Bos, C. (l986). Semantic Feature Analysis: An Interactive Strategy for Vocabulary Development and Reading Comprehension, *Journal of Reading,* 29, 610-616.

Blevins, W. (l997). *Phonemic Awareness Activities for Early Reading Success.* New York: Scholastic.

Boyd-Bastone, P. (2004). Focused Anecdotal Record Assessment (ARA): A Tool for Standards Based Authentic Assessment. *Reading Teacher, 58* (3), pp. 230-239.

Calkins, Lucy McCormick. (2001). *The Art of Teaching Reading.* New York: Longman.
    This is the woman who beautifully explains the reading workshop and its relationship to the writing workshop as she shares wonderful snapshots of mini lessons, conferring, conferencing, independent reading, guided reading, book talks, prompts, coaching, and classroom library use. Exceedingly readable and direct.

Campbell, Robin. (2004). *Reading and Writing for Real Purposes.* Portsmouth, NH: Heinemann.
    This work focuses on how children who deftly absorb and interconnect symbols and sounds of their universes can be supported in K-1 classes to extend this ability into phonics learning. Campbell demonstrates how immersion in a highly literate classroom filled with print and language stimuli allows kids to build accurate letter-sound relationships. The book provides a framework for teaching phonics using proven field-tested Campbell strategies.

    Among these strategies are: early mark making, read-alouds, playing with language in rhyme and song, writing and reading in a variety of genres, exploring environmental and classroom print, and using students' own names. Samples of student work are included.

Chancey, C. (l994). Language development, metalinguistic awareness, and emergent literacy skills of 3 year old children in relation to social class. *Applied Psycholinguistics*, 15, 371-394.

Clay, Marie M. (1993). *An Observation Survey of Early Literacy Achievement.* Portsmouth, NH: Heinemann.

Clay, Marie M. (l993). *Reading Recovery: A Guidebook for Teachers in Training.* Portsmouth, NH: Heinemann.

Cooper, J. David. (2004). *Literacy-Helping Children Construct Meaning.* Boston, MA: Houghton Mifflin. (5th Edition).
 This book explains with numerous charts, tables, templates, and excerpts form actual texts, what the balanced literacy approach to the teaching of reading and writing is. It offers the new teacher: exact schedules, strategies, guidelines, assessment tools, bibliographies, research, and even scripts for conferring with children.

 Cooper is a clear and crisp writer who does not overwhelm the reader, but rather engages the reader. Even veteran teachers would return again and again to this text for support and refreshing insights.

Cox, Carole. (2005). *Teaching Language Arts.* Boston, MA: Pearson.
 A compendium of state of the art lesson plans, web resources, online case studies, teaching ideas and extensive templates. All of these materials are aligned to the balanced literacy reading and writing workshop model.

 The book also includes teaching ideas for the ELL reader, children with learning disabilities, and speakers of non- standard dialects. The book also features snapshots of second language learners as well as bi-literacy web resources.

Cullinan, Bernice E. (l998). *Three Voices-An Invitation to Poetry Across the Curriculum.* New York: Stenhouse. K-6 and beyond.
 Two classroom educators and a noted researcher in children's literature demonstrate how poetry can be used in the classroom to teach various aspects of reading and to nurture lifelong literacy. Thirty-three grade and age appropriate strategies are included which have been field tested in classrooms across the country.

Ezell, H. K., & Justice, L. M. (2000). Increasing the Print Focus of Adult -Child Shared Book Reading through Observational Learning. *American journal of Speech Pathology*, 9, 36-37.

Flesch, Rudolf. (l985). *Why Johnny Can't Read* New York: Harper and Row.

Fountas, Irene C., & Gay Su Pinnell. (2001). *Guiding Readers and Writers 3-6.* Portsmouth, NH: Heinemann.
 This work includes 1000 leveled books with guidelines for using them as part of a reading and writing workshop. The book explains how to use various genres in the classroom and how to use visual graphic organizers for the teaching of reading and writing.

Fountas, Irene. C., & Gay Su Pinnell. (1999). *Matching Books to Readers Using Leveled Books in Guided Reading K-3.* Portsmouth, NH: Heinemann.
This major contribution to the field has a list of 7, 500 grade and age appropriate books. In addition the authors include word counts to be used for keeping running records, text characteristics, guidelines for leveling of additional books and suggestions for developing classroom library collections.

Other works by these researchers also published by Heinemann include:

Voices on Word matters: Learning about Phonics and Spelling in the Literacy Classroom (1999) and *Word Matters-Teaching Phonics and Spelling in the Reading/Writing Classroom* (1998).

Fry, Edward Bernard, Kress, Jacqueline, Fountakidis, Dona Lee. (2000). *The Reading Teacher's Book of Lists.* San Francisco, CA: Wiley Press.
This book is an invaluable one for the working classroom educator. It includes ready to use lists that cover a multiplicity of teacher needs. Among them are: spelling demons, readability graphs, phonics, useful words, reading math, vowel lists, anagrams, portmanteaus (do you know what they are and how well they can work in word study?), web sites, classic children's literature, etc. Even a veteran teacher educator will find useful and new resources. Also wonderful for developing independent word study investigations and literature explorations.

Ganske, Kathy. (2000). *Word Journeys-Assessment-Guided Phonics, Spelling, and Vocabulary Instruction.* New York, NY: Guilford Press.
This book offers a practical approach for assessing children's spelling. The author has created a DSA (Development Spelling Analysis) tool which teachers can use to evaluate individual children's spelling progress and to differentiate instruction. The book includes snapshots of children at different levels of spelling development.

Hall, Susan. (1994). *Using Picture Books to Teach Literary Devices.* Westport, CT: Oryx Press.

How to Help Every Child Become a Reader. Just Publishing. K-6 and beyond.
This accessible text draws on materials developed by the US Department of Education to share research, resources, referrals and suggestions for supporting all children to become lifelong and engaged readers. It offers specific suggestions and resources for assisting struggling readers including those with special needs and those from ELL backgrounds.

Labov, L. (2003). When Ordinary Children Fail to Read. *Reading Research Quarterly,* 38, 128-31.

Macmillan, B. M. (2002). Rhyme and Reading. A Critical Review of the Research Methodology. *Journal of Research in Reading,* 25(1), 4-42.

Makor, Barbara. *Primary Phonics Readers.*
Short storybooks that K-2 can own and read independently.
> They feature phonetically controlled texts, sounds and spellings that are grade and age appropriate and high interest child-centered themes. As children progress through the series of twenty titles, they review and enhance their mastery of phonetic elements, sight words, and sequences at a more rapid pace. This material is compatible with the majority of phonics programs.

Munro, J. (1998). Phonological and Phonemic Awareness: Their Impact on Learning to Read Prose and Spell. *Australian Journal of Learning Disabilities*, 3, 2, 15-21.
> Paperback Nursery Rhyme Sampler-Whispering Coyote Press-Essential for a Prek-1 classroom and useful even in grades 1 and 2; these classic nursery rhymes promote phonemic and phonological awareness and children's ownership of their reading through song and movement.

Routman, Regie. (2000). *Conversations: Strategies for Teaching, Learning, and Evaluating.* Portsmouth, NH: Heinemann.

Routman, Regie. (1994). *Invitations: Changing as Teachers and Learners K-12.* Portsmouth, NH. Heinemann.
Routman, Regie. (1996). *Literacy at the Crossroads: Crucial Talk About Reading, Writing, and Other Teaching Dilemmas.* Portsmouth, NH: Heinemann.

Routman, Regie. (2002). *Reading Essentials.* Portsmouth, NH: Heinemann.

Statman, Ann. *Handprints-Leveled Storybooks for Early Readers Educators Publishing Service*-Grades K-2.
> These fifty titles which come with five teacher's guides were leveled using the Fountas and Pinnell Guided Reading Leveling System. The stories reflect real world situations and people young readers know. They include: sentence structure, pictures and cues that focus strategic reading. Print size, sentence positioning, and word spacing is appropriate for the level of the particular storybook. The titles build a strong sight vocabulary through the use of high frequency words. Language used within the series progresses from natural to formal book language.

Schumm, Heanne Shay. *The Reading Tutor's Handbook.* Free Spirit. K-6 and beyond.
> This guide offers step by step instructions, templates and handouts for providing children with differentiated reading support. It is not only helpful for teachers, but also can be shared with paraprofessionals, teachers, interns, and parents as a support framework for the classroom reading program.

Taberski, Sharon. (2000). *On Solid Ground: Creating a Literacy Environment in Your K-3 Classroom.* Portsmouth, NH: Heinemann.

Terban, Marvin. *Time to Rhyme-A Rhyming Dictionary*. Boyd Mills Press. Grades 1-3.

> This book is easily enough formatted so that it can be used to introduce children in the early elementary grades to the use of a rhyming dictionary as a reference tool. Its simple word groupings encourage writing which can also reinforce and reciprocally enhance reading skills through the reading and writing workshop.

Vail, Patricia. *Reading Comprehension-Students Needs and Teacher's Tools*. Educators Publishers Service K-6 and beyond.

> This is a compendium of explanations of specific instructional practices, terms, student projects, learning games and resources which are critical for successfully teaching reading.

ALPHABET BOOKS

A major genre of fiction and non-fiction for the teacher of reading is the alphabet book. These books' appeal, concepts, and efficiency as models for reading and writing merit them a special section in this bibliography. Even those whose text is simple enough for Prek-2, can serve as anchor books and models for writing workshop in grades 3-6.

Aigner-Clark, Julie. (2002). *Baby Einstein- The ABCs of Art*. Illustrations by Nadeen Zaidi. New York: Hyperion Books.

Beaton, Clare. *Zoe and Her Zebra*. Barefoot Books. Prek-1.

> This board book features a character young children can identify with named Zoe. Her adventures are told in a simple, repetitive text with a soft literally "touchy" felt art.

Bunting, Eve. *Girls A to Z*. Boyd Mills Press. PreK-1.

> This book uses the alphabetic format to promote the opportunity for girls to select various professions and careers ranging from astronaut to zookeeper. Bunting's text is breezy and rhymes.

Cheney, Lynne. (2002). *America- A Patriotic Primer*. New York: Simon and Schuster Books. Illustrated by Robin Priess Glasser.

Cheney, Lynne. *A Is For Abigail: An Almanac of Amazing American Women*. New York: Simon and Schuster Books. Ages 4-8.

Glaser, Milton. (2003). *The Alphazeds*. Miramax. Ages 4-8.

Grimes, Nikki. *C is for City*. Illustrated by: Pat Cummings. Boyd Mill Press. K-3. This alphabet rhyme book doubles as a guide to city activities. With its built in invitations to readers to search for alphabetical items, it is perfect for use as an informal assessment tool or an interactive/paired reading anchor text.

Inkpen, Mick. (2000). *Kipper's A to Z*. San Diego: Harcourt. Ages 3-7.

Isadora, Rachel. (1999). *ABC Pops! (Picture Books)*. Disney Press. Ages 4-8.

Johnson, Stephen. (1995). *Alphabet City*. Penguin Books. All ages.

Kelley, Marty. *Summer Stinks*. Zino Press. Prek-1. This work describes the summer season in terms of things which "stink" about it, including ants, bugs, and sweat. Fun to read and add to as the alphabet letters are learned and vocabulary is built up.

Martin, Mary Jane. *From Anne to Zach*. Boyd Mills Press. In this captivating book which can serve as a touchstone text for model collaborative authoring, children learn the letters of the alphabet through other children's names.

Melmed, Laura Krauss and Frane Lesser. (2003) *Capital! Washington DC from A to Z*. New York: Harper Collins.

Musgrove, Margaret. (1976). Illustrated by Leo and Diane Dillon. *Ashanti to Zulu. African Traditions*. New York: Dial Books for Young Readers. This is a Caldecott-winning book which uses the alphabetic format for a richly detailed and researched study of 26 African Peoples. It includes a map and pronunciation guide and illustrations that were researched in the Schomberg Center and the American Museum of Natural History. Even the frame design for each illustration reflects the African Kano knot which signifies endless searching.

Paratore, Colleen. *26 Big Things Hands Do*. Minneapolis, MN: Free Spirit. What is delightful about this alphabet book is that it presents the alphabet letters as positive actions children can perform with their own small hands to help others. These actions include: applauding, giving gifts, planting, and volunteering. Of course, alphabet study can continue with adding other "helping actions" to the word wall or substituting them in the text.

Pelham, David, (1991). *A is for Animals*. New York: Simon and Schuster

Seeley, Lorna. *The Book of Shadow Boxes*. Peachtree.
Within the shadow of each letter's shadow box lies a hidden treasure for the young reader to find. The book is intricately and exquisitely designed and conceptualized by Ms. Seeley. Its visual fascination extends well beyond the elementary grades as it of course fosters not only the alphabetic principle, but also reading comprehension and literacy response.

Sneed, Brad. (2002). *Picture a Letter*. New York: Penguin Books.

Seuss. *ABC*. Random House. Ages 2-up.

Thornhill, Jim. *The Wildlife ABC and 123: A Nature Alphabet and Counting Book*. Maple Tree Press. K-1 with additional nature notes on the species for the teacher/parent.
In addition to fostering the alphabetic principle, the book nicely mixes geographic, multicultural, and scientific knowledge into a beautifully designed text. It uses children's fascination with nature to foster reading and math literacy.

Zschock, Martha and Heather. (2002). *Journey Around New York from A to Z*. *Beverly*. Mass: Commonwealth Editions

Zschock, Martha. (2001). *Journey Around Boston from A to Z*. Beverly Mass: Commonwealth Editions.

TRADE BOOKS

These books foster particular aspects of reading skills, fluencies and competencies.

Blackstone, Stella. *Where's the Cat?* Barefoot Books. Prek-k.
This book which focuses its primary school readers on searching for a lost cat provides excellent use of repetitive language and encourages interactive reading.

Campbell, Bebe Moore. (2003). Sometimes *My Mommy Gets Angry. New York, New York: G. P. Putnam's Sons.*
This is a moving story about a young girl whose mother suffers from mental illness. It is told in a way that is easy to read, along with beautiful illustrations. The main character is Annie. Sometimes her mother is very happy and other times very angry and sad. Annie has learned what to do when her mom is having a bad episode. She has books to read, a special stuffed animal and some secret snacks. Annie also has a strong support system in place with friends, neighbors, her teacher and grandmother.

This book is a good introduction to the issue of mental illness. It is especially important in that students see how this young girl is able to cope with this difficult part of her life. "Sometimes by mommy has a dark cloud inside of her. I can't stop the rain from falling, but I can find sunshine in my mind."

Teachers can introduce students to this issue with this poignant book. Students can brainstorm different scenarios and discuss how they can be resolved. They can discuss who their support network includes and what it takes for a person to be strong enough to weather such a storm.

The book is a much needed resource for children in times where Annie's situation is far more common than is generally known. Annie's capacity to make effective, affirming social decisions makes the work an inspirational touchstone for other peers who need to confront their parents' emotional crises. Children might be inspired to author poetry or create deliberately fictionalized narrative accounts about how they have confronted various crises.

In offering an upper elementary grade and age appropriate narrative of a peer dealing with an emotionally ill parent, this book provides readers confronting similar family and caregiver issues with an opening for discussion and for hopeful outreach. Just reading this account may well be the first step necessary to assist a youngster in acknowledging a "hidden problem" and getting crucial adult assistance in dealing with the crisis.

Garza, Carmen Lomas. (1990). *Family Pictures Cuadros de familia*. Children's Book Press.

This book tells the story of the author's childhood growing up in a Hispanic community in Texas. The book is written in both Spanish and English, accompanied by the author's most incredible paintings. The paintings are unique, somewhat folksy, colorful, and totally entrancing. They bring you into Carmen's world. Once inside it, you don't want to leave.

There is so much to explore in this book; it works well with the study of "myself and family", community, communities around the world, Mexico, family traditions and customs. It emphasizes social and emotional learning and how a young girl can find her way in the world. The traditions followed by her community and family were not necessarily accepted or understood by white America. Yet these values gave her the strength to be her own person and to rely on both her relationships and rich inner life to express herself.

There are so many activities that this book inspires. Children can study the origins of the piñata, and make one. They can make a cookbook of recipes from Mexico or from their own homes. Children can also be encouraged to design their own book of family pictures. They can emphasize special occasions that they celebrate or focus on family traditions which reflect their cultural backgrounds. The richness and lushness of the paintings invites the readers to construct meaning and to create their own narratives, procedural accounts, poetry, and dialogues inspired by one or more of the paintings.

Picture walk through the illustrations. Given the Spanish/English text, this strategy can be an engaging spatial entry point for descriptive and narrative spoken and written presentations. The lushly detailed illustrations of family rites and celebrations can be springboards for children's literary and artistic renditions of equivalent family pictures and events which are prompted by Carmen's selections.

Use of dual language text for the book validates children's and family member's responses in languages other than English. Obviously, this book and its format are inspirational for ELL/Bilingual learners and for special needs learners who can be captivated by the paintings.

The power of this book lies in its accessing and modeling the magic of family rites and rituals for a broad spectrum of linguistics, intrapersonal, spatial, and kinesthetic learners from monolingual, bilingual and special needs backgrounds. Common to all of its audience members are the social and emotionally celebratory components of Family Pictures.

Glaser, Shirley, & Glaser, Milton. (2003). *The Alphazeds Words*. Hyperion Books. This book is incredible in so many ways! It is an alphabet book that can be read by or to little ones and not so little ones. It starts with an empty room. One by one, each letter of the alphabet enters the room, each with its own distinct look, fantastic illustrations and typography by the designer Milton Glaser. Each of these letters also has its own distinct personality. A is angry, B is bashful, J is jealous, and so on. The room gets quite crowded. How do all of these different personalities manage to get along and coexist? Not too well apparently, as there is shouting, pushing, hitting and kicking. In the midst of all the chaos, the light in the room goes out and there is silence.

"When the light came back on, something
extraordinary had happened. Four letters
had gotten together to comfort one another.
Together they had managed to create something
larger and more important than themselves.
They had made the first word."

This is a great lesson on how each of us can be an individual, yet when we work together, something wonderful can happen. This book illustrates an incredible lesson in social and emotional maturity, and helps the child realize that it isn't just about "me."

There are many different activities that a teacher can use with this book. The children can work in groups to make their own alphabet book of emotions. They can then present the book as a group, discussing the roles each of them played, and how they each used their unique talents to make the book.

Older children grades 3 and up, can research and present as a group some important discoveries that were made more special because they involved people working together. They can also work on a project about cooperative learning, perhaps surveying class and schoolmates on how they feel they learn the best.

Hest, Amy. (1985). *The Purple Coat.* New York: Macmillan Publishing Co.
In the autumn of every year, Gabrielle travels with her mother to New York City to visit her Grandpa who owns a tailor shop. Once there, he always makes her a new coat, but this year Gabrielle decides the usual navy blue coat won't do. The Purple Coat follows Gabrielle in her attempt to establish her own identity.

Lionni, Leo. (1980). *Inch by Inch.* Astor-Honor Publishing Co. Inc.
In *Inch by Inch*, an inchworm (which is a caterpillar, or larval stage, of the fall cankerworm, which becomes a moth) keeps itself from being eaten by various birds by proving its worth as a measuring device.

Lupton, Hugh. *The Story Tree- Tales to Read Aloud.* Barefoot Books. K-3
These seven multicultural stories are accessible enough to children to encourage their eventually taking over the read aloud sharing on their own. This book is also a good one for family literacy sessions and for parent volunteers to read aloud in the classroom.

Martin Jr., Bill, & John Archambault. (1966). *Knots on a Counting Rope.* New York, New York: Henry Holt and Company.
This beautifully illustrated book reaches out in so many different directions, and we can all learn so much from it. Knots on a Counting Rope is the story of a Native-American boy who is blind and is learning from his grandfather how to survive in this world. Boy-Strength-of-Blue-Horses insists on hearing the story of his birth over and over again.

Every time his grandfather retells the story of the boy's birth, he adds a knot to his counting rope. Each time he hears the story, Boy- Strength-of-Blue-Horses gains more confidence in himself. The story emphasizes the Native-American tradition of storytelling, and there are numerous art, math and social studies lessons that offshoot from this book.

Of course, the telling and retelling of the story celebrate the young blind hero's strengths and weaknesses and ability to set goals with optimism. Stories of one's birth related by others are powerful demonstrations of social skills of the highest order.

This book also deals extensively with social and emotional learning. Children learn that those with disabilities need to be treated with sensitivity while learning to find their place in the world. One way in which children's social and emotional learning is strengthened is by understanding themselves and those around them. In order to facilitate this, each child will interview at least one family member about when he/she was born. The accounts collected with appropriate photos or memorabilia can then be shared in class and perhaps even authored into a *Knots on a Counting Rope* style book format.

Children can also retell the story of the boy using the counting system of cultures other than Native American. This literary response will incorporate cultural study, respect and empathy into ongoing reading and writing workshop efforts.

McCully, Emily Arnold. (1992). *Mirette on the High Wire*. G.P. Putnam's & Sons. Mirette helps her mother run a boardinghouse for acrobats, jugglers, actors and mimes. Her life changes when she discovers a boarder crossing the courtyard on air. She begs him to teach her how he does it. He refuses to teach her, but she begins practicing on her own. As she improves, he begins to help her. In the end she helps him overcome his fear of the high wire.

Rabe, Bernice. (1981). *The Balancing Girl*. E.P. Dutton. Margaret, a girl in a wheel chair is excellent at balancing all kinds of objects. Margaret shows her friend Tommy how good she is at balancing at the school carnival.

Ringgold, Faith. (1991). *Tar Beach*. New York, New York: Crown Publishers. This book is one of my favorites, and it is moving in its words, art, and the beautiful story it tells. This is an effective book to use for younger grades to connect with myself, my family and my community. It can also be used in connection with a mapmaking unit. The children can be encouraged to make a map of their neighborhood from an aerial view.

A starting point for a discussion would be why the author portrayed New York from such a vantage point. In this beautiful book, the narrator, Cassie Louise Lightfoot, lets her dreams and ambitions take her to places in New York City that she ordinarily would not be able to be part of because of her circumstances. As a result of her self-motivation and self-awareness, Cassie is able to go as far as her dreams will let her. In this book Cassie also shows strengths in the areas of emotional sensitivity, as well as inter and intra-personal relationships.

Children can author their own Tar Beach equivalent night fantasies and then share them with one another through an exhibit or big books. Although Cassie's family is obviously poor since they have to picnic on their roof, Cassie's dreamlike lushly illustrated flight over Harlem validates the beauty of their family life and of the city landscape which is accessible to all. This is an invaluable lesson in the importance of the wealth inherent in the appreciation of family connections and the beauty of nature and public architectural designs! A song of family and of the city!

Schories, Pat. *Breakfast for Jack/Jack and the Missing Piece*. Front Street.
These wordless stories help pre-literate children, ELL learners new to this country and special needs children explore the basic elements of story-character, setting and plot. The lack of words allows the children to "construct their own meaning," and create their own different stories which "fit" the illustrations.

Steinberg, Laya. *Thesaurus Rex*. Barefoot Books.
This book introduces a dinosaur with an interest in words whose story is told through a wonderful rhyming text which can be used for fostering phonemic awareness and for choral readings.

Uhlberg, Myron. *The Printer*. Peachtree.
This story celebrates the conventions of print in that the boy narrator's father is a deaf man who speaks with his hands and as a job chooses to turn lead type letters into words and sentences. An excellent book to support family literacy and an appreciation for the conventions of print.

Van Allsburg, Chris. (1988). *Two Bad Ants*. Houghton Mifflin Co.
In *Two Baxd Ants*, news comes to the ant world of a great discovery in a far away place. A delicious crystal has been found. A group of ants set out to bring back this crystal to their queen. Two ants are overwhelmed by the treasure and stay behind in this dangerous alien world. It is a tale of choices, consequences and the discovery of life's real treasures.

Walter, Mildred Pitts. (2004). Illustrated by Larry Johnson. *Alec's primer*. Lebanon, NH: University Press of New England.

> This is the true account of a Virginian slave who was taught to read by his owner's daughter. He later fought in the Civil War on the Union side and became a landowner himself in Vermont. The beautifully written narrative is complemented by the vibrant paintings of Larry Johnson which include authentic period details.

Webliography

Reading Online
http://www.readingonline.org
This online web resource which is sponsored by the International Reading Association is full of specific reading teaching ideas, lessons and new research. It includes summaries of conference presentations and even tips on how to use technology to teach reading.

Balanced Literacy
http://www.thekcrew.net/balancedliteracy.html
Established in 1996, this site is organized according to the components of the balanced literacy approach. It also has an excellent listing of professional books that can assist with various aspects of teaching reading.

Carol Hurst
http://www.carolhurst.com/index.html
This is a terrific resource for exploring the children's literature works which are at the crux of author and genre study. It can be used for material to supplement period studies and discussions of authors' lives. Older children will be able to explore it on their own.

Read, Write, Think
http://www.readwritethink.org/lessons/
This resource maintained by the NCTE, National Council of Teachers of English, has a growing database of age and grade specific literacy lesson plans. It also includes all the graphic organizers cited in this book and many more, ready to download.

Inspiration Software
http://www.inspiration.com
http://www.inspiration.com/freetrial/index.cfm
This is the home site for the Inspiration and Kidspiration mind mapping software. These online templates and capacities assist the reading teacher with customizing the various graphic organizers discussed throughout the book, and with gaining the ability to design customized graphic organizers for a particular theme, study or student group. A free trial version of this resource which is child friendly can be downloaded.

Visual Thesaurus
http://www.visualthesaurus.com/online/
This is really both an online dictionary and a thesaurus.

Resources for Read Aloud, Shared Reading, and Independent Reading available on the Internet include the following:

http:// www.mightybook.com/library_4to6.htm.
This is a library of books read aloud by the computer. Children can listen to these books or practice reading with a buddy as the computer broadcasts the text. Of course, this type of read aloud would only be used IN ADDITION to the vibrant read-aloud of the teacher.

http://www.enchantedlearning.com/Rhymes.html
These are online nursery rhymes ready for reading to the children and posting throughout for room or for literacy center display.

SEDL-RCI Framework of Reading
http://www.sedl.org/reading/framework/assessment.html
This is an excellent resource for readings in the theories and methods of foundations. There are topic aligned links to specific theorists which can be included at the close of your lesson planning and may be reviewed before certification tests.

TOOLS TO HELP YOU TEACH THE FOUNDATIONS OF READING AND SUCCEEDING IN CONSTRUCTED RESPONSE CERTIFICATION EXAMINATIONS

Appendix 1- The Record of Reading Behavior- A close up look at a key assessment tool.

Often in the constructed response question on a foundations of education certification test or on a general elementary certification test; the educator is asked to analyze a record of reading behavior or to construct an appropriate one from data given in an anecdote. Furthermore with the current climate of accountability, it is a good idea for new teachers and for career changers to examine closely the basic elements of recording reading behavior.

While there are various acceptable formats for emergent literacy assessment used throughout the country, the one selected for use here is based on the work of Marie Clay and Kenneth Goodman. These two are key researchers in the close observation and documentations of children's early reading miscues (reading mistakes).

It is important to emphasize that the teacher should not just "take the Record of Reading Behavior " and begin filling it out as the child reads from a random book prior to beginning of the observation. There are specific steps for taking the record and analyzing its results.

1. Select a text
If you want to see if the child is reading on instructional level, choose a book that the child has already read. If the purpose of the test is to see whether the child is ready to advance to the next level, choose a book from that level which the child has not yet seen.

2. Introduce the text
If the book is one that has been read, you do not need to introduce the text, other than by saying the title. But if the book is new to the child, you should briefly share the title and tell the child a bit about the plot and style of the book.

3. Take the record
Generally with emergent readers' grades 1-2, there are only 100-150 words in a passage used to take a record. Make certain that the child is seated beside you, so that you can see the text as the child reads it.

If desired, you may want to photocopy the text in advance for yourself, so you can make direct notations on your text while the child reads from the book. After you introduce the text make certain that the child has the chance to read the text independently. Be certain that you do not "teach" or help the child with the text, other than to supply an unknown word that the child requests you supply. The purpose of the record is to see what the child does on his or her own.

As the child reads the text, you must be certain to record the reading behaviors the child exhibits using the following notations.

In taking the record, keep in mind the following: Allow enough time for the child to work independently on a problem before telling or supplying the word. If you wait too long, you could run the risk of having the child lose the meaning and his/her interest in the story as he or she tries to identify the unknown word.

It is recommended that when a child is way off track, you tell him or her to "Try that again" (TTA). If a whole phrase is troubling, put it into square brackets and score it as only one error.

The notation for filling out the Record of Reading behavior involves noting the child's response on the top with the actual text below it.

Comprehension Check

This can and should be done by inviting the child to retell the story. This retelling can then be used to ask further questions about characters, plot, setting and purpose which allow you to observe and to record the child's level of comprehension.

Calculating the Reading Level and the Self-correction Rate

Calculating the reading level lets you know if the book is at the level on which the child can read it independently or comfortably with guidance or if the book is at a level where reading it frustrates the child.

Generally, an accuracy score of 95-100% suggests that the child can read the text and other books or texts on the same level.

An accuracy score of 90-94% indicates that the text and texts likely will present challenges to the child, but with guidance from you, a tutor or parent, the child will be able to master these texts and enjoy them. This is instructional level.

However, an accuracy score of less than 89% tells you that the material you have selected for the child is too hard for the child to control alone. Such material needs to be shared with the child in a shared reading situation or read to the child.

KEEPING SCORE ON THE RECORD

Insertions, omissions, substitutions, and teacher told responses, all count as errors. Repetitions are not scored as errors. Corrected responses are scored as self corrections.

No penalty is given for a child's attempts at self correction that results in a finally incorrect response but the attempts should be noted. Multiple unsuccessful attempts at a word score as one error only.

The lowest score for any page is zero.
If a child omits a line or lines, each word omitted is counted as an error. If the child omits a page, deduct the number of words omitted from the total number of words which you have used for the record.

Calculating the Reading Level

Note the number of errors made on each line on the Record of Reading Behavior in the column marked E (for Error).

Total the number of errors in the text and divide this number into the number of words that the child has read. This will give you the error rate.

If a child read a passage of 100 words and made 10 errors, the error rate would be 1 in 10. Convert this to an accuracy percentage, or 90%.

Calculating the Self Correction Rate

Total all the self-corrections.
Next, add the number of errors to the number of self-corrections and divide by the number of self-corrections.

A self correction rate of 1 in 3 to 1 in 5 is considered good. This rate indicates that the child is able to help himself or herself as problems are encountered in reading.

Analyzing the record

This record should assist the educator in developing a detailed date specific picture of the child's progress in reading behavior. It should be used to help the educator individualize instruction for the specific child.

As the errors are reviewed, consider whether the child made the error because of semantics (cues from meaning), syntactic (language structure), or visual information difficulties.

As self-corrections are analyzed, consider what led the child to make that self-correction. Check out and consider what cues the child does use effectively and which the child does not use well.

Consider the ways in which the child tackles a word which is unknown. Characterize that behavior and consider how the teacher can assist the child with this issue.

If a child can retell at least three quarters of a story, this is considered adequate for retelling.

Analysis of reading behavior records can and should support the educator in designing appropriate mini lessons and strategies to help the child with his or her recorded errors and miscues.

Sample Test

1) **The major difference between phonemic and phonological awareness is:**

A) One deals with a series of discrete sounds and the other with sound-spelling relationships.

B) One is involved with teaching and learning alliteration and rhymes.

C) Phonemic awareness is a specific type of phonological awareness that deals with separate phonemes within a given word.

D) Phonological awareness is associated with printed words.

2) **The theorist in early reading (emergent reading) who has identified five tasks for phonemic awareness is:**

A) John Munro

B) Brian Cambourne

C) Marilyn Jager Adams

D) Lucy Calkins

3) **An oddity task is one in which children:**

A) Identify the odd number in a mathematical series and talk about how they did it.

B) Perform a creative exercise designed for differentiated learning styles.

C) Recognize which sound is odd in a series of like sounds.

D) Design a different activity for themselves.

4) **All of the following are true about phonological awareness EXCEPT:**

A) It may involve print.

B) It is a prerequisite for spelling and phonics.

C) Activities can be done by the children with their eyes closed.

D) It starts before letter recognition is taught.

5) **Ms. James is seated with a child by her side. The child is reading aloud from an open book. Ms. James is teaching in a school that has embraced the Balanced Literacy Approach. Therefore it is most likely that Ms. James is writing and recording:**

A) The child's use of expression in reading aloud.

B) The child's errors and miscues.

C) Her observations of the child's attitude toward reading.

D) The child's feelings about the particular passage being read.

6) **Most of the children in first-year teacher Ms. James's class are really doing well in their phonemic awareness assessments. However, Ms. James is very concerned about three children who do not seem to be able to distinguish between spoken words that "sound alike," but are different. Since she is a first year teacher, she feels her inexperience may be to blame. In truth, the reason these three children have not yet demonstrated phonemic awareness is most likely that:**

A) They are not capable of becoming good readers.

B) They are bored in class.

C) They may be from an ELL background.

D) Ms. James does not pronounce the different phonemes clearly enough.

7) Ms. Ramsey has forgotten her credit cards and has limited cash in her wallet. She is buying supplies for her reading classroom that she wants to have annotated with the children's names by the first day of school. She should buy all of the following with her cash except:

A) Folders.

B) Markers.

C) Rulers.

D) Index cards.

8) Ms. Rivers is preparing for a parent teacher conference. She does all of the following EXCEPT:

A) Collects individual child running records.

B) Puts away all the book bags and leveled pots so the classroom will be more spacious.

C) Puts out by each child's seat the child's weekly log and spelling folder.

D) Sets up work samples by each child's place.

9) In terms of a balanced literacy classroom, a "leveled bin" indicates:

A) A plant set at child's eye level for descriptive writing purposes.

B) A bin with books the child has selected.

C) A bin with books leveled by the teacher.

D) A bin with all kinds of reading materials including magazines and packaging on a child's level.

10) Mark Garner has been told that he will have to support some special needs readers in his classroom in addition to the rest of the students. He can expect to have:

A) Gifted children who are accelerated in reading skills for their grade and age.

B) Children who have disabilities and will need special support in accessing the content and methods he uses with the rest of the class.

C) Children who come from native language backgrounds other than English.

D) Children who display the capacities and needs detailed in a and b.

11) Julia has been hired to work in a school that serves a local public housing project. She is working with kindergarten children and has been asked to focus on shared reading. She selects:

A) Chapter books.

B) Riddle books.

C) Alphabet books.

D) Wordless picture books.

12) It is 4 PM, yet Francine is still in her classroom. The seats in her classroom are filled with adults of various ages who are holding books. They are seated two by two with both holding copies of the same book. Francine probably is:

A) Explaining to parents how she will teach a particular story.

B) Demonstrating shared reading with a buddy for volunteer parents.

C) Hosting a parents organization meeting for her grade level.

D) Distributing old books from the class library to parents.

13) The work of Chard and Osborn (l999) in establishing guidelines for children with reading disabilities has shown that it is essential for them to:

A) Read wordless picture books.

B) Learn at least 10 sight words.

C) Work intensely on the alphabetic principle.

D) Focus on using syntactic clues.

14) A key theorist whose work has helped teacher's document children's oral reading progress throughout the school year is:

A) Jerome Bruner.

B) Daniel J. Chard.

C) J. David Cooper.

D) Marie Clay.

15) The first grade class is on a neighborhood walk. As the children approach the neighborhood Kentucky Fried Chicken chain, Danny reads from the store window "Kentucky Fried Chicken Hot and Crunchy." Danny has never read or been taught to read this before. The most likely explanation for Danny's being able to read this is that he is:

A) An advanced reader who is self improving.

B) His parents have taught him to read the signs and materials at the Kentucky Fried Chicken store.

C) He is in the logographic phrase of phonics learning.

D) This was just a lucky guess on his part.

16) An observer enters Julia's first grade classroom. Children are working with oaktag strips and placing the word letters on these strips on a sentence strip holder. Then they seem to be involved in some kind of counting. The observer is confused. This activity is taking place during the reading block. Julia explains:

A) The children are counting letters.

B) This is word sorting and the children are grouping words by length, common letters and sound.

C) The children are combining mathematics counting and word study.

D) The children are doing a strategy sheet based on a particular word family.

17) As he walks up and down the hallway, Mr. Adams, the new Assistant Principal, continually hears Ms. Brown telling her children to go to the wall. Mr. Adams looks briefly at the literacy block schedule and continues on his walk through the building. He realizes that Ms. Brown's children are at work on:

A) A new hall display.

B) Taking down an old display and then redoing it for a new theme.

C) Adding words to their spelling word wall.

D) Measuring the height of plants for a mathematics lesson.

18) Randy is proud of how many new vocabulary words he has learned. He enjoys playing with a device his teacher has, since it helps him to show all the words he can create from various letters. The device is a:

A) Word strip.

B) Letter holder for making words.

C) Word mask.

D) None of the above.

19) Ability grouping means:

A) Grouping of children according to the results of an IQ test.

B) Grouping of children with similar test results for instructional purposes.

C) Grouping of children according to their oral reading accuracy rate.

D) Grouping of children wit similar needs for instructional purposes.

20) Tim is not in the same ability group as his best friend Alex. He starts to cry even though he is a second grader. The teacher comforts him by telling him the truth that:

A) He is just as smart as Alex.

B) He can play with Alex during recess.

C) Ability groups change as the children's needs in them change during the year.

D) Tim is smarter than his best friend Alex.

21) "Beautiful Beth is the Best Girl in the Bradley Bay area." This sentence could be used to help children learn about:

A) Assonance.

B) Alliteration.

C) Rhyming pairs.

D) None of the above.

22) Greg Ball went to an author signing where Faith Ringgold gave a talk about one of her many books. He was so inspired by her presence and by his reading of her book *TAR BEACH*, that he used the book for his reading and writing workshop activities. His supervisor wrote in his plan book, that he was pleased that Greg had used the book as an/a _____ book.

A) Basic book.

B) Feature book.

C) Anchor book.

D) Focus book.

23) A delegation from the United Kingdom has come to the United States and since they are considering adapting the balanced literacy approach, they are very interested in seeing the small group demonstrated. Mr. Adams knows that he should bring them into Greg's room when Greg is doing which activity?

A) A mini lesson.

B) A conference with individual students.

C) A time when children are divided into small and independent study groups.

D) A read-aloud.

24) As the visitors from the United Kingdom tour the school, they are pleased to hear a sing-song chant "Don't fall asleep at the page, don't forget the _____" Mr. Adams explains to them that the first graders are learning about pointing at words and moving from the left to the right, this is called:

A) Directionality

B) Return sweep

C) Top to bottom

D) Line for line reading

25) **Andrew is just starting school, but it looks like he will be successful in reading because:**

- A) He comes from a family which cares about his progress.

- B) He is phonemically aware and knows his alphabet.

- C) He has been in pre-school.

- D) He is well behaved.

26) **Gracie seems to be struggling with her reading, even in first grade, although her mother works at a publishing firm and her dad is an editor. Her speech is also full of mispronunciations, although her parents were born in the school neighborhood. Gracie should be checked by:**

- A) A reading specialist.

- B) A speech therapist or an audiologist

- C) A pediatrician.

- D) A psychologist.

27) **Ronald's parents are hearing impaired. He probably will need:**

- A) Extensive work with the use of picture cues

- B) Work with songs, rhymes and read alouds to promote phonemic awareness.

- C) No extra work or support.

- D) None of the above.

28) **Maria was an outstanding student in her elementary school in Brazil. Now she is nervous about starting fourth grade in the US, although she learned English as a second language in Brazil. She and her parents should be relieved to know that:**

- A) She will get extra help in the United States with her English.

- B) There is a positive and strong correlation between a child's native language and his/her learning of English.

- C) Her classmates will help her.

- D) She will have a few months to study for the reading test.

29) Paul is a new teacher. He has just started his logs and assessments for his children's phonemic awareness. He asks a reading teacher to look over his log, but the log is returned to him:

A) Paul gave the log to the wrong colleague.

B) The colleague would not help him out by reviewing it.

C) The log did not have the dates the child's behavior was observed and had no stated performance standards.

D) The log didn't have a cover letter from Paul.

30) The term graphophonemic awareness refers to:

A) Handwriting skills.

B) Letter to sound recognition.

C) Alphabetic principle.

D) Phonemic awareness.

31) A stationery store owner in the neighborhood of the school is amused by the fact that the children on a school walk, are rushing up to various store signs and street signs. The children are probably exploring:

A) The alphabetic principle.

B) The principle that print carries meaning.

C) Letter sound recognition.

D) Phonemic awareness.

32) As Ms. Maxwell enters a first grade class, the teacher is busily writing down what the children are saying. The teacher is probably doing this to:

A) Demonstrate how to copy down speech.

B) Make a connection and promote awareness of the relationship between spoken and written language.

C) Authenticate the children's comments.

D) Raise the children's self esteem.

33) A district observer notes that fifth graders are showing younger peers in the third grade how to hold a book and walk around with it, they assume:

A) That the fifth graders are particularly theatrical.

B) That the fifth graders are proud of how they read stories aloud.

C) That the fifth graders are training the younger children in book holding.

D) That this has nothing to do with instruction.

34) Environmental print is available at all of the following except:

A) Within a newspaper.

B) On the page of a library book.

C) On a supermarket circular.

D) In a commercial flyer.

35) Book handling skills include ALL of the following except:

A) Putting a cellophane or plastic cover on a book.

B) Identifying the back cover of the book.

C) Reading the book jacket.

D) Reading dedication page and the title page of the book.

36) The best way for a primary grade teacher to model directionality and one to one word matching would be:

A) Using a regular library or classroom text book.

B) Using her own person reading book.

C) Using a big book.

D) Using a book dummy.

37) As far as the balanced literacy movement is concerned the "WHOLE" is:

A) All the reading themes to be covered that day.

B) The whole class meeting for the mini lesson.

C) The complete unit to be covered over the month.

D) All of the reading and writing work to be done in connection with one book.

38) The "TO, WITH, BY" continuum means:

A) The teacher works with the children.

B) The children work Independently.

C) Everything is led by the teacher and taught to the children.

D) The teacher first teaches to the children, then works with them and ultimately the children learn by themselves.

39) Factual book features children should learn include:

A) Captions.

B) Glossaries.

C) Diagrams.

D) All of the above.

40) When they are in 6ᵗʰ grade, children should be able to independently go through an unfamiliar collection and:

A) Use only the table of contents.

B) Use the first line indices, and find a poem by author and subject.

C) Use only the glossary.

D) None of the above.

41) At a faculty meeting Ms. Riley found out that she might have crisscrossers in her class and that Mr. Brown had them and he was happy about it:

A) Crisscrossers are students who have skipped a grade.

B) Crisscrossers are students with excellent skills in reading and in Math.

C) Crisscrossers are second language learners who have a positive attitude toward first and second language learning.

D) Crisscrossers are second language learners who are only positive about English Language Learning.

42) Cues in reading are:

A) Vowel sounds.

B) Digraphs.

C) Sources of information used by readers to help them construct meaning.

D) None of the above.

43) As part of a study for a unit on the history of Massachusetts, Mr. Gentry is using the early childhood book *26 Letters and 99 Cents* by Tina Hoban. He wants his readers to study it and create a more detailed guide to their state using its concept. This is a technique frequently used in:

A) Reading and writing workshop.

B) Writing process instruction.

C) Readers workshop.

D) Technical writing.

44) A key theorist who supports a phonics centered approach is:

A) Marie Clay.

B) Sharon Taberski.

C) Shelley Harwayne.

D) Rudolf Flesch.

45) To decode is to:

A) Construct meaning.

B) Sound out a printed sequence of letters.

C) Use a special code to decipher a message.

D) None of the above.

46) To encode means that you:

A) Decode a second time.

B) Construct meaning from a code.

C) Tell someone a message.

D) None of the above.

47) There are two basic types of text structure:

A) Fiction and non-fiction.

B) Primary and pre-k.

C) Expository and narrative.

D) Wordless and text rich.

48) While the supervisor is pleased overall with Barbara's first year of teaching, he feels that given the fact that two of her students are transfers from Mexico and one student has a hearing impairment, she has to plan for:

A) Extra homework for all of them.

B) Extra time for the hearing impaired child.

C) A buddy to work with the two students from Mexico.

D) Differentiated instruction to meet these students varied special needs.

49) The district is emphasizing that all students in grades 3-6 must focus this month on the reading of functional documents. Ms. Ramirez just smiles and scoops up a handful of free newspapers which she gets on subscription. This is Wednesday and there is a food section. She plans to use:

    A) The main news stories.

    B) The sports pages.

    C) The recipe pages.

    D) The comics.

50) Ms. Ramirez also wants the children to share their functional reading skills with their families, so she asks that they take the newspapers home to focus on the:

    A) Advice columns.

    B) Fill in coupons.

    C) Metropolitan news briefs.

    D) Weather section.

51) Mr. Adams was pleased with Ms. Ramirez's reading lesson, but he realized that she would have visually represented the comparisons she was trying to get the children to make better, if she had used:

    A) a big book.

    B) More expressive language.

    C) A better literary example.

    D) A graphic organizer.

52) Margaret is the winning Ps 123 orator. She loves reciting poetry by Shel Silverstein. Who would guess that she is also a poet in her first language? Margaret's first language is definitely:

    A) English.

    B) French.

    C) Spanish.

    D) NOT English.

53) **A teacher is asking children to look at the beginning letters of words. She then asks the child to connect the beginning letter to the text and story and to think about what word would make sense there. This is an example of:**

   A) A balanced literacy approach.

   B) A phonemic approach.

   C) A phonic approach.

   D) AN ELL differentiated approach.

54) **The teacher is watching the children go from oral speech into writing. The teacher says, "Great job:"**

   A) A good decoding.

   B) A good recoding.

   C) A good encoding.

   D) All of the above.

55) **By November the first graders have a vocabulary of words which they can correctly pronounce and read aloud. These words are their:**

   A) Sight vocabulary.

   B) Recognition vocabulary.

   C) Personal vocabulary.

   D) Working vocabulary.

56) **As the child is reading and has made an incorrect attempt, the teacher prompts:**

   A) That is a mistake, do it again.

   B) No, you are stupid. .. why can't you get it?

   C) Does that make sense to you?

   D) Forget it, this is too hard for you.

57) **Asking a child if what he or she has read makes sense to him or her, is prompting the child to use:**

   A) Phonics cues.

   B) Syntactic cues.

   C) Semantic cues.

   D) Prior knowledge.

58) **When you ask a child, if what he or she has just read "sounds right" to him or her, you are trying to get that child to use:**

   A) Phonics cues.

   B) Syntactic cues.

   C) Semantic cues.

   D) Prior knowledge.

59) By definition, which children in a classroom will have trouble with syntactic cues?

    A) Those from families who do not have household libraries.

    B) Those not in a top reading group.

    C) Those from ELL backgrounds.

    D) All of the above.

60) "Self correct" in reading means:

    A) The teacher corrects on the record the errors the child makes.

    B) The child goes back and corrects errors made in a running record.

    C) The reading specialist teaches this to the child.

    D) a and b.

61) A natural role for a highly proficient reader would be:

    A) To assist the teacher with cleaning the classroom and organizing the student folders.

    B) To develop charts for the teacher by copying needed poems for full class study.

    C) Tutor and support struggling readers.

    D) Work on his/her own interests while the teacher works with the rest of the class.

62) A theorist who believes that there is a finite body of approved literature children should be taught on various grade levels and has produced books about what everyone needs to know to be literate on various grade levels is:

    A) Rudolf Flesch

    B) J. David Cooper

    C) John Dewey

    D) E. D. Hirsch

63) Children "own" words when all of the following happen except:

A) They find these words on their own.

B) The teacher provides a mandated word list.

C) They use the words in their own writings.

D) The words appear in literature that interests them.

64) A discussion circle can convene:

A) After the children have finished reading a text as a group.

B) Before the children read a text as a group.

C) While the reading of the text is going on.

D) All of the above.

65) To promote word study, children can:

A) Be required to go to the dictionary at least once or twice a day.

B) Collect and share words of interest they find in their readings.

C) Do vocabulary work sheets from a basal reader or commercial vocabulary book.

D) Do all of the above.

66) In order to get children to compile specialized vocabulary, they can use:

A) Newspapers.

B) Internet resources and approved web-sites that focus on the special interest.

C) Experts they can interview.

D) All of the above.

67) If children are engaged in creating a museum within classroom project to exhibit their work, they are:

A) Not doing any reading or writing.

B) Doing many authentic reading, writing, and researching tasks.

C) Not likely to visit a real museum.

D) All of the above.

68) Teachers should select at least ___words for pre-reading vocabulary discussion:

A) 12.

B) 15.

C) 2-3.

D) 8-10.

69) The teacher should choose words for pre-story discussion and exploration based on:

A) The teacher's interest.

B) Whether the teacher feels the children have prior knowledge of or experience with the words.

C) A pre-existing grade level required vocabulary list.

D) Words that will impress his or her supervisor.

70) Two steps a teacher might take before selecting words for study are:

A) Reading the story and story mapping.

B) Asking advice from a veteran teacher and the grade leader.

C) Looking in a teacher's guide and copying out the words listed there.

D) All of the above are correct

71) A teacher discovers after considering his class's prior knowledge of the story material that he would need to teach 12 words at least before he starts teaching the story to the whole group. This indicates:

A) The children will need a read-aloud.

B) The children will need independent reading.

C) The children will need guided reading.

D) The children will need shared reading.

72) **The teacher is very concerned about identifying a book that is "just right" for Jay to read independently. This means that Jay should be able to read this book with:**

    A) Below 92% accuracy

    B) 100% accuracy

    C) 95-100% accuracy

    D) 92-97% accuracy

73) **Jay really wants to read a book that he can only read with 94% accuracy. He could get to read this book as:**

    A) An independent reading.

    B) A guided reading.

    C) A shared reading.

    D) All of the above.

74) **When taking a child's running record, the kinds of self corrections the child makes:**

    A) Are not important, but the percentage of accuracy is important.

    B) May show something about which cueing systems the child relies on.

    C) Can be meaningful if analyzed over several records.

    D) Both b and c

75) **A "decodable text" is:**

    A) A text that a child can read aloud with correct pronunciations.

    B) A text that a child can answer comprehension questions about with a high percentage of accuracy.

    C) Text written to match the sequence of letter-sound relationships that have been taught.

    D) None of the above.

76) **Once a teacher has carefully recorded and documented a running record:**

    A) There is nothing further to do as long as the teacher keeps the running record for conferences and documentation of grades.

    B) The teacher should review the running record and other subsequent ones taken for growth over time.

    C) The teacher should differentiate instruction for that particular student as indicated by growth over time and evidence of other needs.

    D) Both b and c

77) The reliability of a test is measured by:

   A) The number of children who can pass it.

   B) The number of children who fail it.

   C) The degree to which it measures what it is supposed to measure over time.

   D) None of the above

78) A quartile on a test is:

   A) A quarter of the grades grouped.

   B) The division of the percentiles into four segments each of which is called a quartile.

   C) 25 of the tests scored.

   D) b and c

79) Validity in assessment means:

   A) The test went off without any previewing of the questions or leaks on its contents.

   B) The majority of test takers passed.

   C) The correct time was allowed for the children to complete the test.

   D) The test assessed what it was supposed to assess and measure.

80) Vocabulary should be introduced after reading if:

   A) The children have identified words from their reading which were difficult and which they need explained.

   B) The text is appropriate for vocabulary building.

   C) The teacher would like to teach vocabulary after the reading.

   D) a and b

81) The teacher is working on a life science unit in grade five and using many print and electronic sources for information. Some of these words have a linear and some of them a hierarchical relationship to one another. The teacher has spent much time explaining how the words connect with one another. At this point, it would be a good idea to:

   A) Use a root family diagram or tree.

   B) Work with the base words.

   C) Use hierarchical and linear arrays.

   D) Start semantic mapping for a particular concept.

82) **Direct teaching of a concept or strategy means:**

    A) The teacher teaches the concept or strategy as part of a genre lesson.

    B) The teacher teaches the concept as part of the writing workshop.

    C) The teacher explicitly announces to the class that this strategy will be taught.

    D) The teacher teaches the strategy to a small group of children or to an individual child.

83) **The word "bat" is a ___word for "batter-up":**

    A) Suffix.

    B) Prefix.

    C) Root word.

    D) Inflectional ending.

84) **"Ballgame" is a _____word. Its meaning is derived from the combination of "Ball" and "Game":**

    A) Contraction.

    B) Compound.

    C) Portmanteau.

    D) Palindrome.

85) **In a balanced literacy classroom, new vocabulary would most likely appear on:**

    A) An experiential chart.

    B) A class newspaper.

    C) The word wall.

    D) Outside the room on a bulletin board.

86) **An effective way to build vocabulary and to make connections with mandated science and mathematics material is to teach Greek and Latin roots using:**

    A) Semantic maps.

    B) Hierarchical arrays.

    C) Linear arrays.

    D) Word webs.

87) **As a parent walked through the first grade floor of her school, she kept hearing repeated clapping. Most likely the children were:**

    A) Clapping to show respect for one another.

    B) Rehearsing for how they would clap at a play.

    C) Clapping out syllables of multi-syllabic words.

    D) All of the above.

88) As part of study about the agricultural products of their state, children have identified 22 different types of apples produced in the state. They can use a _____ to compare and contrast these different types of apples:

A) Word web.

B) Semantic map.

C) Semantic features analysis grid.

D) All of the above.

89) Based on individual conferences with many children, the teacher realizes that although they are all self-improving readers, they need help in better use of the context to define words. The teacher decided to try the use of:

A) A dictionary to look up words.

B) A thesaurus to use with the dictionary.

C) Contextual redefinition training.

D) Instruction in how to effectively use a dictionary.

90) The parents of Ramon, a child who has grown up in Puerto Rico and studied English there as a second language, ask that the teacher provide him with individual support in context redefinition. Ramon is scoring above grade level in reading. His mother, who is also a teacher of reading, argues that:

A) He should get extra help because he has just transferred from another country.

B) Being walked through the process of using contexts is helpful for an ELL student.

C) He needs to work with a peer on this skill.

D) None of the above.

91) A bound morpheme is:

A) A prefix.

B) A contraction.

C) An inflectional ending that can be added to a base word to change its case, gender, number, tense or form.

D) A root word.

92) A second grader is writing his first book review. He has conferred with his teacher several times while he was writing the book review. Now he is rehearsing it with the teacher before he reads it aloud to the class. The child's learning of how to compose and deliver a book review has been:

A) Done independently.

B) Assisted by family support.

C) Done in a cooperative group setting.

D) Scaffolded by the teacher.

93) One of the many ways in which a child can demonstrate comprehension of a story is by:

A) Filling in a strategy sheet.

B) Retelling the story orally.

C) Retelling the story in writing.

D) All of the above.

94) A strategy is:

A) A practice or routine the teacher can continually refer to.

B) A practice or routine a child can continually refer to or use.

C) A sheet or template for a practice the child can continually fill out.

D) All of the above.

95) The Stop and Think Strategy means that the child reader will:

A) Read through until the end of the story or text.

B) Ask himself or herself if what he or she has read makes sense to him or her.

C) Stop after reading some text and write down his/her concerns.

D) All of the above.

96) Taking responsibility for a child's own learning, will usually involve the child in:

A) Reading and writing on his/her own.

B) Developing a personal literacy project which will later be shared with the teacher and peers and family.

C) Putting away books and materials when directed.

D) a and b.

97) "Sounds right" can sound wrong to:

A) Any reader who is not a fluent or early reader.

B) AN ELL reader.

C) A struggling reader.

D) None of the above.

98) "Bias" in testing occurs when:

A) The assessment instrument is not an objective, fair and impartial one for a given cultural, ethnic, or special needs participant.

B) The testing administrator is biased.

C) The same test is given with no time considerations or provisions for those in need of more time or those who have handicapping conditions.

D) All of the above.

99) Norm-referenced tests:

A) Give information only about the local samples results.

B) Provide information about the local test takers did compared to a representative sampling of national test takers.

C) Make no comparisons to national test takers.

D) None of the above.

100) If you get your raw score on a test, you will get:

A) The actual number of points you scored on the test.

B) The percentage score of the number of questions you answered correctly.

C) A letter grade for your work on the test.

D) An aggregated score for your performance on the text.

101) The data coordinator of the district who is concerned with federal funding for reading will probably want to start aggregating scores immediately because:

A) It is interesting to crunch more data.

B) By aggregating, the individual scores can be combined to view performance trends across groups.

C) This will help the district determine which groups need more remedial instruction.

D) b and c

102) A standardized test will be:

A) Given out with the same predetermined questions and format to all.

B) Not be given to certain children.

C) If given out in exactly the same format with the same content, may be taken over a lengthier test period (i.e. 4 hours instead of three or two).

D) All of the above.

103) Mr. Mandrake is subbing for Ms. Matley. He sees by the schedule that he is supposed to start the day after the morning meeting with a Read-Aloud. He notes a large picture on the easel and grabs the book just two minutes before the Read-Aloud is to start. He shouldn't heave a sigh of relief because:

A) He needs to be familiar with the book so that he can plan the read-aloud.

B) He does not know if the class has already heard this book.

C) He has not planned vocabulary, themes, or activities to go with the book.

D) All of the above.

104) The science fair is coming up and Ms. Gardner is trying to find time in her busy schedule to work on her class's earth worm diary project. With all of the mandated tests and assemblies, she has not found time to start her students on their earth worm research. Within the context of reading instruction, she can:

A) Begin a thematic study unit.

B) Start with a read aloud of the *Diary of an Earth Worm* by Doreen Cronin.

C) Scaffold the research process by going online with her children using an approved search engine to find matches for earthworm sites.

D) All of the above.

105) Annie's mother has been invited to class to serve as a guest reader. She scoops up her favorite books from her family bookshelf and rushes off to school. When she gets to Annie's classroom, she is greeted and ushered into a rocking chair and given a special hat to wear. The explanation is:

A) The children are excited to have a volunteer and are bored with their teacher day in and day out.

B) This is a class designated author's chair and an author's hat has been worked on by the whole class for anyone who comes to read to them or who reads his/her own writings.

C) Both a and b

D) None of the above.

106) Four of Ms. Wolmark's students have lived in other countries. She is particularly pleased to be studying Sumerian proverbs with them as part of the sixth grade unit in analyzing the sayings of other cultures because:

A) This gives her a break from teaching and the children can share sayings from other cultures they and their families have experienced.

B) This validates the experiences and expertise of ELL learners in her classroom.

C) This provides her children from the US with a lens on other cultural values.

D) All of the above.

107) As Ms. Wolmark looks at the mandated vocabulary curriculum for the 6th grade, she notes that she can opt to teach foreign words and abbreviations which have become part of the English language. She decides:

A) To forego that since she is not a teacher of foreign language.

B) To teach only foreign words from the native language of her four ELL students.

C) To use the ELL students' native languages as a start for an extensive study of foreign language words.

D) To teach 2-3 foreign l language words that are now in English and let it go at that.

108) As Mr. Adams exits his school building, he notices that Mr. Mark, a new teacher, is leading a group of happy looking fifth graders back into the building. They are carrying all kinds of free pamphlets and circulars from a local coffee house. Mr. Adams immediately asks Mr. Mark why the class went to that coffee house during the lunch break. When he hears Mr. Mark's answer, he is delighted:

A) Mr. Mark says they went looking for environmental print and words with a café and latte root.

B) Mr. Mark says they didn't spend any money and got free hot chocolate.

C) The children will have to summarize a pamphlet as homework.

D) All of the above.

109) Mr. Adams has complained to Mr. Mark that there are too many newspapers piled up in his classroom. Mr. Mark has responded that he does not want to throw away these piled up newspapers because:

A) They can be used for letter—sound correspondence.

B) They represent environmental print.

C) They can be used to create print-meaning signs.

D) All of the above.

110) In Ms. Francine's class, dictionary use is a punishment. Mr. Adams is:

A) Pleased with the way that Ms. Francine approaches dictionary use

B) Unconcerned with this approach to the use of the dictionary

C) Convinced that the teacher should model her own fascination and pleasure in using the dictionary for the children.

D) Delighted by the fact that children are being forced to use the dictionary.

111) Dictionary study:

A) can begin in grades 1 or 2.

B) can begin in pre-K using the lush picture dictionaries.

C) should start on grade three level.

D) a and b.

112) An excellent research project that can combine dictionary study with science research would be:

A) A student authored dictionary terms and phrases about earthworms.

B) A teacher developed specialized dictionary of words and phrases about. earthworms.

C) A collection of articles on earthworms put together by the school librarian.

D) b and c.

113) A veteran teacher waited for her adult daughter outside of her daughter's first class in the Teaching of Reading. As she and her daughter talked about the first session of the course, the teacher never heard an explicit mention of the teaching of reading. All she heard about was:

A) Learning about narratives.

B) Dealing with text structures.

C) Constructing meaning.

D) All of the above.

114) Making inferences from the text means that the reader:

A) Is making informed judgments based on available evidence.

B) Is making a guess based on prior experiences.

C) Is making a guess based on what the reader would like to be true of the text.

D) All of the above.

115) Sometimes children can be asked to demonstrate their understanding of a text in a non-written format. This might include all of the following except:

A) A story map.

B) A Venn diagram.

C) Storyboarding a part of the story with dialogue bubbles.

D) Retelling or paraphrasing.

116) A very bright child in a grade one class came from a family which did not a have a strong oral story telling or story reading tradition in its native language. This child would need support in developing:

A) Letter-sound correspondence skills.

B) Schemata for generic concepts most children have in their memories and experiences based on family oral traditions and read a loud.

C) Oral expressiveness.

D) b and c.

117) The concerned parent whose child had a visual impairment wanted as much help for him as the teacher and the school district could give her. She begged: "Please, he didn't attend pre-school, he has no prior knowledge." Strictly speaking this is:

A) Correct, since he didn't get pre-school experiences.

B) Incorrect, since prior knowledge covers everyone's experiences.

C) Incorrect, since he did have prior knowledge experiences but these didn't match those of many of his peers, so he would need to enhance his prior knowledge.

D) b and c

118) **Mr. Mark is a brand new teacher who is not from the neighborhood where his school is located. He is a bit nervous as this is his first teaching assignment. He does not yet know how to relax enough to get his students to activate prior experience. He should:**

A) Try a free recall question: Tell us what you know about...

B) Try an unstructured Question: Let's talk About...

C) Use word association: What do you associate X with?

D) All of the above.

119) **Among the literary strategies that teachers can use to activate prior knowledge are:**

A) Predicting and previewing a story.

B) Story mapping.

C) Venn diagramming.

D) Linear arrays.

120) **Ms. Angel has to be certain that her fourth graders know the characteristics of the historical fiction genre. She can best support them in becoming comfortable with this genre by:**

A) Providing sequel and prequel writing opportunities using that genre.

B) Reading them many different works from that genre.

C) a and b.

D) Having them look up the definition of that genre in a literary encyclopedia.

121) **Author's viewpoint questions stump Gary. His teacher can help him by asking him during their reading conferences:**

A) If Gary-feels the book he is reading, is it just right for him.

B) What the author would say about what the character is doing in the story.

C) How the story can be changed to another genre.

D) If Gary-wants to read more books by this author.

122) Ms. Clark is seen by outside observers from her district, seated in front of her class of sixth graders with a notebook in her lap and an easel. She reads aloud from a book and then writes down a series of questions. As she reads along, she sometimes writes down the answers to her own questions. This is most likely:

A) A sign that Ms. Clark is uncertain of her own comprehension capacity.

B) She is modeling self questioning for the children.

C) She is aware that she is being watched and wants to make a good impression.

D) All of the above.

123) Bill has been called up to the teacher for an individual conference. She asks him to retell one of the books he has listed on his weekly log. He begins and is still talking 7 minutes later. Most probably, Bill:

A) Told the entire story with all its details and minor characters.

B) May or may not have really gotten the main points and perspectives of the story.

C) May have really liked the Story.

D) None of the above.

124) Ms. Ancess used to take time to have her children memorize major poems and even had an assembly for parents and school staff where the children dramatically recited various poems. Now that she is worried about the children's reading scores, she doesn't want to waste time with this memorization. Actually if she still includes this high interest, child-centered experience:

A) The children can use their oral fluency and her modeling as a bridge for enhanced comprehension.

B) The children can get a sense of "ownership" of the words.

C) Children and parents will have a "break" from worrying about the test.

D) None of the above.

125) To help children with "main idea" questions, the teacher should:

A) Give out a strategy sheet on the main idea for children to place in their reader's notebooks.

B) Model responding to such a question as part of guided reading.

C) Have children create "main idea questions" to go with their writings.

D) All of the above.

Answer Key

1. C	47. C	93. D
2. C	48. D	94. D
3. C	49. C	95. B
4. A	50. B	96. D
5. B	51. A	97. B
6. C	52. D	98. D
7. B	53. C	99. B
8. B	54. B	100. A
9. C	55. B	101. D
10. D	56. C	102. D
11. D	57. C	103. D
12. B	58. B	104. D
13. C	59. C	105. B
14. D	60. B	106. D
15. C	61. C	107. C
16. B	62. D	108. D
17. C	63. B	109. D
18. B	64. A	110. C
19. D	65. D	111. D
20. C	66. D	112. A
21. B	67. B	113. C
22. C	68. C	114. A
23. C	69. B	115. D
24. B	70. D	116. B
25. B	71. C	117. D
26. B	72. D	118. D
27. B	73. A	119. A
28. B	74. D	120. C
29. C	75. A	121. B
30. C	76. C	122. B
31. B	77. C	123. A
32. B	78. B	124. A
33. C	79. D	125. D
34. B	80. D	
35. A	81. C	
36. C	82. C	
37. B	83. C	
38. D	84. B	
39. D	85. C	
40. B	86. D	
41. C	87. C	
42. C	88. D	
43. A	89. C	
44. D	90. B	
45. B	91. C	
46. B	92. D	

Rationales for Sample Questions

1. This is a sheer memorization question. By definition, phonemic awareness falls under the phonological awareness umbrella. All of the other choices do not deal with the DIFFERENCE between the two types of awareness.

2. Another memorization question which can only be answered by either knowing Adams's theory or by knowing that the other theorists listed did not present that theory. Anywhere from 10-15% of the questions on the certification tests are based on knowledge of the theorists and key terms associated with their theories.

3. This question involves the test taker's knowing that in reading the term "oddity task" involves identification of an odd sound within a series of like sounds. Choice A dealing with mathematics plays on that discipline's definition of odd which would not be tested on a foundations of reading exam. The other choices are "common sense definitions" of oddity which are not appropriate answers for a test in reading.

4. The key word here is EXCEPT which will be highlighted in upper case on the test as well. All of the options are correct aspects of phonological awareness except the first one, A, because phonological awareness DOES NOT involve print.

5. This question requires knowledge of running records and familiarity with error recording and miscues. The test taker has to know that this is the standard format for a running record of reading behaviors and that choices "C" and "D" deal with attitudes and feelings which are not part of the running records used as part of the balanced literacy approach.

6. Choice A is not correct. All children are capable of becoming good readers and the other choices, given Ms. James's dedication, are not the most likely reason these three children (a minority of the class) are struggling.

7. The answer is "B" because all of the other options are essential for record keeping. The key word here is "EXCEPT."

8. The answer is "B" because the teacher does not want the room to appear more spacious, but wants parents to have a feel for the book bags which indicate the primacy of reading.

9. The answer is "C" and this is a memorization question.

10. All the answers are correct.

11. Given the fact this is a kindergarten in a public housing project, she will be most successful with wordless picture books, since there is no guarantee the children have had prior exposure to the other types of books listed. The answer "D" will allow them to construct a story from the pictures.

12. The answer is "B" because the question details that the adults are seated two by two holding copies of the same book. This is the buddy reading style.

13. The answer is "C" and this is a memorization question.

14. The answer is "D", Marie Clay, and this is a name you "have to know" from this guide or your courses.

15. This is a classic manifestation of "C", the logographic phrase of phonics learning.

16. The answer is "B", and again this answer would grow out of teaching experience and familiarity with manipulatives or reading this guide.

17. The answer is "C" because in today's balanced literacy classroom, a wall is a word wall.

18. The answer is "B" and this is a familiar device in today's reading classroom.

19. The answer is "D" and this is a key definition which should be memorized.

20. The answer is "C" by definition; also a teacher would never get into the other personal comments which are offered as choices with a second grader.

21. This is a question that any English literature or Reading major can answer. The answer is "B."

22. This is another question using current terminology. While all the other choices make sense, "C" is correct because a book that is used to teach reading and writing is called an Anchor book.

23. "C" is the only correct answer choice because small refers to group size.

24. The answer is "B" and this term is in the Glossary.

25. This IS a deliberately tricky question. Each of the choices has merit. The best choice is "B" because that one is confirmed by current research.

26. This one is "B" because Gracie is a neighborhood child and shouldn't be having these difficulties with pronunciation.

27. This is one you can work out. The answer is "B" because obviously Ronald's parents will not be singing with him and doing lots of read alouds.

28. All of these choices have an element of truth in them, but go with "B" which reflects research results.

29. The answer is "C" because all logs need to have dates and standards.

30. The answer is "C" and it is a definition question.
If you missed it, re-read through the Glossary.

31. The behavior described here only matches one reading activity, "B."

32. This is another deliberately tricky question. All of the answers may appeal to you, but, choice "B" is the theoretical way to describe what the teacher is doing when he or she writes down what the children are saying.

33. This is a standard part of "book holding", so that the answer is "C."

34. The key word here is "EXCEPT" and environmental print is not defined as print in a library book, so choice "B" is the right one.

35. Ironically "A" is correct because book handling as defined in reading, does not include putting covers on books.

36. Key word in this question is "best" and the answer is "C" because this type of a book is best for teaching and display.

37. This is another deliberately tricky question, since all of the answers make sense, but only "B" is correct because that is the definition of "WHOLE" in balanced literacy.

38. The answer is "D" and is another definition question.

39. The answer is "D." All of the above is the correct answer because captions, glossaries and diagrams are but three of the text features that students need to be able to identify in a text. Other text features include headings, charts, maps, indexes, and tables

40. This is a question, you can reason out. The most complex task described here is "B.".

41. This is a definition question and the answer is "C."

42. This too is a definition question and the answer is "C."

43. The answer is "A." The fact that Mr. Gentry wants his class to use this for both reading and writing , should help you pick the right choice even if you don't know the answer.

44. The answer is "D." Flesch was a proponent of the phonics approach to reading in his book "Why Johnny Can't Read" which was essentially a critique of the American educational system. Neither of the other three choices propose explicit teaching of phonics to help children master reading.

45. The answer is "B" and a definition question.

46. The answer is "B" and is a definition question. If you are missing many definitions, perhaps make flash cards of the Glossary words and study them intensively.

47. The answer is "C," Expository and Narrative. Fiction and non-fiction are genres, Primary and pre-K are grade levels, and Wordless and text rich are types of books for young children.

48. This is a tricky question because all of the choices have an element of truth in them. But the best choice is "D" because it includes the special approaches Barbara will have to take with her ELL and special needs students.

49. Functional literacy refers to knowing things that students have to do on a day to day basis. Reading a recipe is classified as functional literacy because students learn how to read directions to perform a task. The answer is "C."

50. Coupons, like want ads are functional the families can fill in or act on. The answer is "B."

51. The answer is "A" because the BIG BOOK is a good visual display tool, ' .

52. This is a deliberately misleading question; all the test taker can know for certain is that Margaret's first language is NOT English. You know she is an ELL student because the question talks about her "first language." The answer is "D."
53. The focus on letters and sounds is "C" a phonics approach.

54. This is another definition question; read the definition section carefully before the exam. The answer has to be "B."

55. The term is "B" recognition vocabulary. This is a definition you have to know.

56. Obviously, "B" can not be right. Generally, a caring teacher would not say "D," but "C" is the preferred wording in use now in reading classrooms.

57. Semantic cues are the hints that students can discern from the reading to help them make sense of the text. In some cases, the message of the text depends on the other words around them, so students learn how to determine the meaning from context clues. The answer must be "C."

58. This is another one of those answers using the language of linguistics in reading. The answer has to be "B," syntactic clues.

59. This question can actually only have a single correct answer. It is "C" because by definition a child from an ELL background does not have a strong accurate sense of what "sounds right" in English.

60. There is only one correct answer here and it is "B." This is a key principle of the running record.

61. While all of the choices are possibilities, the concept of the highly proficient reader tutoring leads to answer "C."

62. The answer is "D" and this has to be memorized and known.

63. Again the test taker has to find the choice which is incorrect and it is choice "B" when the teacher puts up a mandated word list.

64. By definition, a discussion group can convene only "A" after the children have read a work.

65. All of the answers will promote vocabulary, so the answer is "D."

66. The answer is "D" because all of the responses are correct.

67. There is only one correct answer here and it is logical, "B."

68. The correct answer is "C," 2-3 words. Teachers should select a small number of words for pre-teaching to allow the students time to comprehend the text and achieve the objectives related to the reading. For example, in a non-fiction text, these words could be key terms related to the main topic. Even students with an extensive oral vocabulary may not be able to recognize words in print because they are not words that they normally encounter in their reading. The activities the teacher plans in relation to the words will help the students internalize the strategies more readily when only a few words are selected each time.

69. This is another one where the correct answer is "B" and only "D" is an unlikely choice.

70. This is one you can reason through and choose "D" easily.

71. This is one you can reason through, if you know that generally during READ ALOUD you do not stop to explain many words. You would not want to give material for independent or shared reading where so many words had to be explained. Hence the correct choice is "C," guided reading.

72. The answer is "D" because those are the "just right percentages."
73. The answer by definition is "A" because if "just right." is synonymous with the independent reading level.

74. The answer is "D" and related to taking a child's running record.

75. This is choice "A" which is the definition of decodable.

76. Students learn at different rates, therefore students in any class will be at varying levels of learning. By differentiating instruction and incorporating assessment **for** learning rather than assessment **of** learning, teachers can help students succeed. When teachers assess student growth over time and monitor the areas in which they are experiencing difficulty, they can alter the instruction and the activities to match student needs. The answer is "C."

77. This is a definition question and the answer is "C."

78. While this is also a definition question, choice "B" is one that a linguist would choose.

79. "D" is the answer here and it also makes good sense to the test taker.

80. This is a question the literate test taker should be able to "reason" through. Vocabulary introduced by children and a good text with opportunities to expand vocabulary are needed. Answer "D" which includes both "A" and "B" is the right choice.

81. The astute test taker should get this right whether he or she actually knows these materials or not. "Hierarchical" appears in both the question and in the correct choice "C."

82. The answer is "C" and this is a definition question.

83. The answer is "C."

84. Answer "B."

85. The answer can only be "C" and should be part of the test taker's theoretical background.

86. The answer is "D" and historically these have been used to teach Greek and Latin roots.

87. This is related to phonics and the answer is "C."

88. The answer here is "D" and all of these graphic organizers would work with the topic of apples.

89. The answer is "C" and the trick is to notice the "better use of context" in the question and match it up with "C," contextual redefinition training.

90. The answer is "B" and it is one that is confirmed in theory and is referenced in this guide.

91. The answer is "C," a definition question.

92. This is easy to see that it is "D", scaffolded by the teacher. The child has been assisted by the teacher as he prepared the book review.

93. The answer is "D" since all the options are good ones.

94. The answer is again "D" since all the options work.

95. This is a tricky question and requires that the test taker know the very specific definition of the STOP and THINK strategy to know that the only correct answer is "B."

96. Again this has to do with the way "responsibility for your own learning" is now defined and the answer is "D."

97. This is a truism of ELL education and the answer is "B."

98. This is one where the correct answer of "D" is also the commonsense response that a literate test taker would select.

99. There is only a correct answer here by definition and "B" is it.

100. Again these are all definitions which the test taker should memorize before the test (see the Glossary in this guide). The correct answer is "A."

101. Again this is a definition answer and the correct choice is "D."

102. This is all about what a standardized test means and answer is "D."

103. The answer is "d," but this is a question anyone who has gotten through the coursework or taught, should have no problem with.

104. This is a question someone who has taught or gone through course work should ace to get "D." Remember going online with children and using approved search engines is fine.

105. The best answer is "B" and involves knowing about the "author's chair" concept.

106. This a question where the correct answer "D" makes good common and educational sense.

107. This is a question where you can reason your way to the correct answer, "C." "A" sounds chauvinistic and unrealistic and "B" is limiting and teaching only 2-3 words is not a good use of instructional time.

108. This is a question where the correct choice is "D" and makes good teaching and learning sense.

109. This is a question where choice "D" makes good sense to a teacher who knows the value of having newspapers for class projects.

110. The word "punishment" in the question should alert the test taker to the answer that the only choice "C" can be right.

111. This is a question that any literate test taker who has been in a children's book section recently can answer. Choice "D" is correct.

112. This question is tricky in that only choice "A", which deals with a student product, is correct. The others are all adult centered.

113. The only answer here is "C" which emphasizes "constructing meaning," the current phrase for "reading."

114. This is a definition question that a literate test taker can answer based on the general definition of inferences. The answer is "A."

115. Answer "D" is correct. Retelling and paraphrasing can be in oral form whereas the other choices all involve writing or the use of pencil and paper. By asking students to retell a story, the teacher can determine the level of comprehension. Of course, this has to be modeled for the student, especially paraphrasing, so that the student relates the important facts or events and does not include any information that is not necessary.

116. Although the question appears to be a very technical one, it actually can be easily and correctly answered by seeing how choice "B" echoes the fact that most children would have schemata based on family oral traditions.

117. This is a question which a caring and literate test taker could correctly answer and get "D" as a response. Everyone has prior knowledge of some sort.

118. Again this is a common sense question and "D" is the correct choice.

119. This is a question that a literate test taker could answer and the best choice is "A" because in their predictions, children evidence prior knowledge.

120. The answer is "C. "Online encyclopedias meet the information technology outcomes that align with language arts outcomes. When students are taught to avail of the online encyclopedias, it can save enormous amounts of space in the classroom as well as trips to the library. Students can complete all their work on the computer without having to stop and thumb through a regular encyclopedia to find the information they need.

121. This is a question where the correct choice "B" is the only one that mentions an author.

122. The only answer here is "B" because this is a technique children are taught and Ms. Clark is modeling it. "C" is insulting to Ms. Clark and "A" is insulting as well.

123. The only obvious choice after 7 minutes of talk is "A."

124. Choice "A" is the best theory answer here.

125. This is one where all the options are right. The answer is "D."

Constructed Response Questions

Constructed Response Question One

Jean is a first year teacher who is taking over the classroom of a thirty-year veteran teacher who is retiring. Jean goes in to meet with the teacher. The teacher, Ms. Banks, talks about the importance of teaching the young first graders the concepts of print.

She gives Jean a list of these concepts and suggests that Jean create some assessment format so that she can be certain that all of her first graders learn these concepts. She also tells Jean that she will be volunteering her time in a neighborhood preschool program close to her home and so she will be taking her private books and materials with her. She suggests that Jean go over the list of concepts of print and consider the needs of her class as she prepares for teaching this crucial set of skills. Before Jean leaves the classroom, Ms. Banks tells her that the kindergarten teacher has let her know that three children who will be in her class next year are from ELL backgrounds where their families are not involved in oral story telling or reading from native language texts.

Ms. Banks' concepts of print list:

- STARTS ON LEFT

- GOES FROM LEFT TO RIGHT

- RETURN SWEEP

- MATCHES WORDS BY POINTING

- POINTS TO JUST ONE WORD

- POINTS TO FIRST AND LAST WORD

- POINTS TO 1 LETTER

- POINTS TO FIRST AND LAST LETTER

- PARTS of the BOOK: Cover, Title Page, Dedication page, Author and Illustrator

Jean thanks Ms. Banks for all of this help and asks if she can send Ms. Banks some of her teaching ideas for Concepts of Print and the ways she plans to differentiate instruction for her ELL students before the end of the year. Ms. Banks smiles and says she feels good to know that her classroom will be taken over by Jean. She promises to review Jean's response.

Constructed Response Answer One

First, as far as assessment for the key skills of concepts of print, I have decided that it is very important that I have a record of when and how well each of my students masters these concepts. After much thought, I realized that I will be keeping assessment notebooks for all of my students as part of my general reading and teaching. Therefore, I plan to print out all the key concepts of print on an 8" x 11" piece of paper in a grid format. This sheet will be included with other assessment grids for each individual child.

After conferencing with the child and I determine the child has demonstrated mastery of a particular concept, I will check it off on the grid and date that mastery. If I have other comments to make about the child's level of mastery or fluency, I will make an anecdotal notation about the child as well. I think that this will guarantee that I have a detailed checklist record and anecdotal record of all my children's individual progress on concepts of print.

I plan to use big books and many of the latest picture books, including Caldecott award winners in demonstrating and sharing with children many of the concepts of print. I will do much of my instruction mini-lessons. In fact I intend to use some of my own favorite alphabet books to introduce these conventions. With a book like Clare Beaton's, *Zoe and her Zebra*, I can easily and naturally cover the title page, cover, illustrator, and also manage to engage the children in the use of repetitive language.

Once I have shared that delightful book with the children as a read-aloud, we will be able to return to it again and use the repetitive language of it in its big book format to demonstrate for the children how they can point under each word as if there is a button to push. I can also demonstrate for the children how they should start at the top of the text and move from left to right. I will model going back to the left and under the previous line in a return weep.

After modeling this as part of the mini-lesson, the children can be divided in small groups or pairs and take other big book and practice the "point under each word" and the "return sweep" as part of "shared reading" or buddy reading. I should be able to identify some highly proficient readers who will be happy to serve as 'buddy' reader/tutors for the ELL children. I will ask that these "buddies" take time in small groups to work on another book from the alphabet book collection to share with the class as a whole. The use of the alphabet books also helps me to get some time in on the alphabetic principle.

I will also do a classroom writing workshop using the original alphabet book I use for the read-aloud, say *Zoe and Her Zebra* as a model for creating our own story. Perhaps we will call it *Barry and his Boxer*. In this way we will have a concrete literary product that demonstrates the children's mastery of and fluency in the concepts of print as they create an "in style of" story about a peer using illustrations, title page, dedication page, numbering of pages, back and front cover and other concepts of print.

I think that using individualized assessments, a group/class collaborative writing project, and an anchor alphabet book will help me successfully teach the concepts of print and address the needs of my ELL learners as well.

Constructed Response Question Two

Marianne has been selected as one of a team of teachers who will start teaching in a brand new school building that has been under construction for several years. While Marianne, a grade three teacher, is thrilled to be moving into new facilities, she is a bit overwhelmed to have to "set up her room" all over again at the new site. Her administrator, Mr. Adams, tells her that there are five new teachers with no previous experience teaching primary school age children who will be on staff. He tells her that these educators could really use help setting up their classrooms.

Marianne smiles and decides that she would very much like to use her set-up of her own grade three classroom as a workshop and demonstration for setting up a literacy teaching environment for these new staff members. Mr. Adams thinks that is a great idea and asks Marianne for an agenda and for a general description of what she will cover in her three hour workshop so that he can give it to the district office.

Marianne is happy to comply because she realizes that she will be assisting new colleagues and getting ten helping hands to help her set up all the materials she has accumulated over a twenty-year career.

Constructed Response Answer Two

The concept of sharing with new colleagues how to set up a classroom is very exciting to me. I know, based on my experiences, how crucial a well-planned and conceptualized space is for young learners' literacy learning. Therefore this is an agenda for what I will cover in my three hour in service session for my new colleagues.

First, I will discuss how whatever the size of the classroom space, it must be sectioned off into the following areas: a meeting area, with a sofa or "soft" setting; a chair, easel and basket to store book bags; a conference table; children's tables; and bin/basket main area for trade books; and another space for computers.

I may even give out a diagram of my classroom from my old school and some pictures. We will discuss collaboratively how I will set up my own new space as well as how they will want to set up their own spaces to allow for different uses of space within their own classrooms.

I will get into the issue of whether or not they want to have a traditional desk or use smaller tables for everyone. I think that they will need time to consider their own teaching styles in this regard. All teachers need to set up a space where they can easily confer with children and have access to individual assessment notebooks, reading folders (plus poetry/spelling, reading response, and handwriting notebooks) for all their students. I intend to show them how to prepare these folders for each child and how to store them so they can get to them when they need to make additional annotations for each child. Given the fact that I am working with new colleagues, I suspect that this will take at least an hour and a half of our time. I am also going to model for them a weekly reading log.

Most important of all, I am going to spend the major amount of time talking to them about the book bins as I place mine around the classroom. I will show them how to label the books using the Fountas and Pinnell levels and how to arrange the book bins with the spines out so that the children can see the books. Together we will examine how the bookcases should be close to the walls and the expository books should be separated from the narrative texts. I will also get together my audio-cassettes and book sets so that they can see how I set up my read-along center for all my children. I will share some dual language tapes I use with ELL students as well. I have some extra "author's hats" and author's chair slipcovers I will share with them.

I also intend to show them how to select big books for the easel display and anchor books to be shown there as well. By the way, I will also coach them how to write away for supplies and how to store supplies in common areas so that some children are not missing necessary materials for class activities.

Even though we are focusing on literacy, I am going to show them where to store mathematics materials, other texts, and art supplies. I will end the session by making sure that they know where to place their chart wall and the word wall. If I have time, I will sit down with each of them and start them on the word wall and some key charts for their first day. They will leave my room with an actual experience of setting up a literacy environment, plus viable teaching and reading suggestions for the first day. Most importantly, I will be available for an in-school classroom consultation, if necessary.

Tips and Reflections for tackling the Constructed Response Questions:

- Use as many phrases and words from the question as possible in your response.

- Be specific. Mention specific books, authors, theorists, and strategies you have studied. Even though this is a test about the teaching of reading, make specific use of children's trade books and literature if appropriate.

- Use as many details as you are given in the question to make your response. Write no more than 5-7 moderately brief paragraphs. The more you write, the larger the margin for error. Check your spelling, grammar and check to see that you answered everything that was asked, but no more than what was asked. Be positive and proactive about your ability to respond to whichever situation is presented.

- Stick with strategies, teaching ideas, and methods that are tried and true.

- Reread your writing at least twice for spelling and grammatical errors.

Additional Professional Citations

Block, Cathy Collins. (2002). *Comprehension Instruction: Research Based Practices.* New York: The Guilford Press.

Calkins, Lucy McCormick. (2001). *The Art of Teaching Reading.* New York: Longman.

Cambourne, Briane. (2002). "Conditions for Literacy Learning." *The Reading Teacher*, 55, (8): 758-62.

Cambourne, Briane. (I993). *The Whole Story: Natural Learning and the Acquisition of Literacy in the Classroom.* Auckland, NZ: Ashton, Scholastic.

Cunningham, Patricia M. (2000). *Phonics They Use: Words for Reading and Writing.* 3rd Edition. New York: Addison Wesley Longman.

Evidence Based Reading Instruction. (2002) Articles from International Reading Association. Newark, Delaware: *International Reading Association.*

Hoyt, Linda. (2002). *Make it Real-Strategies for Success with Informational Texts.* Portsmouth, NH: Heinemann.

Kimball-Lopez, Kimberley. (I999). *Connecting with Traditional Literature.* Boston: Allyn and Bacon.

Moustafa, Margaret. (I997). *Beyond Traditional Phonics.* Portsmouth, NH: Heinemann.

Owocki, Gretchen. (2003). *Strategic Instructions for K-3 Students.* Portsmouth, NH: Heinemann.

Owacki, G, and Y. Goodman. (2002*). Kidwatching-Documenting Children's Literacy Development.* Portsmouth, NH: Heinemann.

Quindlen, Anna. (1998). *How Reading Changed My Life.* New York: Ballantine Books, I998.

Routman, Regie. (2000). *Conversations.* Portsmouth, NH: Heinemann.

Schultz, C. (2000). *How Partner Reading Fosters Literacy Development in First Grade Students.* Action Research project, Saginaw Valley State University, University Center, Michigan.

Short, K., J. Harste and C. Burke. (I996). *Creating Classrooms for Authors and Inquirers.* Portsmouth, NH: Heinemann.
Trelease, Jim. (2001). *The Read-Aloud Handbook.* 4th Ed. New York: Penguin.

Wilde, Sandra. (2000). *Miscue Analysis Made Easy: Building on Student Strengths.* Portsmouth, NH: Heinemann.

Wilde, Sandra. (2000). *Reading Made Easy*. Portsmouth, NH: Heinemann.

XAMonline, INC. 21 Orient Ave. Melrose, MA 02176

Toll Free number 800-509-4128

TO ORDER Fax 781-662-9268 OR www.XAMonline.com

MICHIGAN TEST FOR TEACHER EXAMINATION - MTTC - 2007

PO#   Store/School:

Address 1:

Address 2 (Ship to other):

City, State Zip

Credit card number_____-_____-_____-_____   expiration_____

EMAIL _____

PHONE   FAX

13# ISBN 2007	TITLE	Qty	Retail	Total
978-1-58197-968-8	MTTC Basic Skills 96			
978-1-58197-954-1	MTTC Biology 17			
978-1-58197-955-8	MTTC Chemistry 18			
978-1-58197-957-2	MTTC Earth-Space Science 20			
978-1-58197-966-4	MTTC Elementary Education 83			
978-1-58197-967-1	MTTC Elementary Education 83 Sample Questions			
978-1-58197-950-3	MTTC English 02			
978-1-58197-961-9	MTTC Family and Consumer Sciences 40			
978-1-58197-959-6	MTTC French Sample Test 23			
978-1-58197-965-7	MTTC Guidance Counselor 51			
978-1-58197-964-0	MTTC Humanities& Fine Arts 53, 54			
978-1-58197-972-5	MTTC Integrated Science (Secondary) 94			
978-1-58197-973-2	MTTC Emotionally Impaired 59			
978-1-58197-953-4	MTTC Learning Disabled 63			
978-1-58197-963-3	MTTC Library Media 48			
978-1-58197-958-9	MTTC Mathematics (Secondary) 22			
978-1-58197-962-6	MTTC Physical Education 44			
978-1-58197-956-5	MTTC Physics Sample Test 19			
978-1-58197-952-7	MTTC Political Science 10			
978-1-58197-951-0	MTTC Reading 05			
978-1-58197-960-2	MTTC Spanish 28			
978-158197-970-1	MTTC Social Studies 84			
			SUBTOTAL	
FOR PRODUCT PRICES GO TO WWW.XAMONLINE.COM			Ship	$8.25
			TOTAL	

Breinigsville, PA USA
28 April 2010
237041BV00001B/1/A